Listen to This

American Made Music Series
Advisory Board

David Evans, General Editor
Barry Jean Ancelet
Edward A. Berlin
Joyce J. Bolden
Rob Bowman
Susan C. Cook
Curtis Ellison
William Faerris
John Edward Hasse
Kip Lornell
Bill Malone
Eddie S. Meadows
Manuel H. Peña
Wayne D. Shirley
Robert Walser

University Press of Mississippi
Jackson

Listen to This

Miles Davis and *Bitches Brew*

Victor Svorinich

www.upress.state.ms.us

The University Press of Mississippi is a member
of the Association of American University Presses.

Frontis image on page iii: Miles Davis, 1970s, courtesy of Photofest

Copyright © 2015 by University Press of Mississippi
All rights reserved
Manufactured in the United States of America

First printing 2015
∞
Library of Congress Cataloging-in-Publication Data

Svorinich, Victor, author.
 Listen to this : Miles Davis and Bitches brew / Victor Svorinich.
   pages cm. — (American made music series)
 Includes bibliographical references and index.
 ISBN 978-1-62846-194-7 (cloth : alk. paper) — ISBN 978-1-62846-195-4
(ebook) 1. Davis, Miles. 2. Davis, Miles. Bitches brew. 3. Jazz—History and criticism. 4. Jazz musicians—United States. 5. Popular music—United States—1961–1970—History and criticism. 6. Popular music—United States—1971–1980—History and criticism. I. Title.
 ML419.D39S86 2015
 788.9′2165092—dc23   2014024080

British Library Cataloging-in-Publication Data available

For my father, Big Vic

Music is strange. Why does it change so frequently? Is it because my life is always changing? My life could never be an open book, so there are many secrets in my life. People don't understand mode, Dorian mode, Phrygian mode, electronics, etc., just like they don't understand us. But it's ok, since they don't understand my music, they get surprised. Isn't it great that you can experience surprise through music?

—Miles Davis (as told to Kiyoshi Koyama for the shelved liner notes to *Agharta*, 1975)

Contents

Acknowledgments xi
Album Notes xiii
Beginnings 3

1 Climate 9

2 Development 21

3 Preparation 39

4 Music 51

5 Post-Production 97

6 Aftermath 111

7 Beyond *Brew* 135

8 Miles in 3-D: Images of *Bitches Brew* 161

With No End (An Epilogue) 173
Notes 177
Music Credits 195
Index 197

Acknowledgments

Almost everyone in my life has made this possible including my parents Vic and Nancy, my wife Anna, my aunt Debbie Biber, Les Kennedy, Lewis Porter, the crew at Columbia/Sony, the University Press of Mississippi, the photographers, and all the other contributors found throughout this book. THANK YOU

Album Notes

Miles Davis: *Bitches Brew* (Columbia GP-26)

Recorded: August 19–21, 1969, Columbia Studio B, New York City.

Release Date (U.S.): March 30, 1970*

Track Listing:
1. C0103313: Pharaoh's Dance 20:04 (Josef Zawinul) Zawinul Music BMI
2. C0103745: Bitches Brew 26:58 (Miles Davis) East St. Louis Music/Jazz Horn BMI
3. C0103750: Spanish Key 17:31 (Miles Davis) East St. Louis Music/Jazz Horn BMI
4. C0102951: John McLaughlin 4:22 (Miles Davis) East St. Louis Music/Jazz Horn BMI
5. C0103747: Miles Runs the Voodoo Down 14:01 (Miles Davis) East St. Louis Music/Jazz Horn BMI
6. C0103746: Sanctuary 10:57 (Wayne Shorter) Miyako Music BMI

Personnel:
Miles Davis, trumpet
Charles (Don) Alias, drums
Harvey Brooks, Fender bass
Chick Corea, electric piano
Jack DeJohnette, drums
Dave Holland, bass
Bennie Maupin, bass clarinet
John McLaughlin, guitar
Jumma Santos (Jim Riley), percussion

---

*Many sources list the record release as April 1970. Discographer Peter Losin narrowed it down to the March 30 date.

Wayne Shorter, soprano sax
Lenny White, drums
Larry Young, electric piano
Joe Zawinul, electric piano

Additional personnel:
　Produced by: Teo Macero
　Engineers: Stan Tonkel (August 19, 21), Frank Laico (August 20),
　　Ray Moore
　Cover painting: Mati Klarwein
　Art director: John Berg
　Original liner notes: Ralph Gleason

Listen to This

Beginnings

I don't play rock. I play black.[1]
—Miles Davis, 1969

Running the Voodoo Down

Between 1969 and 1975, Miles Davis went through the most productive period of his career. In no other seven-year span had he produced as many studio and live recordings. This was yet another period marked by the intense experimentation and innovation that was already a hallmark of his then thirty-year career. He was on a mission. The high-water mark of this expedition happened during three summer days in August of '69: the double album *Bitches Brew*. The backdrop: New York City in the late 1960s, Woodstock wrapping up two hours north the morning before, a group of some of the greatest musicians, and a whole lot of baggage.

Bitches Brew is a reflection of and response to what was happening at the time in Davis's life and everyone else's. It is a social commentary on African American culture during a very turbulent time in America, delivered by one of the most prominent voices in jazz. Between the civil rights movement, race riots, black militant movements, changes in the African American artistic culture, and weighty personal matters, Davis had much to draw and reflect upon. His previous work never had to contend with the kind of disillusionment, anger, and fear that dominated the late-sixties social landscape. Davis's record certainly has a sense of hostility and change. "This music came at the end of the 1960s . . . after all the chaos," wrote Davis biographer Quincy Troupe. "*Bitches Brew* summed up an era that was going out, with something new on the verge of coming in."[2] This summation is neither mass-audience friendly nor a small-niche production. This commercially hyped and heavily produced album delivered social commentary on a grand scale by a consummate artist who explored the complexities of the issues of the times in a profound manner.

Tuesday, August 19, 1969, could have been any other morning for Miles. Making recordings was nothing new to him, for he had been doing it frequently for the past twenty-five years. He had been an established celebrity for a long time. But the atmosphere around him was changing rapidly. Record companies were looking to cash in on the youth culture entranced with rock and roll. "There were four-hundred thousand people at the concert [Woodstock]," wrote Davis. "That many people at a concert makes everybody go crazy, and especially people who make records."[3] While rock was white hot, jazz was dying. For the first time, the cool Miles was feeling the pressure. His label was scrambling to capitalize on the new wave and was in an all-out war with Warner Brothers trying to sign new acts and promote the ones they had to young concertgoers. Meanwhile, Davis's sales were crashing and his concerts took place in half-filled clubs—not Woodstock. Somehow, he had lost the public's ear. "So this was the climate with Columbia and me just before I went into the studio to record *Bitches Brew*."[4]

Dark Magus

Miles Dewey Davis III was born on May 26, 1926, in Alton, Illinois, and moved to East St. Louis the following year. His father, a dentist, provided his son with an affluent upbringing. The family even owned a large farm in Arkansas where young Miles rode horses. Upon graduating high school in 1944, he moved to New York City to study music at Juilliard and carve a niche for himself. However, entranced with the fast, thriving bebop club scene, Davis soon dropped out of school in pursuit of a career on stage. Although Juilliard was a top music conservatory, Davis became bored and felt the program was too "white" and could never give him the education he could find on the streets. "Shit, I could learn more in one session at Minton's [Playhouse] than it would take me two years to learn at Juilliard."[5] He obsessively followed his hero Charlie Parker in hopes of playing with him and making the scene.

Gigging fanatically, Miles eventually made a name for himself and began cutting his own records. In the late forties he befriended composer/arranger Gil Evans and began work on the album *Birth of the Cool*, which became a cornerstone of the cool jazz movement. During the 1950s, Davis signed with Prestige, followed by Columbia Records, beginning a thirty-year relationship with the label. He would continue projects with Evans, construct his first legendary quintet featuring John Coltrane, and release records that spearheaded the modal jazz movement (most notably *Milestones* and *Kind of Blue*).

Davis's success on the road and in the studio (his efforts with Evans sold exceptionally well, and *Kind of Blue* would eventually become the best-selling jazz album of all time) led to a fertile period as the 1960s rolled in. Experimenting with different groups and projects, he eventually formed a second quintet that is still a benchmark for small jazz groups to this day. The union lasted around four years (1964–68) and featured young jazz faces Wayne Shorter, Herbie Hancock, Ron Carter, and Tony Williams (who was still a teenager upon arrival). By this point, Davis began leaning toward a band sound. The music needed to be organic, spontaneous, free, and collaborative. This sixties quintet would devise little sketches as a launching pad and let the music unfold in the moment. The results were anarchic, chaotic, bewildering, transcendent.

Miles could never be considered a satisfied man. His restlessness and foresight created the innovations in his life. Nothing was ever good enough, and when he found something inspiring it left his life quicker than it took to be found. There was also a sense of smugness in him that allowed what was to happen after all his past accolades. In the late sixties R&B, soul, and the Motown Sound were all over the airwaves, but it was rock music that truly reached its zenith. The sound once puttering around in juke joints, gin mills, and the dinky Sun Studios spread like wildfire. It went beyond top record sales, concerts, and massive festivals; it defined the sixties temperament. What made rock so appealing? Well, it had the edge. Rock is dissonant, dangerous, impure. After fifty years, we have forgotten the vulgarity of distorting a signal to get that rock guitar sound. But it was also its exoticism. Rock music is black music just as it was in Elvis Presley's day. The beats, the lyricism, the blues phrasing and forms all came from African American culture, be it West Africa, the plantation, the honky tonks, or the jazz clubs. Some of the biggest rock bands of the sixties—the Beatles, the Rolling Stones, the Jimi Hendrix Experience, Cream, Led Zeppelin, and so on—not only copped their sound from the old bluesmen, but covered (and sometimes even plagiarized) their repertoire. Whether it got the recognition it deserved in its day or not, black America dominated popular culture. Well, Davis made sure it got the recognition.

Electric Ladyland

Davis was just as restless with his women as he was with his music. In 1968 he met and married Betty Mabry, a young (twenty-three to his forty-two) model, musician, and socialite. It was the second of three Davis marriages (all ending in divorce) and it was a whirlwind, lasting less than a year. The ink was yet to dry on his divorce papers with Frances Taylor when Miles and Betty got married (divorced in February, married in September).

Betty was wired into the New York club/art/fashion/music/decadence scene, befriending all the glitterati of the late sixties. It was easy to see why Miles was attracted to her. She was young, fast, gorgeous, and had an obvious charisma. "She was indomitable," noted Carlos Santana. "You couldn't tame Betty Davis."[6] Betty's charms worked on Miles, for she seemed to call all the shots. She took him to all the clubs, turning Miles on to all the exciting new musicians. He started taking care of himself, quit smoking, ate right, and got hard-core with boxing. As on any other day, Miles would scuttle off to Gleason's gym to spar and exercise after each *Brew* session. Betty was hard to keep up with and certainly high maintenance.

Davis even started dressing in the latest sixties fashions. Gone were the days of the stiff, old Brooks Brothers suits. It all started at a little boutique with no name on East 9th in New York's East Village, three blocks up from the Fillmore East. The shop was opened a few months before the *Bitches Brew* sessions by a pair of Moroccan ladies, Colette Mimram and Stella Douglas, who imported exotic ethnic garb that would become the staple of late-sixties/early-seventies rock star fashion. The place was the local hangout for the rich, the chic, and all the local rockers from down the street including Hendrix, Johnny Winter, Gregg Allman, and Santana. Betty, being on top of anything glamorous, befriended the two owners and introduced Miles to New York's roaring late-sixties fashion scene. Miles was one of their first customers, buying a Luna Felix amber-beaded necklace.[7] Douglas introduced Miles and Betty to Hendrix, who happened to be dating Mimram at the time. "Jimi looked over and saw Miles, and they looked up in surprise, as if to say, 'Oh, you?' They started teasing each other."[8] Miles was hooked.

At the clubs, Miles experienced the power of electrified rock—high power, high volume, unadulterated. He met some of Betty's rocker friends and got close with Hendrix and Sly Stone. In the end, however, Betty was a bit too brash and immature for Miles's tastes and could no longer be trusted—he accused her of stealing his money and sleeping with Hendrix.[9] That was that.

Despite the turbulence in their relationship, Betty was a major factor in Davis's next musical phase. His exposure to these new artists had a one-eighty effect on him. Acoustic was out and electric was in, for the rest of his life. As he had with Parker in the forties, he would chase Hendrix, Stone, and James Brown. It was pop music, yes, but why was it popular? Well, it was good. It was fresh, strong, unyielding, and somewhat familiar; it was black music.

1. Climate

It was honest. It was honest.[1]
—Bob Dylan

Great art reflects the times in which it is created. In the twentieth century artists were faced with extremes in violence and progress. Wars, weapons of mass destruction, dictatorships, the civil rights movement, and breakthroughs in technology shaped a social landscape that led to a massive response from Picasso, Eliot, Stravinsky, as well as modern-day romantics like Jimi Hendrix, Janis Joplin, Otis Redding, Sly Stone, and countless others. Formality and consonance gave way to innovation, self-expression, emotion, raw energy, and at times an abstract modernity where artists convey images that no longer represent the visual world. Often, what seems radical at first appears definitive when gazed from a distance.

The King

I can't overemphasize how shocking he looked and seemed to me that night.[2]
—Roy Orbison on tour with Elvis Presley, 1955

Elvis Presley was a southern boy, born and raised in the Bible Belt during the mid-twentieth century. He was a quiet kid who came from a small, poor family. Most accounts of his early life describe him as "average"—decent grades, a bit of a loner, unpopular, occasionally troublesome. He enjoyed singing, but no one pegged him to go very far with it. His eighth-grade music teacher gave him a C. Still, inspired, he began cutting his first records at Sam Phillips's Sun Records Studios in Memphis while still a teenager. Like Presley, Phillips was a fan of many African American musical styles, most particularly the blues, but he knew the difficulties of popularizing this music in the segregated South. "If I could find a white man who had the Negro sound and the Negro feel, I could make a billion dollars." Then came Elvis. According to Phillips, at the end of a session recording sulky ballads, Presley picked up a guitar and started wailing "That's All Right," an old Arthur Crudup blues number, making Phillips scramble frantically to get it on tape.[3] The rest is history.

At first, many great artists appear to go against the world they live in. When Presley first gained his success, he appeared to be everything that his culture was not. The Eisenhower fifties was a conservative era. There was Perry Como, the nuclear family, TV dinners, long poodle skirts, and segregated buses. Elvis came in playing black music, swimming in sexuality. He was the voice of the repressed fifties teenager. He was the voice of youth for every generation after him.

What makes a voice for a generation? In the fifties Presley's voice conjured up rebellion against a conservatively constructed world. He was the perfect purveyor for the message. He had the simple, quiet good looks, and an insecure demeanor underneath all the energy, glam, danger, and lust. "I'd never seen anything quite like him, he just *had* it. I had never heard of Elvis Presley when I went out there,"[4] said Jimmie Rodgers Snow when touring with the King in the fifties. Behind the innocent farm-boy imagery, Presley had a voice and stage presence that was ferocious. It was like nothing else.

Musically, he was no revelation. Black musicians were essentially doing the same thing as Presley. After all, most of his repertoire was lifted from old blues and R&B singers. "The colored folks been singing and playing it just like I'm doin' now, man, for years more than I know. They played it like that in the shanties and their juke joints, and nobody paid it no mind 'til I goosed it up,"[5] said Presley. The R&B records of other performers Phillips was cutting were also geared to young audiences, but those musicians did not have the magnetism of Elvis . . . and they were black.

Judas

Bob Dylan was a hero of the early-sixties folk movement—a scene unscathed by pop music and rock and roll. It was the Antarctica of the music world. Rock and roll was greasers, teenyboppers, drunken dancers, and hooligans.[6] Folk artists were the purists, the protesters. They were there as a voice against everything wrong in the world—the consumerism, commercialism, deficits in human rights, the extremes in violence.

Brought up in a Midwestern, Jewish, middle-class community, Dylan spent his youth listening to country, blues, and fifties rockers like Elvis, but eventually, he turned to folk. Although folk music lacked the certain emotions and force found with the rock and rollers, folk musicians were storytellers whose energy was in their lyricism. "The thing about rock and roll was for me anyway it wasn't enough," said Dylan. Folk music tackled the tired, the weary, the poor; it had the ability to reach down, find faith, and overcome adversity.[7] With a guitar on his side, he made his way to New York in search of an audience for his voice. What he found was a culture so absorbed in itself, it made him sick. "I knew I wasn't going to stay there. I knew it wasn't my thing. Many times I spoiled it. Many times I went against it. Anytime they tried to think I was like them. I knew I wasn't like them."[8]

In 1965 Dylan dropped his acoustic guitar and released "Like a Rolling Stone" and other electric songs with great success. His album *Highway 61 Revisited* went gold and "Like a Rolling Stone" topped the charts. Dylan hit the road performing half acoustic and half electric sets, and the reception was startling. Younger listeners were into it, but older fans were cooled by this electric Dylan. His appearance at the Newport Folk Festival was a low-water mark on his American tour where he was greeted by incessant booing throughout his whole set. To the Newport faithful, Dylan's rock antics erased the sincerity so embedded in his artistry. Already tired of this self-absorbed, self-righteous scene, Dylan made it clear he was not going to bow down to them. And how pure were their souls anyway? "Lightnin' Hopkins had made electric records for twelve years, but he didn't bring his electric band from Texas," said Dylan guitarist Mike Bloomfield. "No sir, he came out at Newport like they had just taken him out of the fields, like the tar baby."[9]

Things got worse when the band hit Europe in 1966. Dylan was met with a hail of boos and jeers throughout the electric sets in France. It eventually got the best of him. Between songs, Dylan lashed out "Don't worry, I'm just as eager to finish and leave as you are" to the Olympia audience. "I'm doing this for you. I couldn't care less. I wouldn't behave like this if I came to see you," was hollered back to a feisty Paris crowd. The most infamous stop was Free Trade Hall in Manchester, England. As the electric set started, hundreds of concertgoers began walking out. Those who stayed began a barrage of heckling and booing. The loud cry of "Judas" toward the end of the set was the clincher. "I don't believe you. You're a liar," shot back Dylan. He then instructed his band to "play it fucking loud" and hurtled into "Like a

Rolling Stone." It was almost mocking—loud, snarling, condescending. He carried the youthful arrogance of rock and roll. He was pissed off.

Manchester was the last stop on the European tour as Dylan headed back to the States to finish the American leg. Two months later, Dylan allegedly suffered a motorcycle crash, forcing the cancellation of the remaining dates. Despite a speedy recovery, he would not tour again for another eight years.

"Like a Rolling Stone" describes a world filled with disillusionment, loss, and hostility. The tune seems eerily autobiographical. Like the song's subject, Dylan himself must leave behind a world that is no longer his. Dylan's alienation sums up a counterculture plagued with social upheaval, leaving everyone "with no direction home."

What's Going On? There's a Riot Goin' On

While Dylan was finding his own voice and making a stand against folk purity, racial tensions in America peaked while Americans tried to understand why thousands of young adults were being slaughtered in Vietnam. Malcolm X was assassinated, then Martin Luther King, leading to rioting across the country. More troops to Vietnam. Things were a mess; by the end of the sixties the hippie dream was dying.

Born Sylvester Stewart in 1943, Sly Stone grew up in a deeply religious family in the northern San Francisco Bay town of Vallejo. His Christian parents encouraged music, enabling Sly to learn a multitude of instruments. By the late sixties, Haight-Ashbury became the hippie epicenter, home to the idealism, Santana, Jefferson Airplane, the Grateful Dead, the drugs. Stone got his start at a local radio station playing soul and modern rock. Running around the Bay Area, he gathered a crew that would become Sly and the Family Stone, a soul-funk-rock band that would help define his generation.

By the mid-sixties, black musicians directly developed a voice in America's popular culture and got some of the recognition they deserved. Artists such as Brown, Otis Redding, Sam Cooke, Wilson Pickett, and Aretha Franklin paved the way for young Sly to permeate his infectious grooves through America. In 1967 Redding was one of the star attractions at the Monterey Pop Festival. Two summers later, Stone was a sensation at Woodstock (with Hendrix, of course, dominating both shows). He was quick to recognize his popularity and newfound sense of entitlement. The month before Woodstock, Stone was asked to close the Newport Jazz Festival, which turned out to be a total disaster. Performing "I Want to Take You

Higher," Stone ignored cues that he was over time and kept screeching "Higher! Higher!" turning the crowd (who were now rushing the stage and spilling into the box seats and photography pit) into a frenzy. "Pandemonium was like a drug to Sly Stone," wrote Newport founder George Wein. "Instead of calming his fans, he was enticing them." Nobody told Stone what to do. Shortly after Newport, Wein approached the singer for another show only if he behaved himself and kept to his allotted time. Stone wanted no part of Wein. "Man, why are you calling me?" he told Wein. "Why don't you talk to my manager?"[10] Stone, too, had the charisma—the flashy persona, the wild stage antics, the funky, catchy dance vibes, the psychedelic shadings of the counterculture surrounding him, and the exoticism. The kids went wild. He just *had* it.

Like so many other great ones, Stone burned out before he could fade away. His lifestyle by far surpassed his exuberant persona. He spent money and took drugs in excess. His Bel Air mansion was nestled across the street from that of the *Beverly Hillbillies*. But by the early seventies, the Family Stone began to dissipate. Their live appearances became less frequent as Stone put on a perennial disappearing act. He cancelled twenty-six out of eighty shows in 1970. He blew off television appearances. The drugs and disillusionment of his day would eventually get the best of him. Open-minded psychedelia turned to shut-in cocaine to three decades of crack. By the new millennium and pushing seventy, Stone had been in and out of rehab and reportedly was homeless in the Los Angeles area.

Stone will always be remembered for his foot-stomping, feel-good sixties hits, but he will be forever immortalized for his lashing of the surrounding counterculture. After his string of pearls, he would release *There's a Riot Goin' On* in 1971—a dark funk masterpiece as a response to Marvin Gaye's rhetorical question *What's Going On* that was asked earlier that year. The album yielded one hit single, "Family Affair," and sold well but was hardly a commercial breakthrough by Stone standards. The legend and notoriety of it was more of a creeper. The album cover eerily recalls the message sent by Davis on *Bitches Brew*—one of tension and release. *Riot* sports an American flag with the blue replaced with black and suns for stars in order to represent unity for people of all colors.[11] The heart of the record clearly illustrates the harsh dissonance associated with African American existence during this time. This was Stone's state of the union address.

Good certainly turned to bad as the seventies lurched in. "The war is over. They won," proclaimed a righteous Lester Bangs in Cameron Crowe's *Almost Famous*. The decadence and cynicism of the sixties and seventies would later get the best of Miles Davis, who went into a drug-addled exile of his own in 1975. Gaye, too, would spend the next decade searching for the answer to his own question in a pile of cocaine, leading up to his demise by the hand of his own father. The King's exit may not have been a by-product of counterculture cynicism, but it can certainly be credited to the wheels of the system he helped design. Despite failing health including multiple drug overdoses and a coma, he was a relentless touring machine in the seventies. Early warning signs came in 1973, when Presley collapsed out of a limo before a concert in Maryland. The show was a disaster for the falling star. "He was so fucked up. It was obvious he was drugged. It was so bad. The words to his songs were barely intelligible. . . . I remember crying,"[12] said sideman John Wilkinson. The ax finally fell in 1977.

Super Bad

James Brown, "Mr. Dynamite," "The Hardest Working Man in Show Business," the "Godfather of Soul," "Soul Brother Number One," was born in utter poverty in Barnwell, South Carolina, in 1933. His parents split up when he was two, leaving him with his womanizing father, who shipped him off to his aunt who ran a whorehouse. Soon he was a man of the streets, finishing his formal education in the seventh grade, and taking life into his own hands. You can say Brown had a checkered past, but then again, trouble always seemed to find him; his rap sheet covered the better part of five decades. Beyond his street hustlin' scruff, Brown was a hard-core criminal, having been arrested and imprisoned numerous times for armed robbery, assault, domestic violence, and drug violations, to name a few. He was dangerous, the "bad boy."

Brown was always into the blues, R&B, and gospel growing up and developed an interest in singing and becoming an entertainer. He got an early start in his musical career working the chitlin' circuit down south. Through hard work, he found a name for himself and managed to carve out a massively successful career spanning some sixty years.

In concert, Brown was magic. He had the whole package: originality, the dance moves, the funky beats, the swagger, the glam, the voice, the talent. He just *had* it. By the late sixties he had assembled some of the finest and most influential bands in music history. His sets would be electrifying impromptu jams leaving both audiences and band mates bedazzled. Most of the material was long, free-form, and unsegmented, with Brown calling the shots at any given moment. With a click of his shoes, a tap of his toes, or a screech from the voice, he commanded his band and the direction the music would go. With all the high-flying, spur of the moment action, it was not easy being in a Brown band—and he ruled with an iron fist. To say that Brown was a perfectionist or a disciplinarian would be an understatement. Every costume had to be just so. All the musicianship needed to be perfect. If not, he would distribute fines. Cruel, but it had to be that way. Similar to Davis, Brown thought that if the leader is frail in any way, the band will be weak. You had to be tyrannical.

Brown, too, was a socially conscious man. After all, he was a black man from the South raised in the same racist, segregated conditions as the rest of his peers. Hits such as "Say It Loud—I'm Black and I'm Proud" and "Talking Loud and Saying Nothing" illustrate Brown's stance as a Negro in the modern world. More importantly, like Stone, Hendrix, and Davis, Brown enjoyed commercial success without the barriers of race, or for that matter, any barriers at all. His music and style spoke to generations of fans regardless of color or gender. Nevertheless, his music is black music. It is dense and abstract, like a new language. It is soul, funk, blues, jazz, R&B, even West African. His lyricism is ghetto talk, jive. At its core, it recalls the chitlin' circuit, the honky tonks, the streets, and the demons so associated with Brown's past. It was his voice, his music.

The Electric Gypsy

Back at Woodstock that Monday morning before *Bitches Brew* got under way in New York, twenty-six-year-old Jimi Hendrix was closing shop with a twisted, violent rendition of the perennial event standard "The Star Spangled Banner." It had been a rough weekend for Jimi. He was supposed to play the night before, but weather conditions backed up the schedule and Hendrix insisted on closing the show. After a long trek to Yasgur's farm, Hendrix and his crew shacked up at a nearby cottage awaiting the performance, but the guitarist wasn't feeling it. "He seemed really sick, or really high, and was sweating bullets," explained Leslie Aday, a crew member of Dylan's, who was with Hendrix that night. "As we sat there, he seemed nervous and didn't think he could pull it off."[13] But Jimi got it together. There was a welcome sun coming up that morning after a weekend of torrential rains that pummeled the grounds and spirits of the fans. That Monday morning definitely felt like a bad hangover. The fraction of that massive crowd that stayed for Jimi's set had definitely seen their share of highs and lows that weekend, but Hendrix was worth the wait. He ripped through a two-hour-plus set with effortless ferocity. He made sure to get his standards in, but mostly stuck with long, dark blues jams. The jewel came about three quarters of the way through with his performance of the national anthem, a piece that would eventually define the spirit of the sixties and youth radicalism.

Nineteen sixty-nine was a tough year for being patriotic and being an American. Woodstock came off as a metaphor for all the country's moral woes.[14] Hendrix's performance acknowledges these conditions and sums up the voices of all Americans having to come to terms with them. Similar to Picasso's *Guernica*, his marred lyricism and brutal imagery suggests a country being torn apart. What did Hendrix imply by performing it at a function decrying the state of the union? "All I did was play it. I'm an American. I used to sing it in school," he told Dick Cavett nonchalantly in an interview a year later. When Cavett warned Hendrix of the hate mail he would receive for his "unorthodox" performance, a befuddled and quite sincere Hendrix replied, "Nasty letters? It's not unorthodox. I thought it was beautiful."[15]

There has been an ongoing controversy about Hendrix's cryptic performance for over forty years. Was it a heartfelt, earnest nod to the place he called home or a lashing at the reality his country entrenched him in? Perhaps it is all a moot point, for the writing was already on the wall. Hendrix's rendition only confirms the brutality of war and the feeling of falling apart at the seams in an ultra-modern, ultra-violent world. Perhaps his naysayers were not ready for the reality of the human condition saturated in Jimi's music. Of course, his admirers certainly outnumbered his critics.

Hendrix was already looked upon with scorn by middle-America conservatives still stuck in the Eisenhower fifties. Not everyone was young, liberal, and experimental, and there was still a great part of the population who had not caught up with desegregation laws, Martin Luther King, and affirmative action. Free love and the racket of rock and roll was not the mantra of the majority in the United States. Even at Woodstock, Jimi was one of only three African American artists playing to a sea of white youngsters with a speckle of black kids. Hendrix represented everything the establishment was afraid of: a black, sexually charged male playing uncontrollably loud rock guitar.[16]

Two years earlier, Hendrix had caught the world's attention at the Monterey Pop Festival with his guitar "sacrifice." "I'm gonna sacrifice something that I really love. Don't think I'm silly for doing this. I don't think I'm losing my mind. This is for everybody. This is the only way to do it," he whimsically warned his California crowd before the start of set closer "Wild Thing." Decked out in a pink boa, skin-tight trousers, and other garb that can only be identified as sixties fashion, Jimi brimmed with sexuality and flamboyancy. The weekend's performers all took their seats to see what the fuss was. Brian Jones of the Rolling Stones made a special trip from London just to introduce him to the crowd.

Nineteen sixty-seven was Hendrix's breakthrough year. He had just released his debut album *Are You Experienced?* the month before Monterey with his trio the Jimi Hendrix Experience (Mitch Mitchell on drums, Noel Redding on bass) to great success, peaking at number two on the U.K. charts behind only the Beatles' *Sgt. Pepper's Lonely Hearts Club Band*. Born in Seattle in 1942, Hendrix was a product of a broken home and a sexually abusive, poverty-stricken upbringing. As a result of domestic violence, alcoholism, and general neglect, Jimi was a shy, withdrawn boy who eventually found an outlet in music. Around the time of his mother's death when he was fifteen, a relative gave him a cheap acoustic guitar on which Jimi would start his tutelage. As he got older, he made his rounds through various R&B bands, with varying success. He finally caught a break in 1966 while gigging in New York. As his name started to catch on, he eventually hooked up with producer Chas Chandler, who flew him to England and helped him form the Jimi Hendrix Experience. Word about the wild young bluesman spread throughout all the British Invasion circles that were enthralled with American blues and R&B musicians. The record was cut and Hendrix became a worldwide legend.

A few highlights aside, including an ironic cover of "Like a Rolling Stone," Monterey was not a particularly inspired set for Jimi. His stage performance was somewhat banal and focused too much on shtick as opposed to his raw, untamed musicianship. Jimi seemed a bit nervous, perhaps a little too easy to please, and maybe a tad too high that night. By the set closing, things got somewhat absurd. At the end of "Wild Thing," Hendrix jammed the guitar against his amp, creating some ungodly feedback, then set fire to the instrument. He proceeded to repeatedly smash the guitar onstage and threw the remains to the crowd. In his documentary of the festival, filmmaker D. A. Pennebaker captured the shock and awe on the faces of the concertgoers. Clearly, not even all the youth were ready for Jimi.

Behind the hazy, gentle, almost lackadaisical personality of Hendrix lay this wrecking ball of creativity and musicianship. He had ferocity like no other. "By the time we got him to play at Monterey, he was the hottest act around," recalled Monterey promoter and musician John Phillips. "A couple of years later, he was dead. He just went like a fireball."[17] Just about a year after Woodstock, the excesses of Jimi's life caught up with him. He was both an architect and a casualty of his generation. The side effects of a life in the limelight and a prolonged LSD bender—paranoia, anxiety, pressure, and overall poor health—led to bad business, creative, and personal decisions. Like so many other sixties icons, the drugs finally got the best of him. He died before he got old, aged twenty-seven.

The Prince of Darkness

Looming over the scene was the raspy-voiced, suave, mysterious, irascible Miles Davis. Those who knew him understood the many sides of the man. If he liked you, he could be the kindest, sweetest, most gentle person you would ever meet. He had a way of making special bonds with many of the people in his life that would last decades. He became a father figure to many of his young sidemen. But if you got on his bad side, watch out. Not only was he notorious for being difficult, but at times he was downright violent. He had a temper that rivaled James Brown's. Miles was big on first impressions. "He can be cold on a motherfucker if you come off wrong," explained Quincy Troupe when first meeting him. "First, he might just ignore you altogether. Two, he might turn loose those ray-gun eyes at you. Third, he might just curse you out and put you down verbally in such an unbelievably cruel manner."[18]

Despite his privileged upbringing, the man had one hell of a sense of etiquette, and his attitude and lifestyle sometimes rubbed the wrong people the wrong way. His confrontations with the law gave him a rap sheet like a pimp's. Outside of New York's Birdland in 1959, he had his first major brush with authority. He had the hots for a pretty young blonde and decided to walk her to a cab during a set break. When a suspicious police officer told Davis to move on, he would not back down, leading to a nightstick to the head and a trip to jail for the bloody Davis. More arrests followed. Two months before recording *Brew*, Davis had a gig at the Blue Coronet in Brooklyn. Late that night, he was sitting in his Ferrari with girlfriend Marguerite Eskridge when gunshots blasted the car nearly killing the two. Davis was grazed by a bullet and later taken to the hospital. Accounts of the shooting vary. Some reports say that the shooting was from small-time gangsters looking to extort Davis.[19] According to a conversation he had with the trumpeter, *Brew* cover artist Mati Klarwein said that the incident was a mafia hit because Davis refused to play at a mafia club.[20] When the police arrived, they searched the Ferrari and found marijuana, leading Miles to a trip downtown after his hospital visit. Five months later, sporting a new red Ferrari, Miles was in a no-parking zone with a young woman when a New York cop noticed that not only was he illegally parked, but he had no registration sticker. As Miles rummaged through the glove box, a pair of brass knuckles fell out, leading to another night in jail. "On the way to the station the cop keeps saying 'I've got Miles Davis,' like I was Jesse James."[21]

There's a great shot of Miles at Hendrix's funeral pimpin' with a woman on each arm. The girls, one of whom is Betty Mabry, are grieving intensely. Davis, looking aggravated, is sporting the trendiest regalia. "That funeral was such a drag that I said I would never go to another one after that—and I haven't,"[22] he remarked. The flash, the women, the violence, the darkness. Where did it all come from? Davis had a very strong sense of self, and despite a changing social climate, particularly in matters involving black identity, he knew that whoever he was or whatever he did had to be on his own terms. It all traced back to his charmed childhood. Being from an affluent black family was something quite rare, and there was always a deep suspicion and insecurity that at any moment these privileges could easily be taken away from him. White eyes would always be lurking and trying to nab whatever credit was due to him in order to destroy his social status. This belief would create a protective shield and outlook that would affect all the business and personal relationships he had throughout his life. His attitude can be traced to his father, Miles Senior, who was an avid follower of Marcus Garvey, and would teach his son the values espoused by Garvey such as self-worth and self-reliance that he would carry with him throughout his life. Young Miles's short-fused temper and contempt for whites can also be attributed to his father. Miles Senior had a take-no-shit attitude, especially when it came to whites. In his autobiography, Junior remembered a time when his father chased a white man with a shotgun for calling his son a nigger. He carried this attitude into his private life, although young Miles never recalled any physical harm from him. The sneering eye of discipline from a disappointed and aggravated authoritative figure was far worse punishment. "I would have almost preferred his whipping me to the way he used to look right through me like I was nothing,"[23] recalled Miles.

His mother, Cleota, was a different story. She never saw eye to eye with most of her husband's outlooks, and as a result, they constantly fought. She was less the radical and more of a William Pickens (NAACP) supporter. She was the physical disciplinarian, the one who would do the whipping. Although Miles admitted to having her fashion sense rub off on him, they were never as close as he was with his father. At thirteen, around the time he received his first trumpet from his father (which caused a fight because Cleota wanted him to play violin), he and his mother developed problems communicating. Despite all the advantages, the family was split apart when his parents finally divorced and young Miles eventually moved on.

He also learned from his father that for a black man attaining power was not easy. "To realize you don't have any power to make things different is a bitch,"[24] wrote Davis. It was up to him alone to define his music and himself on his own terms—a leading characteristic of the up-and-coming black power movement. Gaining respect and free will came from empowerment. Davis was successful at attaining power because he maintained his identity while changing his music to reflect the times. Davis wanted to be free to experiment even in a world where experimentation for blacks was certainly constraining. He defied and challenged himself because he could. He had the autonomy and access to be able to ignore what everyone else said about who he was and what he was doing.[25]

Davis's concern was not to capitalize on rock's success, but to fill some of the voids left behind. First off, he needed to brush himself off and get back on top again. He had way too much ego and too lavish a lifestyle to let life pass him by. He was a connoisseur of fast women and Ferraris. Dwindling revenue was a no-no. In order to get back on top, he would have to change the course of music once again.

Like *Bitches Brew*, it is arguable that Hendrix, Woodstock, and all the other sixties highlights were right-place-at-the-right-time occurrences. The success of these artists and events came because there was an audience that was desperately waiting for something like this to happen. Tired of the mundane, the clichéd, and the "pure," young audiences wanted to hear the strange, harsh, dark imagery because it was so much a part of their world. Like Hendrix, Brown, and their counterparts, Davis would also insist that *Bitches Brew* was his music for a younger generation regardless of how radical or progressive it sounded. Presley biographer Peter Guralnick felt that when Elvis changed the line from "you may have religion" to "you may drive a pink Cadillac" in "Baby, Let's Play House," "he defined something of his own, not to mention his generation's aspirations."[26] Like *Brew*, it also may have defined an era. Although Davis wanted to reach a wider and younger African American audience, it was not for the goal of popularity. He wanted to reconnect this audience to the challenging and complex world in which they lived. It was a dark world, and he needed to play the sounds that were nowhere to be found. It was on his terms. It was honest.

2. Development

Miles Davis: The fifteen year success story that happened overnight.
—*Bitches Brew* promo ad

A Fateful Break?

Nothing sounds like *Bitches Brew*. Not even anything that Miles Davis had released before. Davis's cultural surroundings, new influences, and experimentations made a heavy imprint on his new sound; however, *Bitches Brew* was not a revolution. Whether it is Davis, Beethoven, Schoenberg, Jimi Hendrix, or Picasso, something always comes from something. *Bitches Brew* came from a ten-year-plus development period and an abundance of African American culture. Using electric instruments, new rhythmic textures, rock beats, novel approaches to composition and improvisation, and other off-the-cuff tinkerings, it appeared as a radical departure both from Davis's previous efforts and more broadly from the aesthetics of jazz and African American art. But as shocking as the album may sound within his body of work, *Bitches Brew* also incorporated many elements already evident in his second "classic" quintet period (1965–68). There are even aspects of this record that go back to the fifties. The preceding February, Davis recorded *In a Silent Way*, which certainly flirted with modern music and felt like the final destination for this development period; but he needed to push the envelope further.

There is so much that defines *Bitches Brew*. The album explores modal improvisation, extended forms, new uses of timbre, polyrhythm, rhythmic interaction, collective improvisation, atypical instrumentation, etc. Yet there seems to be something eerily familiar about the record. In a sense, *Bitches Brew* illustrates both continuity and change. Many of the traits of this album show how existing elements can achieve a new synthesis that gives the illusion of the radically new, when there is actually a blend of the new and the familiar. Appreciating these continuities casts *Bitches Brew* in a

Bitches Brew Promo Ad. Courtesy of Sony Music Entertainment

new light: as the realization of longstanding developments in Davis's music merged with fresh insight, and not a fateful break or rupture in his art and career.

Birth of the Cool

Chords? We don't play chords. We play sound.[1]
—Miles Davis, 1969

As early as 1950, Davis was moving away from elaborate chord changes as a basis of improvisation in favor of a stripped down, modal approach. Songs with dense chord progressions relied upon harmonic changes to define the tonal center, whereas modal pieces rely only on a pedal point or one tone in order to establish the key center. This style offers the soloist (as well as the entire ensemble) great liberty to explore melody without the restrictions imposed by the bebop-style chord progressions. It also allows the band greater latitude to communicate and shift directions, promoting more of a group sound and dynamic—a significant characteristic of *Bitches Brew*. With its vertically oriented structure, the bebop style confronts the musicians harmonically, whereas modal improvisation challenges the musicians horizontally, or in other words, rhythmically and melodically. This can be traced back to the *Birth of the Cool* sessions in 1950 with the track "Boplicity," ushering in the cool jazz and modal jazz period that later included "Milestones," "So What," and "Flamenco Sketches" from *Milestones* and *Kind of Blue* respectively. Davis also incorporated a stripped-down approach in his collaborations with Gil Evans as in the arrangement of "I Loves You, Porgy" from *Porgy and Bess*, where Evans had him use only one scale.

Davis loved the harmonic concepts of pianist Ahmad Jamal, who utilized a great deal of space in his compositions and arrangements. Jamal was known for stripping jazz standards down to simple pedal points, such as his striking rendition of "Autumn Leaves," where Jamal dismantles the entire harmonic progression and vamps over a single chord. Davis ran with this idea and used it on standards such as "'Round Midnight," "I Fall in Love Too Easily," and of course, "Autumn Leaves." By the mid-sixties, more and more modal pieces, such as "Agitation" and Wayne Shorter's "Masqualero," were finding their way into his live sets. By the end of the decade, modes became the exclusive approach in his bands. With the right rhythmic ideas, he could run with this idea all he wanted. Funk was the perfect fit.

Funk rhythms—such as the ones heard in Miles's late-sixties/early-seventies bands, as well as in James Brown's and Sly Stone's bands—rely on an ostinato that establishes an underlying groove and acts as a tonal center. This would primarily come from the bass, which at times would even serve as the melodic line for the piece. "So What" could be considered an early example of a melodic bass line, but it does not serve as a melodic pattern once the soloists arrive. Once the melody is stated, the bass line morphs into a walk. Tunes such as 1967's "Circle in the Round" and "Water in the Pond" are better early instances of the bass providing a stable, repetitive melodic figure.

Once the groove is established, the remainder of the band could be very free and experimental, venturing in and out of various keys and eventually return to the home key whenever they felt like it. "There was no direct harmony present, meaning chord changes as such," said Dave Liebman, who was a regular in Davis's arsenal from 1972 to 1974. Even though there were centered bass lines, the way Miles and his band would play over it gave the music a distinct polytonal flavor and a complex, multicolored sound.[2]

Sound over Groove

Why announce it? It's only a feeling.[3]
—Miles Davis

Song titles? On the original LP track list of *Miles Davis At Fillmore*, the tracks are labeled as: "Wednesday Miles," "Thursday Miles," "Friday Miles," and "Saturday Miles," depicting the four sets Davis played at the Fillmore East in June 1970. In fact most of his live releases during the seventies had similarly ambiguous song titles. Part of the reason for this was that Miles could not care less about song names, but an unfortunate result was that no one could decipher what was being played. Well over twenty years passed before most of these sets were dissected and supplied with proper titles, and it was not an easy task since the sets had no breaks. Everything moved in one continuous stream-of-consciousness flow.

By 1959 Davis was already tired of traditional song forms, and he eventually abandoned them altogether. Chord changes with an overlying melody became monotonous. Davis insisted that the typical thirty-two bar structure not only made the music too rigid, but stagnant as well because the same sequence keeps on repeating and the improviser is more prone to resorting to old tricks. Even if you assign a certain number of measures for each section or soloist, modal playing essentially has no start or end, leaving plenty of room for the band to stretch out. The next to go was established melodies. Similar to "Flamenco Sketches," "Country Son," "Directions," and most of *In a Silent Way*, *Bitches Brew* has little or no written melody—a trend that ran through his music in the seventies.

With little in the way of chord changes and premeditated melodies, everything began to open up. His live sets became entire suites where most was left to will. By the mid-1960s, there was barely a break between songs. At the end of the sixties, no break. The fragmented melodies that indicated certain songs served as musical cues that separated one jam from another.[4] Right after *Brew*, there were no traditional forms at all. Most groups develop set lists for their performances. Entire tours are preconceived, allowing musicians to prepare for each night's performance. With short gaps and no premeditated forms, Miles's players had to be on their toes, waiting for any small musical cue. Once the gaps were eliminated, more challenges arose; neither the audience nor the players knew what was coming.

Beginning with his classic quintet, Davis's bands were praised for their telepathic communication. Miles even acknowledged this uncanny chemistry with the title of his 1965 album *E.S.P.* As all conventional forms of coherency were ditched, the band had only their wits to go on. It was Miles's ongoing fixation with doing away with patterns. "When you play, you carry them through till you think they're finished or until the rhythm dictates it's finished and then you do something else,"[5] stated Davis in 1967. Miles was pushing toward total spontaneity. Having a great group meant knowing the ins and outs of every band member and being able to react to any situation by instinct alone.

The Sound and the Set Up

Now that everything had loosened up, Miles and his gang had more freedom to explore tone color. Emphasizing good timbre was the vogue of the cool jazz style, and a defining characteristic of Davis's post-bebop sound. It was not about how many notes you could play, but how much you could extract out of each one. Modal jazz pushed it even further. Players could emphasize extended chord tones, or "color" tones as they were commonly referred to (such as the ninth chords that Miles loved), ultimately defining the modern jazz sound.

By the late sixties, Davis was expanding his bands, which broadened the tone color further. Even if he was using smaller groups, he would find ways to make them sound larger. "If I wrote a bass line, we could vary it so that it would have a sound a little bit larger than a five-piece group,"[6] said Davis. The more instruments, the more rich and exotic the texture becomes.

It is not uncommon for any group, whether jazz, classical, or anything else, to add instruments for a wider palette of tone color. Davis, however, had something else in mind. While he was able to further explore timbre with an enlarged band, he was also able to stretch out the rhythmic-harmonic counterpoint for improvisation creating a consistent blend of intertwining rhythms and harmonies being bounced off one musician to another.[7] Davis became fanatical with various instrumentation, and as the ensembles grew, there were even more possibilities for interaction between members. From 1968 to 1970, every recording session had a different setup. The following is a breakdown of some of Davis's groups during this period:

- *Miles in the Sky* (1968): trumpet, tenor sax, electric piano, guitar, bass, drums
- *In a Silent Way* (1969): trumpet, tenor sax, electric piano (2), organ, guitar, bass, drums
- *Bitches Brew* (1969): trumpet, soprano sax, bass clarinet, electric piano (3), guitar, electric bass, acoustic bass, drums (2), various percussion
- *Live-Evil* (1970): trumpet (electric and acoustic), soprano sax, electric piano (2), guitar, bass, drums (2), sitar, voice, various percussion
- *Big Fun* (1969/70): trumpet (electric and acoustic), soprano sax, flute, electric piano (2), acoustic bass, electric bass, guitar, electric sitar, drums (2), African percussion, Indian percussion, bass clarinet[8]

The 1960s saw the dominance of electricity in modern music. Rock pioneers such as the Beatles, the Rolling Stones, Carlos Santana, Eric Clapton, Jeff Beck, Jimmy Page, and most particularly, Jimi Hendrix brought an unparalleled popularity to the electric guitar. Davis's humble flirtations with this new wave started with the electric piano in 1967. Miles was looking for a fuller sound, similar to the orchestral voicings he heard while working with Gil Evans, and thought the Fender Rhodes could do a better job than an acoustic piano. The change did, however, catch his keyboardists off guard. Although pianos such as the Rhodes had been around for a while, the instrument did not take over the jazz circles until the seventies. Herbie Hancock's first encounter with it during a Davis session in 1967 was somewhat bewildering. "I walked in the studio and looked around for an acoustic piano, but didn't see one. So I asked him, 'What do you want me to play?' He says, [imitating Mile's trademark raspy whisper] 'Play that over there.'" After seeing the electric keyboard, which he had never touched before, Hancock asked himself, "He wants me to play that toy?" To his surprise, he found that the instrument had a rich, mellow sound and would continue to use it throughout the seventies with his own groups.[9]

Chick Corea had a similar encounter with the instrument the following year. He showed up for the *Filles de Kilimanjaro* session expecting to play acoustic piano for Miles, but was shocked to see the Rhodes in the room. "I didn't know what it was. I didn't quite know what to do with it. But he was hearing something he didn't describe to me too much. He just wanted me to play it."[10] Soon after *Bitches Brew*, it was no surprise that Miles was using electric pianos exclusively. But the idea did not sit well with Keith Jarrett; when he got the call to join Davis's band in 1970, he had his reservations. "I realized the instruments involved were electric. He realized that I would not normally be doing that, and that I did not do that."[11] Jarrett eventually humbled himself and accepted the invitation, being that it was Miles who asked (and it would be financially lucrative to do so).

Davis's "Water on the Pond" featured Hancock's debut on the (Wurlitzer) electric piano. The Fender Rhodes was introduced on "Stuff" the following year.[12] Not only did the electric keyboard add more color and depth, but it led to a new writing style that lurked on *Bitches Brew*. Hancock remembered, "When the individual band members became aware of the Rhodes, their writing began to change as a result, and in a subtle way, the rhythms began to change."[13] The electric piano created a heavier bottom, and got Miles thinking a little more about his rhythm section.

The Rhythm Section

I like a lot of rhythm…broken rhythm.[14]
—Miles Davis

With bridges, complex turnarounds, codas, and all of that gone, the rhythm section became the center of attention. Both Davis and Shorter began writing pieces that favored a slow-moving line suggesting a dreamy feel—much like what is heard on *In a Silent Way*, *Bitches Brew*, and following works. The themes are more fragmented and there is plenty of space to allow the background to come forward, creating a far more flexible and interactive role with the front line. Take Shorter's "Dolores," the tune the saxophonist thought "planted the seed." After only the first phrase of the theme is stated, there are eight measures of rest in which the rhythm section fills in. This continues throughout the theme.[15] Another head turner is Shorter's "Nefertiti," which contains no soloing with the exception of drummer Tony Williams. Throughout the nearly ten-minute opus, the melody is continuously played behind Williams's unyielding drum work.

Davis saw the relationship between the rhythm section and the front line in a very profound way. Since the beginning of jazz, the rhythm section's role was to support the front line and to accent any developments. Miles saw the roles reversed. The rhythm section would now have a stronger and sometimes leading role, creating the band sound he constantly sought out.

Flirting with Rock

It was not only the electric instruments that inspired Davis, but also the new rhythms that rock brought to modern music. Unlike jazz's syncopated swing feel, rock favors the heavy pounding downbeat, giving the music a strong, forward-feeling drive. In 1965 the rock beats began to manifest themselves in Davis's quintet with Ron Carter's "Eighty-One." The piece's rock-oriented drum pattern suggests a boogaloo influence (a Latin/R&B fusion popular in the sixties) with its eighth-note ride cymbal pattern. While not as forceful as the typical rock beat, the boogaloo was closer to something an R&B band might play. After "Eighty-One," Davis flirted more with direct rock beats, beginning with "Country Son" and most notably "Stuff" from 1968's *Miles in the Sky*. Williams's soul/Motown drum grooves on these tracks had that heavy bottom he first noticed with the Fender Rhodes, and forecast the beats Lenny White and Jack DeJohnette would play on *Bitches Brew*.

There is a difference between how Miles used the beats and how a rock or R&B band might. Rockers and R&B artists tend to use the beat as support for an overlying melody, with little rhythmic interplay between the two. The drummer is really a conveyer, whereas in Davis's bands the rhythm section is more interactive. The other instrumentalists respond to the drummer with various polyrhythms, creating a dense, complex sound, and a unique exchange, where any part can constitute a top. In most rock bands the rhythm section tends to be more static as a whole, leaving the vocalist or soloist on his own.

Besides the many elements of rock that Miles used—the new rhythms, electric instruments, the freshness, the style, the swagger—there were many more that he left alone. Along with the static rhythm section, Davis despised rock harmonies and form. In his music there were no three-minute singles (unless you count the excerpt singles from *Bitches Brew*), no verse/chorus/verse. Rock soloing, mostly premeditated and heavily reliant on blues/pentatonic scales over blues progressions or standard song forms, was also avoided. "I think rock music influenced jazz and the rhythm changed, but harmonically, not at all because jazz musicians tend to play harmony and rock musicians tend to be confused by it,"[16] said Davis producer Bob Belden. While both genres incorporated minimal tonal centers in their pieces, most rock songs utilized a nominal number of scales to solo with, whereas Davis was using all kinds of modes and harmonic experiments (Phrygian, Dorian, chromatic scale, blues scale, etc.).

Voodoo Child

It's that goddamned motherfucking "Machine Gun."[17]
—Miles Davis

There is no question that Jimi Hendrix was the rock god who made the biggest impact on Davis. He had enough talent and style for Miles to overlook the fact that he may have been sleeping with his wife. It turned out that the two had a lot in common and would eventually become good friends. They planned to work together in 1970, but Hendrix's death foiled those arrangements. Jimi did, however, get a chance to play with Davis sidemen John McLaughlin and Dave Holland in an all-night jam session at the Record Plant five months before *Bitches Brew*.[18] Hendrix's presence loomed over Davis's work during the late sixties and early seventies. Miles loved how Jimi blended the language and free-jamming traditions of the old blues men with the ultra-modern—the electric guitar with its cacophony of effects, feedback, and dissonance.

By the late sixties Hendrix's pedal-point blues style dominated Davis's music. 1968's "Mademoiselle Mabry" (which also paid homage to Miles's new wife) is the first piece that had Jimi's stamp. When paired together, "Mademoiselle Mabry" sounds like a cover of Hendrix's "The Wind Cries Mary." Along with the overall mood and tempo, Davis borrowed cadential and melodic figures from Hendrix's tune. On *Bitches Brew* the following year,

Jimi's bluesy, in-your-face bravado can be heard in Miles's echo-drenched intro during the title track, which plays like a tribute to Jimi's reinvention of the guitar. There's also the haunting, deep groove of Hendrix's "Voodoo Chile" imbedded in "Miles Runs the Voodoo Down."

It's no secret that Miles lifted the wah-wah pedal from Hendrix. The device produces a sound close to a trombone used with a plunger, creating a very slurred, bluesy tone similar to early Duke Ellington "jungle music" with Bubber Miley. When used by Hendrix, not only did it achieve this sound, it took the guitar to a whole new dimension. Blended with Jimi's trademark fuzz, tremolo, and other modern effects, the wah-wah allowed Jimi to go to the outer limits, producing a sound that went beyond what anyone thought a guitar could do. Davis's fascination with the wah-wah soon became an obsession. Regardless of any negativity he might receive from the press, he soon had himself, his guitarists, and even his keyboardists using the effect as well. "I got the wah-wah to make me sound more like a guitar. Then the critics started saying that they couldn't hear my tone anymore. I said, fuck them."[19] He started using up to three guitarists all stocked with wah-wahs and other special effects to approximate Jimi's sound (it would take more than one player to get even close to that sound). In the seventies, Miles sought out players like Pete Cosey and Reggie Lucas who had a very Hendrix-like approach. Their solos where not really solos in the conventional sense, but more like effects solos, saturated in distortion and feedback.

Jimi's rhythm section, particularly in his later bands featuring Buddy Miles, also had an immediate effect on the trumpeter. Most would argue that Buddy did not have nearly the technical chops of Jimi's former drummer Mitch Mitchell (Jimi thought so too, and eventually fired him), but there was more to Buddy than what met the eye. He was more of an in-the-pocket groove keeper, whose uncluttered style opened up the rhythm section even more, allowing that "band sound" to resonate.[20] Davis now had a hold on what he wanted.

In a Silent Way

Although *Bitches Brew* is the more celebrated work, *In a Silent Way* is generally regarded as Davis's first jazz-fusion record. Recorded six months before *Brew*, the album is an early attempt at collecting all of the techniques Miles had been experimenting with throughout the decade. Even though it reads like an accumulation, *In a Silent Way* sounds amazingly fresh. It showcases Davis's tinkerings with extended forms in composition, uber-modern production and post-production techniques, rock rhythms, polyrhythms, an expanded rhythm section, modal improvisation, and of course, electric instruments. While *Bitches Brew* illustrates a more expansive approach to these devices, *In a Silent Way* marks the beginning of a journey into a larger world.

At this time Miles was listening to former sideman Cannonball Adderley and his new band, featuring Austrian keyboardist Josef Zawinul. Zawinul joined Adderley's group in 1967 and began making music that was very R&B, soul, rock, and funk based. "Frankly speaking, we were heavily into this stuff with Cannonball's band years before Miles," stated Zawinul.[21] The sound he got out of the electric piano was an eye opener for Miles, who first heard Zawinul playing the Wurlitzer on Adderley's surprise hit "Mercy, Mercy, Mercy" and had to have that sound in his band. So he decided to snag him away from Cannonball's group.

It was not only Zawinul's chops on the electric keyboard, but also his esoteric writing style that grabbed Miles. When he first called Joe in for a studio session on November 27, 1968, Zawinul brought "Ascent" and two versions of "Directions," a piece Davis liked so much he later opened every gig with it. About three months later, Zawinul would bring his musicianship and an early rendition of the title track to the *In a Silent Way* session.

In a Silent Way was recorded in a day. Miles took his band to Columbia's Studio B in New York for a three-hour whirlwind on February 18, 1969. During and after the session, the project and its song titles took on some bizarre names. The first name that popped up as an album title was *On the Corner*, which Davis eventually used for an album in 1972. During the day, they were also using the title *Shhh/Peaceful*. Davis then started calling the album *Mornin' Fast Train from Memphis to Harlem* (or *Choo-Choo Train* for short). It was getting confusing. By June 26, 1969, Davis finally settled on using *In a Silent Way* as the title for his new album.[22]

The album is labeled as two tracks, "Shhh/Peaceful" and "In a Silent Way/It's About That Time," each around twenty minutes in length. Just as with *Brew*, the work seemed to get a new life during post-production, with Teo Macero and Davis rigorously cutting, pasting, and editing the jams.

"In a Silent Way" illuminates Davis's ruthless mindset and work ethic during this time. Zawinul had brought the tune loaded with chord changes and a more elaborate melody, but Miles was not feeling it and tore the piece apart. "I wanted to make the sound more like rock. In rehearsals, we had played it like Joe had written it, but it wasn't working for me because all the chords were cluttering it up."[23] Miles liked the overall feel of the piece but wanted something more like he had on *Kind of Blue*, where the sound was more open and atmospheric, so he trimmed down the melody and stripped the harmony down to one pedal point. Like "Flamenco Sketches," the piece was not penned by Davis but was arranged by him. "Today, many people consider Joe's tune a classic and the beginning of fusion," said Davis. "If I had left that tune the way Joe had it, I don't think it would have been praised the way it was after the album came out."[24] During the rehearsals, Miles did try an alternate version with Zawinul's chords intact and an underlying bossanova beat, and although this version is not without its charm, it clearly did not fit Miles's vision of this project. The take chosen for the record has the gentle, smooth melody playing serenely over one chord (E major) with no underlying beat. Similar to Zawinul's "Ascent" or Debussy's "Prelude to the Afternoon of a Faun" (Prélude à l'après-midi d'un faune), it is a tone poem that floats effortlessly. Joe described "In a Silent Way" as "impressions of [his] days as a shepherd boy in Austria."[25]

When Miles went back to the studio two days after *Silent Way* to work on some odds and ends, he picked up drummer Joe Chambers to record the funky B♭ jam "Ghetto Walk." Miles liked the piece so much that he had originally slated it for *In a Silent Way* along with "Shhh/Peaceful," but the track was eventually cut in favor of "In a Silent Way/It's About That Time." The group also tried another Zawinul tone poem, "Early Minor," at the February 20 session, but later decided to scrap it.

When all was said and done, Miles had something that simply sounded like nothing he had tried before. *In a Silent Way* seemed to close the chapter on many preexisting jazz styles that Davis had flirted with and gave resolution to all his experimentations. Things began moving very quickly. Everything was expanding and evaporating at the same time. Miles was on a roll.

The Lost Quintet[26]

Columbia missed out on the whole fucking thing.[27]
—Miles Davis

The winter of 1969 found Miles with almost a soft spot. With "In a Silent Way" he had just recorded some of his most tranquil work to date. "You have to remember that at that time it was the peak of brutality in America," said Carlos Santana. "The shootings of Martin Luther King and the Kennedys and Malcolm X, and the war in Vietnam, and the riots in the streets.

So this music was very soothing, very healing."[28] On the other hand, it was earth shattering. Miles was thinking out of the box and changing the course of music once again. From a man who without doubt lived for today, this music was so much in the now. Yet by the spring it was yesterday's news. Miles ripped apart the octet and decided to hit the road dead on with a brand new quintet featuring Shorter, Corea, Holland, and drummer Jack DeJohnette. As with *Brew*, he needed fresh blood, so he took guys (except Shorter) who had hardly, if ever, worked with him before.

For drums, he thought of Tony Williams first, but he was already putting together the Tony Williams Lifetime. So he decided to head-hunt DeJohnette from Charles Lloyd's band, much as he did Zawinul from Adderley's group earlier. "I remember Charles saying to Miles, 'Hey man, you're taking my band members,'" recalled DeJohnette regarding Davis's unscrupulous business etiquette. "And Miles said, 'Well you're supposed to when you're on top.' That's not the answer Charles expected."[29] Lloyd's band was a big hit, starting with a strong following in New York, followed by a platinum record, and leading to performances at big houses such as Bill Graham's Fillmore West years before Davis would. Miles was not a fan of the saxophonist, stating that he "never was any kind of player,"[30] but had a taste for some of his musical nuances, his light, floating style, his bandmates, and his success.

Miles initially spotted DeJohnette while the drummer was working with Jackie McLean, shortly before his stint with Lloyd. Miles and McLean obviously had the same taste in drummers, because DeJohnette would soon become one of three McLean alumnus beat keepers in Miles's bands (Tony Williams before him, and Lenny White after).[31] At first, he would only be used as a fill-in for Williams, but once left, DeJohnette would become a permanent fixture in Miles's group.

Miles cherished the deep groove DeJohnette brought to his group. As a drummer, he was able to keep the band in order—a valuable talent, considering the anarchic group play that would ensue. "Miles liked me because I knew how to anchor. I could be as abstract as I'd want to be, but I knew how to lay out a groove, and Miles loved to play with the grooves I laid down."[32] DeJohnette's style came from a heavy rock and soul source, but instead of maintaining a repetitive pattern, he would vary the snare and bass drum hits, giving Davis's backbone plenty of color.[33] It was the perfect engagement, but once DeJohnette decided to bail shortly after *Bitches Brew*, the bands would become too chaotic at times, leaving Miles less than thrilled. After three years of service, the drummer was looking for greener pastures and music even more out there. "One of the reasons I left is because the music was getting more restricted and more predictable. I left, because I wanted to keep doing freer, exploratory things."[34]

Davis spotted Holland in London shortly before recording *In a Silent Way*. The two had never met and Miles was already demanding that the twenty-two-year-old British bassist be in New York in two days for a gig. Miles immediately took to his authentic, no-bullshit, in-the-pocket playing.[35] "I arrived at the club, got ready to go on, and one by one people arrived, but nobody knew me of course," Holland recalled. "I was shy and not wanted to say anything unless I was spoken to. Well, I wasn't spoken to." Miles let Holland fend for himself, and as a result, he flourished in Miles's band. "You heard Dave originally in Ronnie Scott's club, didn't you?" Les Tompkins asked Miles in 1969. "He doesn't play like that now,"[36] was shot back to him.

Corea was also bemused by his own trial by fire. The young keyboardist, who was referred to Miles by Williams (the two were fellow Bostonians who gigged together from time to time), was ecstatic about the opportunity, but when he called up Miles about rehearsals, he found out there was not going to be any and would have to figure out the music while on stage.[37] Part of the reason Miles liked Corea for his group was his ability to find comfort in uncomfortable places, similar to situations boxers are put in. "You see Chick do funny kinds of things because the beat is all messed up," Davis explained. He might play an eleven note phrase—*that* isn't comfortable."[38] The band would do no studio recording as a quintet, only roadwork (hence the "Lost Quintet" label). Aside from the three-day break to record *Bitches Brew*, this new quintet worked together until Miles decided he had enough and expanded his working band at the beginning of 1970.

The live recordings from this time that exist (mostly bootlegs, with the majority of the official titles released long after Davis's death) give the listener a more defined view of Davis's transition from the late sixties to the early seventies. They also reveal what the band was doing without a net. *In a Silent Way* and *Bitches Brew* have so much post-production work that it is difficult to envision the band's power and spontaneity.

To say the Lost Quintet was a trailblazer is an understatement. "Then Miles got caught up in the craziness,"[39] said Santana, juxtaposing the calming effect of *In a Silent Way* with the brutality of the modern world suggested in this new group. He ripped apart his entire repertoire, including the *Bitches Brew* material, which was not even released yet. Along with the new material, he chose songs typical of his fifties sets ("'Round Midnight," "I Fall in Love Too Easily," "Milestones") and his mid-sixties quintet

("Masqualero," "Footprints"). This would be the last time he would ever play pieces from the fifties and mid-sixties. Miles was shedding skin. At one particular show on July 25, 1969, in Antibes, France, the band performed an hour-plus set that included "'Round Midnight," "Milestones," "Footprints," and "Miles Runs the Voodoo Down" without any breaks between songs. If the pieces originally had any chord changes, most were long gone. His new rendition of "'Round Midnight" is particularly sublime. After Davis states the melody with Corea accompanying him with subtle riffs and improvised chords, the band enters and runs through the solos in a naked A♭ vamp at a breakneck tempo. It is lean and mean, with Miles in top form.

At times the band dove into the deep end and took a great deal of chances. DeJohnette described the group as "a lot more avant-garde than people were ready to admit."[40] With limited or no chord changes, dense and abstract rhythms, and revamped musical forms, the songs became almost indistinguishable at times. "He let the world of changing harmonies go, started going into vamps and jungle music, primitive rhythms and abstracted melodies . . . every tune we played was in this incredible abstract form; the meat of the rendition was free improvisation,"[41] said Corea. As with modernist painters, Miles no longer tried to represent the visible world. Although all the elements of Davis's past permeate this band, they take on new meanings. In the fifties, "'Round Midnight" helped prove not only that Davis was one of the premier balladeers of the time, but that he could reconstruct something that was already deemed definitive. Somehow, he proved this once again fifteen years later. What "'Round Midnight" meant to Davis in the fifties is no longer relevant. It takes on another meaning after the Lost Quintet, when Miles never played it again.

Movement

Miles Davis in the past couple of years has totally abandoned the form his music took for a decade.[42]
—Anonymous, *This World*

Sometimes Miles worked at a snail's pace. He would search and search, starting at something like "Autumn Leaves" and would eventually get to *Bitches Brew* in what seemed like a flash.[43] Throughout the journey, Davis had a way of taking the past, present, and future with him. While the music sounded so fresh and on-the-scene, there's a yearning to reconnect to the roadhouse

In a Silent Way and *Filles de Kilimanjaro* Promo Ad. Courtesy of Sony Music Entertainment

music that was so much a part of his adolescent days in East St. Louis. Everything was built upon his past. He took his roots and added Jimi Hendrix, James Brown, Sly Stone, and everything else he had learned since.[44]

In the late sixties Davis was surrounded by cutting-edge, immensely popular African American artists who had made it on their own terms playing uncompromised black music. It was their language and it meant something, which inspired Miles, who despised the "Uncle Tom Nigger." He had much respect for influential and successful black performers such as Louis Armstrong, Dizzy Gillespie, and Sammy Davis Jr., but could not stomach the paths they took to achieve their stardom. "As much as I loved Dizzy and loved Armstrong, I always hated the way they used to laugh and grin for the audiences. I know *why* they did it—to make money and because they were entertainers as well as trumpet players."[45] But Miles would not tap dance for anybody. He was not an entertainer, but a brutally serious artist.[46] In the past, black artists had trouble achieving mass success and credibility based on talent alone. Davis felt that in order to become stars, many blacks had to adjust to the stereotypes given to them by white America. "When he was alive, Bird never got his due. Duke Ellington and Count Basie and Fletcher Henderson never got their due. Louis Armstrong had to start grinning like a motherfucker to finally get his."[47] By the end of the sixties, African Americans were starting to get their due.

It is difficult to imagine Miles Davis walking into Columbia Studios in August 1969 compromising who he was as an artist, because that was never what he did. It is even harder to picture him riding the coattails of the successful new black players around him, because even though he was inspired by them, his music still seemed miles ahead. "Yes he learned a lot from James Brown and Jimi Hendrix and Sly Stone and maybe Santana to a certain extent," remarked Santana. "But he would take all this music and take it to a level where we would have to listen to him."

The social conditions of the time, the creation of *In a Silent Way*, and the subsequent roadwork was a shot in the arm for the trumpeter. Although *Silent Way* would not be released until July 30 and he was still working small clubs that summer, nothing could dampen Miles's brashness. On June 18 Miles requested a rather generous advance from Columbia head honcho Clive Davis via Teo Macero: "I need $20,000. My albums are doing well. I am a star. I am going to do three more albums for him this year and I need money."[48] Although the label was always behind him, they were hesitant to share his optimism. "Wait until September to see accounts," was penciled on the memo. It is likely they wanted to see how the record would do and if Davis would get back in the studio as he proposed. Plus, it did not help that he had already overdrawn his Columbia account. But Miles's word was good. Putting in the work was no big deal because he was experiencing a jolt of creativity like no other time in his life. He also knew what he was doing was going to be big.

3. Preparation

I could put together the greatest rock and roll band you ever heard.[1]
—Miles Davis, 1969

On the Prowl

Bitches Brew was recorded over three days, August 19–21, 1969, at the old CBS Studio Building (Studio B) in New York City. The midtown studio, at 49 East 52nd Street, was a comfy place. Built in 1908, the building was once a guest house for the Vanderbilt family until it was sold to the Juilliard Musical Foundation to house its first graduate school. CBS bought it in 1939 and transformed it into a studio and a home for an array of diverse artists including Frank Sinatra, Paul McCartney, Bob Dylan, George Harrison, and Paul Simon.[2] The studio was alive, with bellowing acoustics, but also controllable with flexibility for a variety of setups. It was less interesting than CBS's 30th Street studio—a converted Armenian church with outstanding acoustics that Miles favored the previous decade—but quite serviceable. The oval shaped 52nd Street room was large (approximately 50' x 40' with forty-foot ceilings) and perfect for Davis's loose, spread-out ensemble.[3]

Once Teo Macero booked the place, Miles proceeded to acquire some new equipment. He put in an order for two Fender electric pianos, a set of Rogers drums, and some bells. The bells, which were never used, seemed like an odd request for the sessions, but Miles was thinking outside of the box and looking to shake things up. By August 8 none of the equipment had arrived, leading to a phone call from Miles to his producer. After getting yelled at, Macero got on top of it and sarcastically notified his secretary Corinne Chertok: "His majesty phoned me today to inquire about the new Fender electric piano and set of Rogers drums he ordered. Where are they and when are they arriving? Please advise. Many thanks."[4] By August 12 Macero was scrambling to meet Miles's demands and sent him a special-delivery letter detailing the studio dates and equipment. He wrote that he would do his best obtaining the electric pianos, but if he could not get his

August 12, 1969

Dear Miles,

I have the following studios booked for you for recording of your new album:

    TUESDAY, AUGUST 19: Studio E, 49 East 52nd Street, 2:30 PM to 5:30 PM

    WEDNESDAY, AUGUST 20: Studio B, 49 East 52nd Street, 10:AM to 1:PM

    THURSDAY, AUGUST 21: Studio B, 49 East 52nd Street, 10:AM to 1:PM

I will try my best to rent two Fender Pianos for these dates. If I can only obtain one, can you bring your Fender to the studio?

Please let me know if the above arrangements are OK for you and the other men. Many thanks.

                              Regards,

P.S. You also mentioned that you want BELLS. Let me know what else you will need for the sessions. Please call me before you leave New York.

cc: Mr. Jack Whittemore

Mr. Miles Davis
312 West 77th Street
New York, New York 10024

Via: Special Delivery

Courtesy of Sony Music Entertainment

hands on any, he asked if Miles could bring one of his down to the studio. Macero knew this would not sit well with Miles, so he had to resort to some bootlicking, informing Miles to call him with whatever else he needed and he would be on top of it. After all the commotion, the studio was finally set with all the equipment waiting.

Miles was insistent on getting the right musicians. He wanted fresh players, not ones who had been around his every move for a decade. These guys needed to be talented, intuitive, and young—their ears had to hear this generation. As a result, the final roster (with the exception of Wayne Shorter) was comprised of musicians who had limited to no experience working with him. He started by grabbing his Lost Quintet (Corea, Holland, Shorter, DeJohnette) touring band that he had formed in March, as well

```
Corinne Chertok
BOB CIOTTI
August 8, 1969


RE:  MILES DAVIS


His Majesty phoned me today to inquire about the new
Fender Electric Piano and Set of Rogers Drums he ordered.
Where are they and when are they arriving?

Please advise.  Many thanks.


cc
```

Courtesy of Sony Music Entertainment

as John McLaughlin and Joe Zawinul from the *In a Silent Way* session that past February. Harvey Brooks, a rock journeyman/staff producer at Columbia at the time, had hooked up with Davis via Macero at an earlier demo for Davis's wife Betty. The bassist, known for his work with Dylan and the Doors, knew nothing about jazz, and *Bitches Brew* would be his door into the jazz world.[5] As for the other new recruits, Bennie Maupin was a recommendation from DeJohnette. Davis hired Lenny White after hearing him play with Jackie McLean, along with some kind words from Tony Williams. Finally, Don Alias and Jumma Santos (a.k.a. Jim Riley) were summoned after Davis heard their work while on tour with Nina Simone. Miles would stand at the side of the stage each night gazing at Alias.[6] "Nina even said, 'I hope he doesn't steal my drummer!' And he did," said Alias. This made Simone furious. The vocalist called Davis and chewed him up so bad, band members in the other room could hear her.[7] But Alias walked away regardless. The opportunity to play with Miles was too hard to pass up.[8] The only musician Miles wanted that he could not get was the young keyboardist Keith Jarrett, who was scheduled to tour Europe for the next two to three months. So he settled on Larry Young, another *Silent Way* cohort, to complete his keyboard section.

The hidden gem in the batch was Maupin, whose bass clarinet haunts the entire album. Detroit-bred Bennie was first and foremost a saxophonist, living in New York's Lower East Side close to DeJohnette at the time. It was a thriving jazz scene in the sixties, with renovated buildings that many musicians called home. On East Third between Avenues B and C, Slugs, a small, smoky jazz club with crude brick walls and sawdust on the floor, was the neighborhood hang out where locals would get together to jam. The club, and its nestled section of Manhattan, soon became the jazz hot spot in the city. "There was music happening everywhere, and I just lived, breathed, and slept music in that period,"[9] said DeJohnette.

The kicker was the highly recognized McLean, a local and regular at the club. People would flock to hear him play, and eventually Slugs was opening its doors to players every night of the week. Soon, the musicians who played there were a "who's who" of the great jazz artists of the era. By the late sixties, Miles would periodically turn up as a talent scout, looking for new recruits (DeJohnette being one of his first targets).

Unfortunately, Slugs and the whole East Village scene dove into the gutter during New York's crime-stricken 1970s. As the neighborhood turned shady, the crowds turned away, and Slugs became a thing of the past. The incident that resonates the most when people think of Slugs is not its sixties heyday, but the slaying of trumpet great Lee Morgan, who was shot on stage by his common-law wife Helen More in 1972.

Maupin and DeJohnette gigged together regularly, so when DeJohnette was called to play on *Brew*, he pulled some strings to get Maupin in the band as well. When he arrived at Studio B that morning, you could say that Maupin had a few butterflies in his stomach, since this was not only his first time playing with Miles but also his first time meeting him in person. The real stinger was that Maupin would not be playing his primary instrument. Miles told Maupin to leave the sax at home and just bring the bass clarinet. This got Maupin scrambling. He was scared to death to show up at one of Miles's sessions rusty, and with no recording experience on the bass clarinet, but he had no choice.[10]

Forming the group was not easy. Getting DeJohnette was especially tough because his wife was expecting a baby at any moment. Despite his rule against bringing significant others on tours and their being present during sessions (which would eventually lead to some fretting among his musicians), Miles agreed to fly in and set up DeJohnette's wife Lydia just so he could have his man on drums. Davis also knew that he would get slammed in the black press for using white players (McLaughlin, Brooks, Holland, and Zawinul) but did so anyway. One of the first to notice was *Jet* magazine, who in a 1970 piece criticized Miles for cutting black players in favor of white. According to Zawinul, Miles's response was simple. "I'd hire one of them brothers if he can play as good as John McLaughlin. You give me one of them niggers and I'll hire him *and* McLaughlin."[11]

In the Dark

Don't play what's there. Play what's not there.[12]
—Miles Davis

Davis held the sessions from ten in the morning to one in the afternoon. Recording in the morning was rare for any musician, and resulted in some grumblings, but he needed his crew fresh and away from the daily distractions they could bring with them. Miles also did not want any disruptions from people hanging around the place, so he closed the studio off to writers, photographers, friends, and ladies.[13]

Despite the early start, Miles built an ambience similar to an all-night jam session. "What's amazing is the mood," recalled Corea. "If I didn't know, I'd say this went down at three in the morning."[14] Miles's loose, rise-and-shine sessions made some feel laid back and others on edge. For starters, the early hours were a bit troublesome for the shaky Shorter. "I was standing right next to Miles and Wayne everyday at that time. Wayne was having some serious issues with alcohol," remembered Maupin. "So even at nine-thirty, ten o'clock I could tell that this guy had been drinking all night because he smelt like a distillery." According to Maupin, Miles was infuriated, but showed some brotherly love to Shorter, telling him to fly straight and letting him go about his business.[15] Shorter responded with some intense playing over the next three days.

Maupin would get to the studio by 9:15, bass clarinet in hand, nervous, and find Miles, who made it a point to get there at least an hour early, setting everything up with Macero and the engineers.[16] As soon as all the players arrived, Davis placed everyone in a tight-knit semi-circle with himself in the middle. Then the tapes started rolling.

Bitches Brew is a study in spontaneity. Exhaustive rehearsing and recording time did not interest Miles since it would only limit his scope. Prior to each session, he would hold a brief meeting with some of the guys to go over some of his ideas. These meetings were hardly detailed. White, DeJohnette, Corea, and Holland got together only to go over the opening section of the title track. Zawinul and Davis met several times at the trumpeter's home to go over the pieces Zawinul had written for the record. He had ten pieces for the sessions, but Davis only wanted "Pharaoh's Dance," which he took the liberty to heavily revise once it was brought to the studio.[17]

As for Miles's own material, very little was premeditated. He had the main themes and forms worked out, and left the rest for the band to produce. Similar to *In a Silent Way*, *Bitches Brew* was a complete experiment. "He was using the studio as a practice ground to formulate new ideas and from that he would see what worked," said Corea.[18] Miles made this a habit going forward. "We did have rehearsals. They were very short and more of a discussion than practice in performance," explained drummer Billy Cobham during *Bitches Brew*'s outtake sessions in January 1970. "There was a theme and form in some way but the structure was not very rigid."[19] Although a few of the tunes were tried out on the road with the quintet that spring and summer, the songs would be revamped, making them almost unrecognizable from previous renditions.

After the initial meetings, these get-togethers mostly consisted of listening to snippets of each day's work. Miles never revealed full playbacks until the record was released the following year. Showing the band the work as they played would be the same as having everything prewritten. "The thing that I remember most about the recording was that they never let anyone listen to anything. We didn't do a take and say, 'OK, let's go back and listen to that,'" said Maupin. "If we did, it would be every bit of about ten seconds. Then he [Davis] would say, 'OK Teo, shut if off.'"[20] If a player didn't like something he played and wanted to try it again, that was unfortunate because it wasn't going to happen.

Even on tour Miles was not into rehearsing. He made it a point to pick guys who could deliver the goods right out of the gate and allow the unexpected to happen. When guitarist Pete Cosey first joined the band in 1973, he remembered a vague get-together with Davis that was comprised only of listening to the previous night's tapes. While the two went over the keys and various shifts in each piece, Cosey was surprised at the band's out-of-nowhere time changes. "I'd listen to a few bars and say, 'What key is that?' and he said, 'E-flat.' Cool, let's go to the next one. And we did that again and again—and this piece is in 5/4 time and I said, 'You move into five there.' And he looked at me and smiled."[21]

During the recording sessions, Davis did not say very much. He would occasionally complain about a headphone level, or yell at Macero, but not much else. At the start of each session, Miles took a little time with each person to go over small things like voicings, but nothing in great detail, making the experience a little frustrating at times.[22] DeJohnette remembered the ambiguous instructions of Davis being in the form of "Play something," and if it did not work, "Play something else."[23] With Maupin, he was even curter. "We had started something with the rhythm section and he looked at me and said, 'why don't you play? I can't think of everything.'"[24]

Davis's uncanny ability to predict the outcome of interaction between particular instrumentalists gave the music life, and it was up to the players to provide substance. He could not start coddling, or writing everyone's parts for them. "Miles as a composer did not invest a lot of time in writing for others as I could see, however he was 'the straw that stirred the drink' in all of the productions that I was involved in. He had very definite ideas of who should play, when this should happen and who to combine with whom,"[25] explained Cobham. If Miles had to explain too much, he had the wrong man for the job.

As a director, Miles was blunt. Similar to Thelonious Monk's recording style, Miles might show up with a few scraps of paper and little else. "If we used any notation it was often a college-type thing with a bass line and some chord movement, and maybe a melody related to that, but it was never something long or extended," recalled Holland.[26] Since very little of the music was notated, he would transmit what he wanted orally, physically, or musically to the players. This was something that he picked up from James Brown, who was famous for using hand signals, dance moves, and various vocal cues to initiate compositional changes. So the band watched Davis carefully and scrambled to figure everything out as it was happening.

Not everyone was comfortable with this way of working. Most of the musicians Davis picked had a fraction of his experience and were essentially left in the dark for three days. They were intimidated by Miles, his directorial style, and the surroundings of a major studio. Maupin's arriving early at the studio each morning was like trying to make a good impression on your new boss. He wanted to soak it all in for fear that it might easily be taken away from him. "Since I had the opportunity to go into Columbia studios for the first time, I said 'Well, who knows? This may be my last time. I want to see how the big guys do it.'"[27] White, who would also get there a good hour early to set up his drum kit, which included a bass drum custom-made from an oil drum, shared the same feelings as Maupin. "I thought every day was the last day."[28] Not only was this his first time recording with Miles, it was the first time he ever recorded with anybody. When asked if he was shaken up by the Prince of Darkness, he stated candidly, "Of course. I was *nineteen* years old. This is my idol. Some people don't get a chance to *meet* their idol. You meet him then you *play* with him? Please."[29] These young musicians were experiencing their dream job and were doing their best to fulfill it, but they soon learned that having Miles as a boss was more than what they bargained for. "The thing about Miles is that everyone loves him, and so everyone had this powerful motivation to make him happy," said

McLaughlin. "Everyone would be in a big circle in the studio, but nobody really knew what he was looking for."[30]

Pointing the Finger

Most of the pieces on *Bitches Brew* are not brief. "Pharoah's Dance" (20:04) and the title track (26:58) alone take up the first two sides. Most of these tracks, however, were recorded in small clumps and assembled later during post-production. Davis would have a certain idea of what he wanted to hear and where he wanted each player within each piece. Then he would start and stop the jams as he saw fit, spontaneously dictating where he wanted each person to play simply by pointing at them. According to Holland, Davis would only provide "sketches of ideas, and we'd play each for ten minutes or so, and then we'd sort of stop, come to an ending of sorts."[31] "We went in and we started playing. He would stop; he would let us play for a while," said White. "Wayne [Shorter] would play then he'd stop then he'd point to John McLaughlin and we'd start up again and John would play. Then we'd stop and he pointed to Bennie Maupin and Bennie would play."[32] This style of writing and physical direction persisted with Miles throughout the early seventies. For the 1972 *On the Corner* sessions, percussionist Badal Roy recalled a similar experience: "I remember one groove I started. Herbie Hancock says, 'oh yeah.' Boom. Miles pointed at me. Herbie started, McLaughlin, the whole band started . . . I still remember we were playing for an *hour*."[33] Without a formal soloing order, the players had to listen very carefully to one another because they had to keep a steady flow even if they didn't know who they would be soloing after. The way Miles was recording, there was no room for clunkers.

Like James Brown, with his hollers and screeches, Miles also had an arsenal of musical cues to dictate certain shifts both on the record and on subsequent tours. While playing in Davis's touring bands after *Bitches Brew*, Michael Henderson mentioned, "Miles would cue everything from the trumpet tempo-wise, slow it down, this is the end, here we come in. If he wanted to stop it or change the melody, all he had to do was give me a cue, and I'd know where to go."[34] Similar to the physical cues, very little was premeditated or explained to the players ahead of time, so the band needed to use their instincts in order to determine what the signals were.

Davis's minimalist style of direction allowed a collective creative process which would ultimately construct the compositions. For Davis, the process *is* the composition. As the title suggests, *Bitches Brew* was an accumulation of musical ideas "brewed" together by the participating musicians, or the "bitches." Therefore, the pieces would not exist without the input from the players themselves. "You get a musician and tell them what to do. And what you tell them to do has to be what they *want* to do," explained Davis. "I mean, you can't tell them something they don't want to do. It won't come out."[35]

Davis began tinkering with this writing style in his mid-sixties quintet. Emphasis was no longer placed on playing the pieces note for note but in expanding upon them and creating new compositions out of them using all the performers at that one moment. "There was that tendency to think that the whole evening was the composition," said Shorter. "As far as everybody in the group thinking that way, it was up to each individual to be on his own to help create images and illusions."[36] When *Bitches Brew* pieces were performed live, it was the same thing. Certain melodies and chord progressions were duplicated, but they were only used as catalysts for reinterpretation. *Bitches Brew* was never intended to be written down. Davis stated, "I knew that what I wanted would come out of a process and not some prearranged shit."[37]

For *Bitches Brew*, Davis served as the conceptualist for the record. He was there to guide the direction of the music (hence the tag "Directions in Music by Miles Davis" on the top of the album cover) and to oversee its development, but it was up to every musician to give the music life. "It means I tell everybody what to do," said Davis about the new tag on his album covers. "If I don't tell 'em, I'll ask 'em. It's my date, y'understand? And I've got to say yes and no. Been doing it for years, and I got tired of seeing 'Produced by this person or that person.'"[38] Yes, Miles needed everyone's input for this record to happen, but he made it clear that this was his recording date and his idea. Miles, however, would find some trouble with this point of view a little later down the road.

Instrumentation

A common denominator of all uncommon musicians.
—*Bitches Brew* promo ad

Play your thing. Play like a nigger.[39]
—Miles Davis to Badal Roy

No one would argue how dense and rhythm-oriented *Bitches Brew* sounds. For the August 19 and 21 sessions, Davis wanted two bassists (Brooks and

Holland), two drummers (White and DeJohnette), and two additional percussionists (Alias and Santos). The August 20 session was the same except with Alias on drums and White omitted.[40] He used two keyboardists (Zawinul and Corea) for all the sessions except "Spanish Key," where he used three (Larry Young is added). This was the first time that Davis used additional rhythm players as well as two rhythm sections playing simultaneously, and he stuck with a similar formula for the next five years. Davis had used this double ensemble to create a certain band dynamic: one static set and one free set. If the piece required some sense of a basic pulse, there would always be at least a bassist and percussionist to provide it. This would allow the group great freedom to create polyrhythms and various textures over the underlying beat. "What I had then was the freedom, because Al [Foster] kept the time, where the 'one' was, and I was able to be Tony Williams. I could switch up time signatures and play through it,"[41] recalled James Mtume while working in Davis's bands following *Bitches Brew*. The more instruments there were, the greater the rhythmic and tonal complexity.

Miles would also choose musicians from diverse backgrounds with extensive experience in odd rhythms and textures. For example, DeJohnette was great for setting up jazzy, syncopated rhythms while White could command heavy rock beats. On tour after *Brew*, Mtume felt very much at home with all this, and when Badal Roy joined in on 1972's *On the Corner*, it only sweetened the deal. The two were able to respond to one another's odd time signatures and cross-cultural styles without a hitch.[42] Although the interplay between Mtume and Roy clicked, it took some time for Roy to adapt to Miles's musical style and in-your-face persona. Even though Roy was new to this country and knew nothing about jazz, Miles was not about to start tutoring him. Says Roy: "He didn't say what groove to play. He said, 'Play your thing. Play like a nigger.'"[43]

Bitches Brew was the only time Miles used two bassists during this period. In the following tours, having only one bassist led to problems, so Miles had to remediate the situation by picking up Michael Henderson. According to Henderson, the bassists Davis used before him (Holland, Ron Carter) that paired with keyboardist Keith Jarrett would typically emulate his directions even if Jarrett decided to go free. This would leave a gap in the rhythm section, break the groove, and make a complete mess. When Henderson entered the band, he was young, inexperienced, and unsure how to handle Jarrett. Miles made it clear to him: "Just don't follow that muthafuckah!"[44] The bassist soon realized that his job was to establish the groove and keep a solid foundation for the group so things would not fly off the handle when the rest of the band decided to go for broke.

State of Confusion

After the *Bitches Brew* sessions, the musicians had mixed feelings about what they had just recorded. It just seemed like incoherent chunks of recorded rehearsals. Some players, such as Holland, did not even know what was captured on tape. "It was like, tape was just running, and half the time I didn't know if we were recording or not."[45] It was only after the album was released that the musicians got to hear what they played and how everything came together. But when they finally listened to it, most of them could not even recognize their own playing. "After each session, Miles invited me to his house to listen to what we recorded. When the record came out, it didn't sound like anything that I heard at Miles's place,"[46] recalled White. Zawinul had a similar experience with the playback. "I really didn't like the sessions at the time. But a short while later I was at the CBS offices and a secretary was playing this incredible music. So I asked her, 'Who the hell is this?' And she replied, 'It's that *Bitches Brew* thing.' I thought, damn, that's great."[47] "I didn't hear any of the music until the recording was released," noted Maupin. While driving through San Francisco, he heard the record for the first time on the radio. "I was saying, 'What is that? It sounds familiar, but I don't know what that is.' I had no idea that the music sounded so beautiful. I couldn't tell anything during the recording sessions."[48] Unbeknownst to the band at the time, something extraordinary happened over those three days. Between the maverick instrumentation, working conditions, musical stylings, and the magnitude of Miles Davis lurking over everything, it was a lot to take in—and Miles was only getting started.

4. Music

A novel by Miles Davis.
—*Bitches Brew* promo ad

Call It Anything

I'd like to say one thing about Miles Davis. One time he said to me, "Hey Wayne, do you get tired of playing music that sounds like music?"[1]
—Wayne Shorter

Call It Anything was one of the working titles used for *Bitches Brew*. It was never really a serious contender, just something Miles mouthed off probably when preoccupied or aggravated. In some way, though, it speaks volumes. What was recorded during those three days in August is difficult to identify or categorize. It is a study in improvisation by a group of jazz artists but does not have the trademark swing. There are electric instruments and rock beats, but it lacks the comfort commonly heard in rock—it is not "I Want to Hold Your Hand." It is soulful but not exactly polished like the great Motown singles. It is funky like Sly Stone or James Brown but way too abstract to be closely linked to those players.

Davis never really put much care into any of his album or song titles. Even *Birth of the Cool*—a title so associated with his persona and genre-defining playing—was penned by someone else. "As for that *Birth of the Cool* shit, I don't understand how they came to call it that. Someone just dropped that label on me."[2] Aside from *Brew*, the only time he had any interest in album covers was when he wanted to show off one of his ladies. Otherwise, titles and labels were a complete waste of time. Part of his disinterest was the old "let the music speak for itself," but the reason was more that Davis's fixation with his work superseded the time and effort to come up with such trivial things. He despised distractions. He had patience for nothing, not his musicians or even his producer. "I had told Teo to just let the tapes run and get everything we played and not to be coming in interrupting, asking questions," said Davis when describing the *Bitches Brew* sessions. "Just stay in the booth and worry about getting down the sound."[3] A technical glitch or a break in concentration for something like a title suggestion was intolerable.

Like how the band felt after the sessions, it is difficult not only to identify or categorize but to figure out just what happened over those three days. As his crew eventually discovered, it takes time to sink in. It is simply a matter of listening. When all was said and done, Davis accomplished a rare feat: he distilled all of his musical and personal attributes and changed the course of music once again.

A Living Composition

Miles's obsession with James Brown and the rhythm section were now in full swing. In Brown's bands, there are a lot of interconnecting rhythmic parts or "Africanisms," such as the complex layering in 1969's "The Funky Drummer," where each musician is playing a separate rhythmic line.[4] Miles figured that he could outdo Mr. Dynamite and create an even denser sound if he kept enlarging his bands, hence the double rhythm section.

Davis's new direction during *Bitches Brew* and for what followed was that everything was part of a whole. Similar to Brown's bands, there were no huge solos. It did not matter when anyone started or stopped. There was no buildup to something or finding the perfect three-minute solo. It was about being in on the action.[5] "Sometimes Miles said, 'This is not working. That's not it. Let's try something else.' But it was never because somebody had made a mistake or something. Miles was hearing the collective," Jack DeJohnette explained.[6] It was about finding the essence of things and not reworking tiny imperfections. Repeated takes would only spoil the spontaneity—the spirit would be lost.

Finding something usually requires looking in the most obvious spots. In order to get everything to work on such a large-scale project, Davis knew that he needed simplicity from each player and not a display of everyone's technical chops. If not, everything could easily fall apart. Davis ran into this problem during "Miles Runs the Voodoo Down." He became frustrated with Lenny White's over-stylized playing and hastily cut him from the piece:

I'll give you a true story. Of all the guys that were on that session, I probably played more funk music than anybody else. "Miles Runs the Voodoo Down" was the only track I didn't play drums on. The reason why I didn't play drums on it was because Miles asked for a beat and Jack [DeJohnette] couldn't come up with one. I was trying to play some real slick stuff and Don Alias said 'I got this beat Miles,' this is a real simple beat. I outthought myself. I thought that Miles wanted to hear some real slick stuff or whatever. So I didn't do what I was supposed to do. I learned a great lesson from that.[7]

By being too slick, White alienated himself from the rest of the band and as a result, nothing could get going. Each musician was just as important as the other and had the freedom to explore many possibilities that could contribute to the composition itself. In a sense, everyone was a co-composer.

Bitches Brew and Improvising: A How-to

There was a team spirit not only in the creation of the *Bitches Brew* pieces but in the soloing as well. Davis had a desire to reengage with the improvising styles that he grew up with such as New Orleans–style jazz, and especially the blues. Just as in early Louis Armstrong records, there is an overall band sense and kinship that pours out. Miles was there to galvanize the sound and give it validity.[8] As powerful a player Davis was, he was not there to outplay his musicians but to direct and shape the flow of sound.

Miles was still big on modes and minimalism. With the exception of "Sanctuary," every piece on the record has very little harmonic movement, allowing all the instruments to breathe. The following list is a breakdown of the keys used on *Bitches Brew*:

- "Pharaoh's Dance": E
- "Bitches Brew": C
- "Spanish Key": D, E, and G
- "John McLaughlin": C
- "Miles Runs the Voodoo Down": F

One criticism that always followed *Bitches Brew* is the lack of linear development within the solos. Certain critics felt that, with its straight rock rhythms and sparse number of chords, the music becomes dull, too open-ended, and loses structure. Jazz enthusiasts admire the complexity in sound that dense chord progressions offer, where a soloist would have to constantly weave through changing harmonies. In his lukewarm appraisal of *Bitches Brew,* John Litweiler argued that rock beats and modes that emphasize color and texture over harmonic structure diminish the depth of improvisation. "The gravitational pull of the modern rock beat upon soloists' accenting discourages anything but the simplest kinds of linear development."[9] In other words, without chord changes and highly stylized jazz rhythms, the decorative elements such as mood and color become the highest common denominator. The scrutiny was something Miles could never shake throughout the rest of his career. In his scathing review of Davis's Avery Fisher performance in 1988, Jon Pareles of the *New York Times* wrote, "Mr. Davis plays trumpet phrases that jab, interrupt, punctuate or, very rarely, sketch a narrative; he'll also engage his band members in dialogues. . . . song forms and linear development have submerged in roiling, open-ended funk."[10]

Much as with a symphony, atmosphere provides another texture to the composition. In order to get this, Davis's (and for that matter, the entire band's) approach to improvisation changed in order to *expand* the development. Using various scales over a centralized tone creates thick harmonic layers when all the instrumentalists are playing simultaneously. Davis ran with this idea all throughout the seventies. "Everybody's got a tonal center and all kinds of things were happening. Major, pentatonic, all kinds of things were happening," explained Azar Lawrence, while playing in Miles's band in 1974. "You were changing different soundscapes, different textures. An augmented or whole tone scale provides a certain texture, a diminished a certain texture, so everybody is working in different textures."[11]

Walking on Thin Ice

Using rock beats raised some eyebrows not only because of its association with pop music but also because it changed the group's interaction with one another. Davis's ultra-dense rhythm section had a colossal effect on what each soloist would attempt. A large number of percussionists, bassists, keyboards, and guitars weaving all sorts of complex polyrhythms forces the soloist out of his box. Therefore, the solos project an interesting *rhythmic* development. Within the group, a constant interaction between the soloist and rhythm section creates a multifaceted tapestry of rhythms. "I believe that Miles drew energy and ideas from the rhythm section and the other instrumentalists in the band," remarked Billy Cobham while working in a post-*Brew* session in January 1970.[12] "He knew how to listen, digest, and react to what he heard from others in performance." Lawrence also picked up on this during his tenure:

> Well, it was real responsive and a lot of suggestions were going on in terms of the keyboard and what the guitars were doing. There was Reggie Lucas and Pete Cosey, and Miles was playing the organ. Therefore, between the two guitars the different textures that were suggested, they would be jumped upon, you would act on it as a lead instrument one way or another because we were all working with a tonal center. That's the pivot point. Then all the colors are pivoting around it. Which one becomes embellished upon depends upon which one the lead instruments decide to define. So all kinds of textures where going on underneath. If the lead instrument picks one course of action of the suggested ones, then that's the one that you're gonna hear. So they're suggesting and pronouncing various different colors at all times.[13]

This is not to say that Davis's solos were only influenced by the rhythm section. As Cobham mentioned, he knew *how* to feed off the rhythm section. It was a constant give and take, so getting cohesiveness was like walking on thin ice. Playing something out of character (much like White's botching) could spell disaster. A musician had to contribute, expect the unexpected, and roll with the punches if necessary.

And it was not always that Davis gave out the musical cues. He encouraged his players to step up to the plate and set a course for the group. Again, he was not looking to do everything for everybody. "The piano or guitar while I'm soloing might suggest a direction that we decided to go on and it may not stick. So I might decide a direction and it will go that way," noted Lawrence. "I might decide a direction and we stay where we were. It's real sensitive and it's real responsive. Lead/follow is all happening at once."[14] Michael Henderson shared the same experience shortly after *Brew*:

> A lot of things he didn't cue. We just went our own with it. I just took the liberties and went on and jumped into stuff, and then he'd always manage to work with it. Having that band and having everyone play off of each other, a lot of the times he'd cue, play off the drums, off of Mtume, off of Reggie [Lucas]. Sometimes, we'd get a cue from one another that had nothing to do with the head that Miles was playing. And then he'd say, "Ah shit!"—you'd take him to another place. Oh yeah, he loved that.[15]

Miles liked what he created. When he was not distracted by petty things such as a player's lack of self-confidence, things would run smoothly and he could coast with his crew. When things went off the handle he had to take charge, too. Of course, he had his own way of doing things—sometimes domesticated, sometimes inscrutable, other times tyrannical. After all, he was the Prince of Darkness.

Day One

"Bitches Brew"

Ok, we're rolling...[16]
—Teo Macero, August, 19, 1969

Throughout the sessions, Miles was in great spirits. Especially on the first day, he is often heard laughing and speaking in a very relaxed, friendly tone with his crew. "He was making everybody comfortable, which I thought was really incredible," said Bennie Maupin. "I thought 'Here's this guy who is supposed to be so mean and so hard to get along with and he's funnier than anybody in the studio.'"[17] Even his usual barking at Macero was at a minimum. With the exception of a few technical glitches that ruffled his feathers, the trumpeter was mostly lighthearted with his producer. Frequently, Miles is overheard saying, "Hey Teo! Can we hear that?" in an enthusiastic voice. When setting up his headphones, he appears to be a bit flustered by what he's hearing (or not hearing). "Hey Teo! How can I hear this, man [plays trumpet]? Will I be able to hear that outta here?" A smart-alecky Macero responds, "You should be." Reflecting the almost condescending tone, Miles shouts back, "Put it *way* up." In the background, Miles is heard laughing and joking with his musicians about the exchange. "Teo tries to be free..."

While rehearsing the title track, which only summed up to a bunch of tiny pieces and false starts, Miles says, "Hey Teo, keep all this. We'll tie it together somehow." Noticing the absurdity of the request, Macero's chuckles are heard in the control room. Even at his most playful, Miles could still be irrational. Some takes later, Miles struggles with the band on a section that would later become "John McLaughlin." "Sounds weird as weird" is mumbled by Davis along with a giggle or two from the band. Yet, he wanted to make the best of what they had and toss the scraps to Macero to gnaw on. "Teo, part of that's nice. Part of it isn't," is thrown at the fumbling producer.

Courtesy of Sony Music Entertainment

With his players Davis showed his human side, but that is not to say he was holding everyone's hands. Although courteous, his instructions were vague, bare bones, and at times snippy. When rehearsals of "Bitches Brew" got under way, Miles is overheard instructing White about what he wants from him. "Lenny, I want you to play some rolls that sound like raaaaaaah." He also tries to explain to Chick Corea what the keyboard should be doing.

Much as in his first gig with Miles, Corea was left to fend for himself. "Hey Chick, listen to him [Zawinul]. See how he plays it." Later he explains, "The chorus line is long notes. You know what I mean? Then you do your thing. Come on," as Miles immediately counts the band back in. When introducing what would become "John McLaughlin," the instructions to Harvey Brooks were to the barren tone of "Harvey, just come in." Then a false start from John McLaughlin seemed to rattle Miles. "Come on, John" was irritably mouthed by the leader. This was day one, track one. It was going to be a long day.

Miles on "Bitches Brew"

Every piece on *Bitches Brew* has various mood changes. There are times when the music is mystic, ambient, and esoteric. Other times, it is shadowy, hostile, and bloodthirsty, making it quite the bipolar performance. Nothing stands in one place for very long, making these lengthy pieces feel rather brisk. This holds true for the title track, where Miles and his band explored a variety scales, rhythms, dynamics, and temperaments, ultimately creating a sullen atmosphere. The opening free-time vamp shows the Prince of Darkness at his darkest. In the introduction, he takes advantage of the lack of beat and harmony with his echo-infused, twisted statement. It makes "Taps" sound cheery. After the intro, the bass line awakens followed by

Bitches Brew (introduction)

Miles Davis

"Bitches Brew" (introduction) © 1969 JAZZ HORN MUSIC; this arrangement © 2013 JAZZ HORN MUSIC

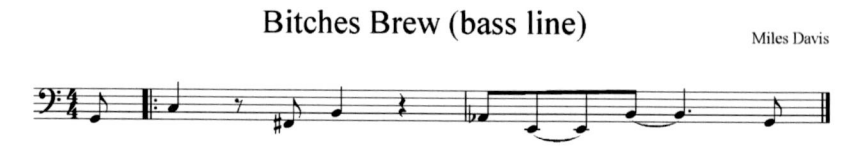

Bitches Brew (bass line)

Miles Davis

"Bitches Brew" (bass line) © 1969 JAZZ HORN MUSIC; this arrangement © 2013 JAZZ HORN MUSIC

Miles's echo-laden finger snaps. Bubbling to the surface is Maupin, whose bass clarinet paints the accents and sets up Miles's first solo before drifting out. "It covers such a broad spectrum in terms of sound and I think that's why Miles wanted me to play so that we could have that perfect contrast that we have on so many of those things," noted Maupin when describing his newly reacquainted instrument. "Because a lot of what I play is like mirror images of things that he played and some just, you know, totally directly away from anything remotely that he played."[18] Without bass clarinet charts or any other formal instructions, Maupin had free roam on the project and starting feeling pretty comfortable. "It was so experimental I just figured I don't have to concentrate on anything other than creating some sounds and listen to what's going on around me and bounce off of that. And then I understood that was what he wanted—he wanted that color."[19]

Davis approached "Bitches Brew" in two distinct ways. His first solo and the beginning chunk of his second are focused on a series of prowling, downward patterns, chromatic passages (he is primarily using a twelve-tone scale), and long tones against an upbeat, well-oiled rhythm section. Even as the music intensifies, his lines remain defiant. Miles sticks with a motif that feeds from the despairing opening section, adding another layer to what the rhythm section is playing and a perfect counterpart to McLaughlin's punchy, jagged solo. After he brings the band to the edge with his climactic finish, the groove simmers back. McLaughlin is still jabbing along as he and the keyboards take center stage in a kind of collective, triple solo. Things come to a halt around seven and a half minutes in as Miles is heard saying, "Keep it like that, keep it tight" (probably to the chagrin of a wincing Macero, for having this caught on the master). Miles calls, "John" (another whoops) as McLaughlin resumes play. Perhaps taken off guard, McLaughlin's solo is brief, featuring a few underwhelming licks before returning to his comfort zone in the rhythm section as Miles steps up again.

Davis's second solo breaks into a whole new direction. This time, Miles storms in with pounding blows that coincide with the dense, stabbing comping of the keyboards. It is hard to say who initiates this mood change because it all happens simultaneously (the keyboard riff happens about one second before Davis). This is more of a collective experience, where the whole band kinetically feels the shift in direction. Everything reaches the boiling point until Miles cools it down and the band kicks back to a groove. Wayne Shorter delivers a brief but menacing solo reminiscent of Davis's first, working longer phrases and getting the most murk you can get out of a soprano sax. Corea's solo is filled with quick flurries of notes and a lot of

Bitches Brew (Miles Davis 1st solo)

Miles Davis

"Bitches Brew" (Miles Davis 1st solo, p. 1) © 1969 JAZZ HORN MUSIC; this arrangement © 2013 JAZZ HORN MUSIC

"Bitches Brew" (Miles Davis 1st solo, p. 2) © 1969 JAZZ HORN MUSIC; this arrangement © 2013 JAZZ HORN MUSIC

empty space—a solo patented for the group sound. Corea too uses a lot of chromaticism, but also relies on a three-triad grouping that Davis suggested (which can also be heard in the piece's introduction). "I don't remember what tune it was, but Miles came up in back of me, he put his arms around me on the piano, and showed me three triads. He played an E major triad, an A♭ major triad, and a C major triad,"[20] recalled Corea. "That was about the closest it ever came to him saying specific notes."[21] A reprise of part one occurs, followed by a jazzy, funky solo by Dave Holland. Miles starts wrapping things up around the twenty-minute mark with an overcast, surreal solo that creates a trancelike quality on the rhythm section. Part one rears its head one last time, capping the twenty-seven-minute opus.

"John McLaughlin"

Like most of the other tracks on the album, "Bitches Brew" was recorded in sections that would later be assembled to form the finished work. It was initially slated as five parts, but only two were used: the introduction, or what Bob Belden described as the "rubato" section using the C pedal point, and the "groove" section that makes up the remainder of the piece. Part five was never recorded, and parts three and four were put together to form "John McLaughlin."[22]

Needless to say, McLaughlin was ecstatic once he found out the piece was named after him. Similar to Holland, McLaughlin was a British import called in by Tony Williams to join his new group, the Tony Williams Lifetime, in early 1969. Little did he know that upon arriving in New York, he would be recording *In a Silent Way* with Miles two days later.

Williams was wrapping up his tenure with Miles at Harlem's Club Baron and invited McLaughlin to the gig the night he arrived in town. Miles already knew that Williams brought McLaughlin into his new group and scoped out the guitarist that night at the club. "For some reason, he recognized me when he came in the door of the club. He looked amazing—as always—wearing a long black cloak, and he walked right up to me and brushed my shoulder with his, saying 'John' in that whispery voice of his . . . That was it," recalled McLaughlin. The next day McLaughlin found himself hanging out at Miles's house and was told to bring his guitar down to the studio the following day.[23] It was not all that easy for the young guitarist being that this was Miles Davis, an idol of his. "He told me he had been listening to me for a long time and that he might be nervous going into the studio with one of his idols," explained Davis. "So I told him, 'just relax and play like you did up at Count Basie's[24] and everything will be all right.'"[25]

Things had been rough for McLaughlin on his first day of work during *In a Silent Way*. Between the nervousness of being thrown into Miles's band and not knowing what to play (of course, he was not given any guitar charts), McLaughlin was a mess. His early bumbling made a first impression on Miles he wished he never made. "After running through the title track from Zawinul's 'In a Silent Way,' Miles wasn't happy with the result and turned to me and said 'Play it alone on the guitar,'" remembered McLaughlin. As he scrambled to figure out what to do, he managed to anger Miles. "Since I had only a piano score I asked him if he wanted the left and right hand together. He said yes, and I said it'll take me a minute to put it together on guitar. He said 'Is that a fact!' . . . Sweat was already running down my back and got worse after that." Miles decided to take it easy on McLaughlin and gave him some friendly, but vague advice instead of a scolding. He told him, "Play it like you don't know how to play the guitar." So McLaughlin tossed the piano music aside and started playing a simple E chord—the very same chord that opens the title track on the record. "On the playback Miles was delighted. I was dumbfounded," said McLaughlin. "It sounded so beautiful, and that

"John McLaughlin" (theme)

Miles Davis

"John McLaughlin" (theme) © 1969 JAZZ HORN MUSIC; this arrangement © 2013 JAZZ HORN MUSIC

John Mclaughlin (solo excerpt)

Miles Davis

"John McLaughlin" (solo excerpt) © 1969 JAZZ HORN MUSIC; this arrangement © 2013 JAZZ HORN MUSIC

was one of Miles's talents—to be able to pull music out of his musicians that they didn't even know was inside them."[26]

Along with *In a Silent Way* and *Bitches Brew*, the two did quite a bit of roadwork and studio dabbling over the next year. By 1970, at the peak of their professional relationship, Miles gave McLaughlin one last piece of advice. "I remember being on a gig with Miles at Lennie's on the Turnpike outside of Boston in 1970," recalled McLaughlin. "It was just me and Miles in the band room and all of a sudden he turns around and says to me, 'John, it's time you form your own band.' Right out of the blue!" Miles had a fatherly love that deeply resonated with these youngsters. "It was wonderful because this guy had more faith in me than I had in myself," explained McLaughlin. "I didn't think I was ready at the time. But I tell you, when somebody like Miles says something like that to you, it really hits you. And it hit me really deep."[27]

"John McLaughlin" is based on a short, funky, old school R&B-type riff that is played spontaneously throughout by the bass and keyboard. It was best to leave it as a separate track since the mood is not nearly as sinister as "Bitches Brew." The barren harmonic and melodic setup allows the

John McLaughlin (Miles Davis solo)

Miles Davis

"John McLaughlin" (Miles Davis solo) © 1969 JAZZ HORN MUSIC; this arrangement © 2013 JAZZ HORN MUSIC

soloist carte blanche to express different ideas. During the rehearsals, Holland explained some of the improvising possibilities to McLaughlin and the keyboardists. It was pretty much a free-for-all. "There's like a G♭ in there as well, you can put an E triad on top of the C minor chord . . . you can put A♭s and B's . . . shit like that." When he lays down the solo, McLaughlin sticks with the C minor blues scale along with some off-color tones to spice it up. The A♭s (G#) and B's indicate an incomplete E triad being used, giving the solo an almost Indian feel when coincided with the C minor blues scale.

With the exception of McLaughlin's "traditional" solo, all other improvising is done collectively. The ever-present Maupin is heard lurking in the corners along with great riffing-off-the-theme interplay from the bass and keyboards. The real star is the "Nefertiti"-like playing from the percussion section. The drums are more in the forefront on the mix, making it a tour-de-force for the beat keepers.

"John McLaughlin" is the only track without Davis and Shorter playing. The two did record solos but they were left on the cutting-room floor. Davis approached the piece much more melodically than McLaughlin, sticking with the C minor and chromatic scales more exclusively, giving the piece a moody, bluesy sound until Davis delivers a series of long fatal blows at the conclusion. As the piece fades out, Miles starts complaining about the headphones again. "Hey Teo, I can't hear nothing over here, man." Without being able to hear himself, it is likely that he was not satisfied with what he played and cut his performance out of the final mix.

"Sanctuary"

Shorter's "Sanctuary," named after a novella by Edith Wharton (Shorter was an avid reader and fan of the author), was an odd choice for the session because it had already been recorded by Davis's band a year and a half before. Its first incarnation came at a session featuring the classic quintet plus a young George Benson on guitar on February 15, 1968. Miles liked the tune so much that he kept it as part of his road arsenal with the Lost Quintet, and even tried to steal writing credit on it. "During the session, Miles asked me about sharing [credit for] his part of 'Sanctuary,'" claimed Shorter. "Miles wanted to get in on it. He said 'You know how it is, Charlie Parker did that too.' I said no."[28]

Miles had always been impressed by Shorter's chops and creativity as a writer. In the late fifties/early sixties, Shorter was the primary composer in Art Blakey's Jazz Messengers. Miles took notice of the young saxophonist

"Sanctuary" by Wayne Shorter © 1971 Miyako Music

while the band was doing a stint at New York's jazz club Birdland and cherry-picked him from the Messengers, forming a professional relationship that would last over five years.[29]

There is no question that the enigmatic Shorter's writing really captures just how complex he is. Along with literary inspiration, Wayne reached back to the simple innocence of his youth when it came to writing. "When I write compositions, I think about those times in my youth and try to recount those moments in music, but adding to that a real purpose for the composition, based on my childhood desires, dreams." There is an essence of metaphysical soul-searching in everything he touches. Shorter is a seeker, constantly looking for meaning in life and ways to express this yearning in his pieces. "I want the sound of noble causes to penetrate the music, and the frivolity of delusions and illusions."[30]

Bitches Brew was the very last project Davis and Shorter worked on together, but the relationship ended on good terms. In fact, Miles encouraged Shorter to lead his own group, much as he did with McLaughlin. "Miles was saying, [imitating Miles's patented whisper] 'Don't you think it's time for you to get your own band?' And I had so many ideas, and the music was coming out like water and everything, and I said, 'Yeah. I think it's time.'" The advice might have come back to haunt Miles since he never found anyone who could fill Shorter's shoes once he left (he went through five different saxophonists in the next five years). But Shorter was out the door anyway. Like Miles, he could not stay still. He did not like staying in a band for more than five years, so he was past due to part ways with Miles.[31]

Perhaps touchy about what had happened the year before, Miles decided that "Sanctuary" was due for an overhaul in the studio. Miles never played somebody else's tune the way it was written, and "Sanctuary" was no exception. On both studio versions of "Sanctuary," Davis actually stays close to the original chord sequence as illustrated on Shorter's handwritten lead sheet. The chords on the later recording are supplied by Joe Zawinul and Corea, who stretch out the bass line and harmony a bit. The bass parts are pedal point, but this is what Shorter wanted. There are no specific voicings for the chords, only markings that call for pedal point ("G♭ Triad," "A♭ Triad," etc.), making it a very free piece. It was originally recorded as a straight tune in ¾ with a definite tempo and specific chord changes, but it ended up being much more open on *Brew*.[32] Shorter's lead sheet has no tempo marking, nor does it have bar lines that would clearly illustrate a ¾ time signature. While the original recording has the waltzy feel, it lacks a steady pulse from Williams, much like most of the *Bitches Brew* version. Without a defined rhythm and constricting chord changes, the rhythm section could go wild, leaving plenty of room for Miles to explore the melody more freely and get more interplay within the band.

The bulk of the revisions are in the structure and mood. The '68 version was a quiet, almost reserved version compared to the unyielding version on *Brew*. The big difference between the two is in the climactic new ending

Sanctuary (Miles Davis Solo)

Wayne Shorter

"Sanctuary" (Miles Davis solo) by Wayne Shorter © 1971 Miyako Music; this arrangement © 2013 Miyako Music

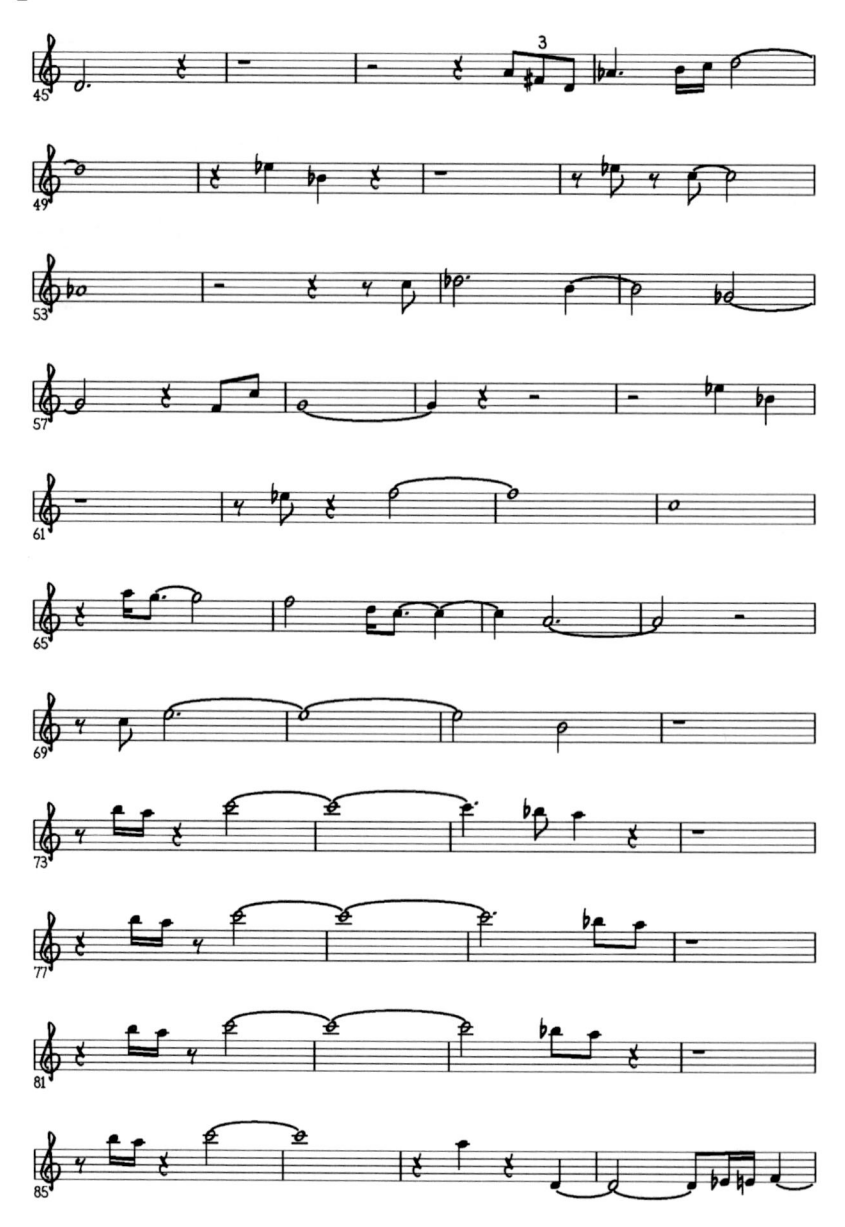

"Sanctuary" (Miles Davis solo) by Wayne Shorter © 1971 Miyako Music; this arrangement © 2013 Miyako Music

"Sanctuary" (Miles Davis solo) by Wayne Shorter © 1971 Miyako Music; this arrangement © 2013 Miyako Music

"Sanctuary" (Miles Davis solo) by Wayne Shorter © 1971 Miyako Music; this arrangement © 2013 Miyako Music

"Sanctuary" (Miles Davis solo) by Wayne Shorter © 1971 Miyako Music; this arrangement © 2013 Miyako Music

that is heard twice (it was only played once—Macero duplicated it during post-production), once about four minutes in and at the end (measure 182). After a gradual build that begins as a desolate duet between Miles and Chick, the trumpeter launches a hollowing three-note phrase, bringing the both the piece and the album to a dramatic climax and haunting close. This grand finale was also a trademark of the ever-changing road renditions that year, where Davis and Corea would set up a calm period before launching into "Sanctuary," which would mark the climax of the performance.[33]

Another revision is the new free-time introduction featuring a solo by Davis. Shorter's melody appears in free time around a minute in (measure 16) followed by a steady beat once the melody is restated (measure 10). During the middle of the second chorus is where the climax melody begins (measure 24), which is actually a vamp from the melody. As things cool off, Miles restates Shorter's introduction followed by another trumpet solo in free time. At approximately 6:45 (measure 117), Davis restates Shorter's introduction and goes through the melody once again. Davis creates a coda by vamping on the last four notes of the piece (measure 163). After this closing section, the melody and blow-out climax along with its little aftermath are pasted to the end, closing the piece out.

Finishing up the Day

The last chunk of the day was devoted to "Pharaoh's Dance" but the effort did not turn out so well. It was initially slated as just a rehearsal to try to organize Zawinul's complex piece, but the band appeared to bite off more than they could chew and were only able to get through a couple of part one's melodies. They noodle with the melodies, underlying rhythms, and harmony as Miles tells Macero to make sure everything is being recorded. As 1 o'clock approached, Macero grew impatient. "Why don't we do this tomorrow?" Macero calls through the intercom. Miles curtly rings back, "We *are* gonna do this tomorrow," but the piece was eventually put on hiatus until the third day.

All the "Pharaoh's Dance" recordings from that day were eventually scrapped. At the very end of the session, the band squeezed in a very brief rehearsal of Zawinul's "Orange Lady" (a track that would be formally recorded that fall on November 19), before Miles decided to call it quits until the next day.

Day Two

"Miles Runs the Voodoo Down"

Even though it is one of the least complex tunes the band tried and it had gotten some road wear prior to the session, Miles's ode to Jimi Hendrix was an uphill battle, taking up the entire August 20 session. Once finished (take 9 was the master), the piece really showed Davis's loose, yet highly structured approach to the entire session. It was originally slated to be performed as it had been on the road that summer, with Miles stating the melody (just a short phrase), a brief keyboard riff from Corea, and then the beat falling into place, but after a handful of false starts, rehearsals, and headaches, it was not working.

It all started with White's "too slick" drum part counteracting another gluttonous part from DeJohnette. Enter Don Alias. Alias was brought in to play congas for the sessions, but decided to lend a hand with the

Miles Runs the Voodoo Down (alt. intro)

Miles Davis

"Miles Runs the Voodoo Down" (alternative intro) © 1969 JAZZ HORN MUSIC; this arrangement © 2013 JAZZ HORN MUSIC

Courtesy of Sony Music Entertainment

"Voodoo Down" dilemma. After listening to the two drummers struggle, Alias "couldn't take it any longer."[34] He recalled hearing some funky beats while attending Mardi Gras that year, blended that with something Buddy Miles might play, and sat down on Lenny's kit to give it a whirl. The beat is extremely sparse, syncopated, tumbly, and somewhat deadpan, leaving room for anything to counteract with it. Miles was thrilled. White was off the track, and now it was time to bring DeJohnette up to speed. This was not easy. Miles, the man of few words, told Alias to play the new beat and have DeJohnette come up with a counter rhythm for it. His first attempt was a bit too much like the over-the-top playing that started the fiasco. Frustration began to mount. During the session, DeJohnette is heard repeatedly saying, "I don't understand." Miles continues to have Alias play the beat again for him, and DeJohnette continues to overdo it. Davis is now reaching his limit. "Jack, when you do that, you fucked that up." Finally Miles vocalizes a faster beat to coincide with Alias. After a handful more attempts, everything gets set in stone and they get their take. The end result is a cool, funky number, catchy enough for Columbia to release an excerpt of it as a single.

Jamming over "Voodoo Down"

With the new sparse backdrop in place along with its stripped-down harmonic framework, the band could begin building up. The tune is jam-packed with group interplay, complex counter rhythms, textures, and good spirits. Despite the difficulties getting this piece going, it really shows the band at its coziest, with all the soloing and comping feeling in the zone. The slow funk vibe worked especially well for McLaughlin, who is at his feistiest here. For all the chomping, sometimes a bit too reserved, pocket playing he did throughout day one, he finally bust outs with barrages of virtuosic lines interspersed with good ol' gut play.

Miles, too, is in great form. Once the hard funk groove kicks things off, Miles is on top of it, forming an immediate alliance with the rhythm section. Reaching back to his St. Louis honky-tonks, he is all blues here. He takes his time before McLaughlin is called in followed by more virtuosic play by a level-headed Shorter. Corea decides to mix things up a little bit when it is his turn by disrupting the hypnotic groove with a frantic chord sequence turning "Voodoo Down" into a frenzy. The percussionists get rattled and respond with a dramatic outburst. Even the bass line gets miffed and joins the cacophony. After enough was enough, the rhythm section brings the

Miles Runs the Voodoo Down (Miles Davis 2nd solo)

Miles Davis

"Miles Runs the Voodoo Down" (Miles Davis 2nd solo) © 1969 JAZZ HORN MUSIC; this arrangement © 2013 JAZZ HORN MUSIC

"Miles Runs the Voodoo Down" (Miles Davis 2nd solo) © 1969 JAZZ HORN MUSIC; this arrangement © 2013 JAZZ HORN MUSIC

groove all the way back down to zero as Davis starts his second solo with a new temperament. He begins with a quiet, creeping, twisted version of the theme, awakening the rhythm section, who bring the groove up a few more decibels. Miles decides to test the waters and commands the final climax of the piece (measure 34), by launching a shrilling trill, summoning the intensity to rise. His phrasing remains bluesy and slurred, but now he orders the band with his screeching dynamics, similar to Corea's keyboard solo earlier. The eruption is brief as Davis draws back with a long fade away, pulling the rhythm section with him (measure 41). Some seconds later (measure 67), Davis has another mood swing and initiates a new groove with a series of detached, choppy notes, which inspires a playful syncopated exchange with the rhythm section. Miles briefly reintroduces the main theme as the rhythm section fades out to end the piece.

Day Three

"Spanish Key"

By the last day, things were running smoothly. The band had finished master takes of "Sanctuary," "Miles Runs the Voodoo Down," and "John McLaughlin," along with some alternative takes that Macero and Miles could chew on later. They had also finished all the parts for the title track, which was now ready for post-production. All that was left was "Spanish Key" and "Pharaoh's Dance." "Spanish Key" was the first attempt that morning and was more or less a slam dunk. The piece was already road tested with the Lost Quintet and did not see a great amount of revision when Davis entered the studio with it. The band appeared to have some morning stiffness when the early attempts were made. On take 1 Miles seems uncomfortable with the rhythm section and flubs a note on the melody. He brings the group to a halt and asks, "Can we break that up more?" They work through some sound tests and a few false starts before they nail two good takes including the master.

"Spanish Key" feels like a road piece. Showing his James Brown swag, Miles loved to use musical cues to incorporate various changes during sets. This carried over to the studio that day, where at least five musical cues are used to signal key changes in "Spanish Key." This was not an easy task for the crew since none of them were identical:

- There is a long scalar passage followed by a keyboard passage which signals the key change to G (measure 53 of 1st solo).

Courtesy of Sony Music Entertainment

Spanish Key (Miles Davis 1st solo)

Miles Davis

"Spanish Key" (Miles Davis 1st solo) © 1968, 1970 JAZZ HORN MUSIC; this arrangement © 2013 JAZZ HORN MUSIC

82 Music

"Spanish Key" (Miles Davis 1st solo) © 1968, 1970 JAZZ HORN MUSIC; this arrangement © 2013 JAZZ HORN MUSIC

Spanish Key (melody)

Miles Davis

"Spanish Key" (Miles Davis melody) © 1968, 1970 JAZZ HORN MUSIC; this arrangement © 2013 JAZZ HORN MUSIC

- Miles plays a shorter phrase, heard at 1:37 (measure 9 of 1st solo) and on one of the rehearsals during Shorter's solo on August 21 at 6:23.
- There is a cue of Davis playing a higher-register fragment of the melody which brings the key to D (measure 13 of melody).
- When Davis performs the opening measure of the melody, the band jumps to the home key of E.
- Finally, there is a jagged run Davis performs at 2:43 (measure 37 of first solo) that shifts the piece to E, flaring up a Spanish tinge (E Phrygian scale is precedent here).

Everything is made-to-order here. No section has a specific length, meaning that a musical cue of any kind could come at any time, making "Spanish Key" a tightrope act.

The piece is a driving, jet-black funk. Davis's opening lines are not anything screeching; he stays quite melodic, and somewhat lurking throughout. The band is content with the groove that is percolating and pretty much leaves Miles to his own business. Things get shaken up in a jiffy when the band modulates to D (measure 39 of 1st solo). Davis begins to react more strongly to the rhythm section, unleashing a halo of shrieking lines, which intensifies the groove further. Maupin's ominous bass clarinet rears its head, initiating a call and response to Miles's spiraling, out-of-control lines (measure 45 of 1st solo). Once Miles has had enough, he announces a musical cue bringing the piece to G, and everything gets back to business as usual as the groove motors on. Corea and McLaughlin are heard trading riffs at one another until the keyboard cue chimes in the next key change bringing Shorter up. Shorter takes his time with this one, blowing through a few key changes, seemingly happy and exploratory with the underlying groove and harmony. His solo unveils a lot of personality throughout—from bluesy, to playful, to somber, to downright esoteric. Davis beckons the next cue, a little more sternly, resulting in another amped-up exchange between Corea and McLaughlin followed by the trumpeter's next solo.

During his second go around, the interplay between the leader and the rhythm section continues, but now Miles becomes more tyrannical. He tries to muscle out the drowning 4/4 funk beat in the rhythm section with a barrage of triplets, before mellowing out the band with a series of smooth, quiet tones. The rhythm section wants the groove back and starts gaining intensity, but Miles will not let go. He decides to answer back with some heavier jabs and some snarling trills, but this does not last long. At around 12:50 (measure 53 of 2nd solo), Davis begins playing long, lush tones followed by a series of more cooling trills, which casts a calming spell on the

"Spanish Key" (Miles Davis 2nd solo) © 1968, 1970 JAZZ HORN MUSIC; this arrangement © 2013 JAZZ HORN MUSIC

band. About a minute later, he tosses out another cue (measure 82 of 2nd solo), moving the key to G and breathing life into the groove as things begin to draw to a close. Maupin gets last dibs and makes a solo appearance that is surprisingly funky (he has mostly been heard in stalker mode throughout the record), until Miles makes last call and closes things out.

"Pharaoh's Dance"

Now that things were wrapping up, it was time to finally tackle "Pharaoh's Dance." The frustration over it that mounted on the first day seemed to carry over to the last. The rehearsal begins on a bit of a sour note with Harvey Brooks M.I.A., thus angering Miles. "Where the fuck is Harvey?" he bellows through the studio. But Miles shakes it off and gets the band right to work. After a few false starts, the band gets part one down.

```
FROM:   Teo Macero
TO:     GIL McKEAN
DATE:   November 5, 1969


RE: MILES DAVIS    "LISTEN TO THIS"    CS 9961


SIDE 1:   Pharaoh's Dance
1.  LISTEN TO THIS                        (ALL)
         STARTS HERE                      (ONE TITLE)
              ENDS THERE

Personnel:

Miles Davis, Trumpet          John McLaughlin, Electric Guitar
Joe Zawinul, Electric Piano   Benny Maupin, Bass Clarinet
Wayne Shorter, Soprano Sax    Leonard White, Drums
Jack DeJohnette, Drums        Larry Young, Electric Piano
Chick Corea, Electric Piano   Charles Alias, Drums
Harvey Brooks, Fender Bass    Jim Riley, Percussion
Dave Holland, Bass


SIDE 2:

1.  BITCHES BREW    Personnel: Same as above except eliminate
                               Larry Young

IMPORTANT:  Be sure to show the following credit where necessary:

            Jack DeJohnette Courtesy of Milestone Records, Inc.

            Many thanks.
```

Courtesy of Sony Music Entertainment

```
                                         Dated: August 20, 1969

Miles Davis
c/o Jack Whittemore
80 Park Avenue
New York, New York 10016

Dear Miles:

        The following will confirm our understanding:

        1. I am the sole writer of the musical composition
entitled "Pharaoh's Dance (Containing Various Movements)".

        2. It is my desire to encourage you to record the
composition on phonograph records, tapes, film, and other forms
of sound devices now or hereafter known and used in the music
business.

        3. In view thereof, I shall pay you fifty percent (50%)
of the writer's share to which I am entitled with respect to
income derived from the production, manufacture, sale or other
use of such sound devices embodying performances by you during
the term of the copyright in and to the composition and all re-
newals and extensions thereof.

        4. It is acknowledged that no license for the mechanical
reproduction, synchronization or publication of the composition
is granted herewith. In the event a motion picture use of a
recording of the composition embodying a performance by you is
contemplated, Zawinul Music, a division of Gopam Enterprises,
Inc., will issue a synchronization license for such use in return
for reasonable consideration.

        5. This agreement sets forth the entire understanding
between you and us, and it shall not be varied except by written
document subsequently signed by the party sought to be charged.
This agreement shall be interpreted in accordance with the law
of the State of New York applicable to arrangements wholly to
be performed therein.
```

The lore of "Pharaoh's Dance" is in its construction. The piece was recorded in so many small portions (nineteen to be exact) that it had Macero scrambling to label what was happening so he could connect everything together later. Based on his abstract sense of the whole project, Davis has to constantly inform his producer about what's going on. "Hey Teo, we just did one section. Make a note of it 'cause you know Saturday when you look at it, it's gonna look funny . . . when the bass clarinet makes an entrance Teo. Put that down." Macero wisecracks back, "I know because I won't be here." With a wit that only Miles can deliver, he shoots back, "You're not here today."

The band continues to work exhaustively on a melody that never makes the final cut. Once the idea is dropped, they chew on part one's second

If the foregoing accurately sets forth your understanding of our agreement, please cause this letter to be countersigned where indicated below.

Very truly yours,

[signature]

Josef Zawinul

Accepted and Agreed:

[signature]
Miles Davis

Accepted insofar as our interests are affected:

Zawinul Music, a division of Gopam Enterprises, Inc.

By: *[signature: Joan Shulman]*

Courtesy of Sony Music Entertainment

exposition. Although a lead sheet from Zawinul exists, much of the rehearsals were done by ear. Holland is overheard teaching the melody line via vocals and bass to McLaughlin and Corea as they try to make sense of Zawinul's challenging piece.

"'Pharaoh's Dance' is about the many slaves, the Egyptian slaves, running around like ants. So I let all the other instruments be teeming around the bass clarinet," explained Zawinul. "Not loud, that's free music to me. Not notes, arpeggios and chords, but an expression of life."[35] Both Miles and Zawinul had the same mindset on how compositions were supposed to be formed—the sum was greater than its parts. Zawinul compared it to painting, where there's a foreground, middle ground, and background. He was not looking for everything to be loud and pulsing all at once, but spread out so you can feel the piece rather than hear it. Zawinul, however, thought that Miles overdid it, and was not crazy about the end result. "I liked 'Pharaoh's Dance.' Miles played it very well, but for me it was a little chaotic." Zawinul felt that Miles took over too much and spoiled some of the collective spirit

88　Music

"Pharaoh's Dance" by Josef Zawinul © 1969 & 1970 by Zawinul Music, a division of Gopam Enterprises, Inc.

Music 89

90 Music

Pharaoh's Dance (Miles Davis 1st solo)

Joe Zawinul

"Pharaoh's Dance" (Miles Davis 1st solo) by Josef Zawinul, © 1969 & 1970 by Zawinul Music, a division of Gopam Enterprises, Inc.

that he conceptualized for the piece. "Everyone contributed a little bit, but he [Miles] knew what he wanted."[36]

Despite the great success the two had together and the friendship they built, Zawinul was turned off by the entire experience. Miles's controlling, bullying way of working never sat right with the keyboardist, and the two drifted apart. Hitching a ride in Miles's Ferrari after *Brew*, Zawinul was quiet the whole trip. When Miles asked why he was getting the silent treatment, Zawinul was blunt. "I didn't like what we did and what is being done."[37] Along with dismantling his work and its essence, Zawinul thought that Miles took more credit than he deserved. "It was a lot of studio time then. I wrote much of that material, all the bass lines . . . well, it doesn't matter how it ended up, but basically it was Miles who got most of the credit for the writing, but many of those things came from me."[38] Zawinul wasted no time telling Davis that he was still the sole writer of the music, regardless of Miles's revisions. On August 20, the day before it was officially recorded, Zawinul sent Miles's manager Jack Whittemore a legal document explaining the terms and conditions of "Pharaoh's Dance," which Davis accepted. Unlike with Shorter, the pair's relationship ended on a bitter note when Zawinul passed on Miles's road invitation and quit working with him for good. "Miles said, 'You want to come on the road with me?' and I said,

92　Music

Pharaoh's Dance (Miles Davis 3rd solo)

Joe Zawinul

"Pharaoh's Dance" (Miles Davis 3rd solo, opening measure) by Josef Zawinul, © 1969 & 1970 by Zawinul Music, a division of Gopam Enterprises, Inc.

"Pharaoh's Dance" (Miles Davis 3rd solo) by Josef Zawinul, © 1969 & 1970 by Zawinul Music, a division of Gopam Enterprises, Inc.

Pharaoh's Dance (Miles Davis 4th solo)

Joe Zawinul

"Pharaoh's Dance" (Miles Davis 4th solo) by Josef Zawinul, © 1969 & 1970 by Zawinul Music, a division of Gopam Enterprises, Inc.

'I'm not gonna do that, man. I want to do my own thing, see what's happening.'"[39] After *Brew*, he and Shorter formed Weather Report.

It's easy to understand Zawinul's antipathy. Davis treated "Pharaoh's Dance" similarly to the way he treated "Sanctuary" and "In a Silent Way"— it was a stomping ground for Miles to do whatever he wanted with it. "Pharaoh's Dance" was originally comprised of two parts. Part one contains a five-measure exposition, an eight-measure section with a B pedal, a transition measure into a four-bar section using a D pedal, and a twelve-measure exposition with a B pedal. Part two has two *very* loosely organized statements, with directions such as "keep developing," "play whenever," "turn statement one in and out with your own free will," and "phrase your own way." It was certainly interpreted loosely by Miles. When all was said and done, many of the sections were omitted and looped in all kinds of ways.

On the track, Davis takes the first solo. His opening phrasing is long and smooth with the rhythm section rolling out a soft red carpet for the leader. The soothing, majestic phrasing is a trademark of Davis's for taming his band. After a studio edit, the rhythm section is heard rumbling things back up. Miles's playing becomes sparse and bitey—a perfect contrast to the underlying straight rock beat. It is almost as if Miles is fighting the beat with his jabbing, syncopated stylings, yet it is just another layer in the thick density of this jam (measure 8 of 1st solo).

After Miles, Maupin takes center stage, wrestling with the deepest reaches of the bass clarinet. His phrasing is confident, as if solid three days of work added an extra coat of tarnish to his sound. The solo gets stabs from the rhythm section, resulting in some interesting interplay until Zawinul interjects some of part one's first statement, fading Maupin out. Around the 8:30 mark, a rhythmic break occurs and statement one of part two begins. Davis only toys with the first three notes along with a couple of flourishes drowned in echo (opening measure of 3rd solo). Thirty seconds later, Davis's next solo is abruptly edited in. The trumpeter is heard weaving through a swarming backdrop of aggressive rhythms. Miles overtakes the backdrop with long, menacing lines with Maupin tagging along (measure 88 of 3rd solo). Miles lets Maupin loose about thirty seconds later and he blows out a hail of shrapnel that summons frantic, spirally lines from Corea. Shorter, who seems somewhat inspired by Maupin, checks in with his own caustic solo, followed by a space-laden, amped-up solo from McLaughlin, who appears to be channeling Hendrix. Zawinul chimes in with some of part one's theme, bringing down the pulse once again.

About fifteen minutes in, the band comes to a grinding halt and begins a hard, steady vamp in B reminiscent of the title track's pounding bass along with cacophonous improvising from all angles. Somehow Miles wedges himself up top, delivering the fatal blows of statement two (opening measure of 4th solo). With his fierce approach and complete disregard of the entire top section, Miles certainly takes liberty with Zawinul's "phrase your own way" instructions.

In "Pharaoh's Dance," as with most of the album, Davis's sound is one with a lot of mileage behind it. His articulation and pronunciation is carved, giving particular detail to all its syllables and nuances, similar to James Brown's characteristic vowel and consonant pronunciations. There is also the sense of a boxer weaving and jabbing that carries over to his bandmates. "He would talk about that, 'Ok, now you've got to set this way . . .' If you play a phrase, you have to know how to set a guy up," explained DeJohnette. "The same thing with boxing. You set a guy up, you feint with a left hook and then catch him with an overhand or uppercut right. It's in the rhythm."[40] "It's the speed, the in and out, the reaction time, the feinting, the move, the combinations," recalled Dave Liebman while working with Miles shortly after *Brew*. "We trained to be fast, fast technically, fast thinking, fast hearing, fast reactions, the ability to perceive what was coming."[41] By the end of "Pharaoh's Dance," Miles finds a way to deliver the knockout blow. Throughout Davis's playing on the track, there is incessant jabbing, a constant touch and dodge. He begins to get the upper hand somewhere in the middle and delivers the onslaught at the very end with the pummeling delivery of the final melody.

Miles Davis with Gary Bartz (left), Jack DeJohnette (rear). Berkshire Music Center, Tanglewood, MA, August 18, 1970. © David Gahr/Getty Images.

At Davis's brownstone, New York, June 1969. Don Hunstein © Sony Music Entertainment.

At Davis's brownstone, New York, June 1969. Don Hunstein © Sony Music Entertainment.

Miles Davis with Teo Macero, June 1969. Don Hunstein © Sony Music Entertainment.

Miles Davis with Teo Macero, January 1970. Don Hunstein © Sony Music Entertainment.

Miles Davis with Clive Davis, 1969. Don Hunstein © Sony Music Entertainment.

Monterey Jazz Festival, September 1969. © Ray Avery/CTSIMAGES.

Newport Jazz Festival, July 5, 1969.
© Teppei Inokuchi.

Miles Davis with Dave Holland. Dallas Memorial Auditorium, July 18, 1969. Photograph by Tad Hershorn.

Miles Davis with Betty Mabry.
Isle of Wight, August 29, 1970.
© Fred Lombardi.

Miles Davis with unknown figure. Isle of Wight, August 29, 1970. © Fred Lombardi.

Miles Davis. Copenhagen, November 4, 1969. © Jan Persson/CTSIMAGES.

Miles Davis with Betty Mabry at Davis's New York brownstone. October 1969. Photo © Baron Wolman.

Miles Davis with his Ferrari. October 1969. Photo © Baron Wolman.

Miles Davis at Gleason's Gym, New York. October 1969. Photo © Baron Wolman.

Miles Davis at his New York brownstone. December 1967. Bob Cato © Sony Music Entertainment.

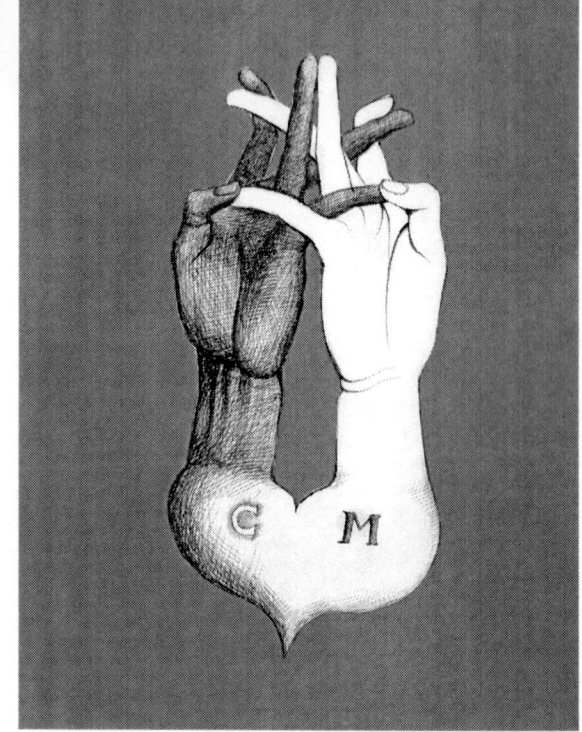

Mati Klarwein, *Tibetan Hand Meditation #84*. © Mati Klarwein Family.

5. Post-Production

I didn't let him intimidate me. You really can't let the artist intimidate you if you really want to be a strong producer. That's why when I get into the studio, I'm a son of a bitch and I don't take lip from anyone.[1]
—Teo Macero, on working with Miles Davis

Razor Blades

Capturing the music on tape was only one piece of the puzzle. With nearly nine hours of recordings to go through, both Miles Davis and Teo Macero had their hands full. Although archaic by today's standards, all recording was done on reel-to-reel, analog eight-track recording equipment, which was state-of-the-art technology in 1969. Columbia was one of only a handful of record labels that had eight-track recording capabilities, and both Miles and Teo utilized it to the fullest.

Once Davis wrapped things up in Studio B, it was up to Macero and his staff to sort out what was captured on tape and construct each piece under Miles's watch. During post-production, special effects, such as the echo on Davis's trumpet during "Bitches Brew," were added along with heavy editing and tape looping of the rehearsals. The most extensive cutting appears on "Pharaoh's Dance," with its nineteen total edits. It was no easy task converting Davis's renegade recording style to vinyl. Macero did not have the luxury of overlapping any of the recordings in order to make smooth matches since so much was recorded in stop-and-go clumps with abrupt endings, leaving very little margin for production continuity. Plus, editing in those days meant taking a razor blade to the tape. As a result, some of the edits are noticeable to the listener.[2] *Bitches Brew* is by no means a flawless record, but considering what they had to work with, it was a miracle the album came together at all.

The Wizard of *Brew*

Teo Macero is to Miles Davis what George Martin is to the Beatles.
—*JazzTimes*

Macero basically fell into his career as a star producer. Growing up in Glens Falls, New York, young Teo worked as a jack-of-all-trades at his father's speakeasy with a passion for creating music. A talented saxophonist, he began writing pieces early in life and decided to make a full run at it, heading to the big city to attend Juilliard in 1948. Macero's writing style leaned toward the avant-garde as well as Third Stream, but he also had an interest in modern jazz, co-founding the Jazz Composers Workshop with Charles Mingus. With some Guggenheim grant money, Macero organized a small series of concerts in the fifties, eventually catching the attention of Columbia producer George Avakian, who offered him a job at the label. He was first assigned as a music editor before getting the call to be a producer in 1957. Teo was leery about leaving his editing post because the money was good and he had never produced a record in his life. But he rolled the dice and it paid off. Over the next fifty years Macero would go on to produce over three thousand albums, including some of the most important recordings of the twentieth century. He oversaw numerous works by Duke Ellington, Thelonious Monk, Mingus, Dave Brubeck, Broadway original cast recordings such as *Bye Bye Birdie* and *A Chorus Line*, the soundtrack to *The Graduate*, and of course, thirty years of Miles Davis.[3]

"Teo Macero was truly one of a kind. In my opinion, he was the prototype musician-producer-composer-arranger bon vivant," noted Bob Belden. "Who else wears an ascot in our current music scene?" Teo was fresher and more suave than many would give him credit for. He was also an honest businessman and very old school, always taking business associates to bourbon-soaked places like Ben Benson's midtown steakhouse for meetings. "I should be dead of a heart attack from the amount of prime steak we consumed at that bistro," said Belden.[4] The quirky, jovial Macero will always be thought of as a tinkerer, and a strong-willed, forward thinker.

"We had our battles. There were times when he wouldn't speak to me and times I wouldn't speak to him," said Macero, who compared his relationship with Davis to that of a husband and wife.[5] Naturally, there were many times in their lengthy relationship that Miles wanted to throw Teo into the street and never look back. Macero could be very obstinate and direct—just like his artist—but Teo too was an artist and knew what it took to get the most out of Davis in the studio. It started with gaining his trust and respect. Macero was not one to be insolent, ask dim-witted questions, or for that matter, say a whole lot of anything in the studio, knowing it was best to be encouraging, accepting, have the artist's best interests in mind at all times, and most importantly, especially when it came to Miles, to stay out of the artist's way. Davis was more or less complacent with Teo's demeanor during *Brew* because Teo listened to him and did his best to keep himself in the control booth and out of the trumpeter's hair.

There were times when Miles was faced with calamities, whatever the size or nature, that would put him over the edge, making Macero a casualty from a barrage of profanities, racial slurs, and damnations. But even when Miles was at the height of his fury, Macero had a way of handling the situation much like a wife handling a heated and mouthy husband. Teo was placating and not defensive, letting Miles know that he got him. Sometimes, Teo was able to soften Miles's hardened persona and bring out the trumpeter's reluctant sense of humor with some playful teasing, such as their exchange during "Pharaoh's Dance" ("You're not here today"), or when the two were working on "Nefertiti" a couple of years earlier. Miles was excited about a take he had just recorded and was wondering what version he liked best from his work that day. At one point Teo joked, "I can put them all together," with Miles dismissing him blithely, "We don't wanna go nuts, Teo." Miles would enjoy taking light jabs at his producer, much like the heckling at the end of "Gingerbread Boy" ("Teo . . . Teo . . ."),[6] or the aforementioned comedic banter between Miles and his crew during "Bitches Brew" at Teo's expense. Even though Miles did trust and respect his producer, he still warmheartedly saw him as Whitey, the fumbling, unhip producer, who could not roll with the black man's cool. He had to keep Teo in check from time to time.

Executive Decisions

"In the studio, I was free flowing. I wanted things to happen spontaneously. I knew from my past experience, what one could do with a raw tape," explained Macero, referring to his hands-off, stand-back approach to producing *Brew*. Typically, a producer's job is to assist in what the music should sound like, but this was never the case with Davis. Miles was way too controlling and demanding for anyone to tell him what to do, especially with his music. During *Brew*, Macero was thought of more like an engineer, and anytime he stuck his nose in too deep, he was immediately scolded by Miles. "I know that in the studio Miles was very firm in telling Teo to keep out of it," said Holland. "Teo would come in the studio to make some suggestions and Miles would be quite rude to him and say something like 'go back in your box' or probably something more explicit."[7] Where Teo was needed the most was not in Miles's studio, but behind the scenes. Macero was a Juilliard-trained musician and composer. He had the right background and mindset to best assist, and not bludgeon, a musician, and work out the logistics of a demanding, major recording project by a high-maintenance artist. For starters, he had to carefully create the setting by booking the studio, track down the musicians, fetch the necessary equipment, and be on top of any thought that popped into Miles's head.

After *In a Silent Way*, Macero had an idea of where Miles was going and what *Bitches Brew* would entail, so he went with Stan Tonkel as the head engineer for the August 18 and 20 dates along with the versatile Ray Moore as the mixing/editing engineer for all three sessions. Tonkel and Moore were staff engineers for Columbia, and had worked in a diverse array of genres including jazz, psychedelic rock, folk, and classical music, and could tackle anything Davis threw at them. Moore had already formed an alliance with Macero, working on a variety of his projects including Davis's *In a Silent Way*, *Nefertiti*, and *Sorcerer*. Moore had an easygoing nature, but could also be very firm in the editing studio, especially when Macero became unreasonable. During mixing, Macero had a habit of listening to the playback at deafening levels, which was unacceptable for Moore. "So I told him I would mix it and he would stay the hell out of the room and when I was finished mixing, he could come in and listen," said Moore. Macero backed off and accepted these conditions even if it meant the he would not be directly involved in the mixing process.[8]

For the August 19 session, Macero worked with Frank Laico, another veteran staff soundman, who began working with Davis on *'Round About Midnight* in 1955. Because the two had such butting personalities and artistic visions, mixing Laico with Macero was like mixing oil with water. Laico was not like Tonkel, a gentle, docile man who would not make waves or object to any of Macero's demands. He was strong willed, and the two frequently butted heads. "I didn't take his bullshit," said Laico. "He was so on to himself." As crazy and self-absorbed as Macero seemed, he did sell records, and the two eventually learned to live with and respect one another. Laico was even tough with Davis. He knew of Miles's troublemaker reputation from the start and always kept a firm stance with him, which Miles dutifully respected. "Miles would be afraid of me because everything he said he thought was the Gospel, but I'd disagree with him."[9] Laico made it clear that Davis was in charge of making the sound while he was in charge of capturing it.

Macero joined forces with the engineers in setting up the microphones and getting a good room sound. One revelation the crew discovered for recording Miles's trumpet was to use a miniature microphone directly attached to his horn. This not only allowed Miles to be heard within a large, cranked up group, but also, Teo could take his sound directly from the source and manipulate it in some clever ways. Miles would be fed into another channel and picked up from an amplifier. "So I had three different sources to work from," explained Macero. "So you could take those sources, keep the main source, and then manipulate the other two sources and come up with *Bitches Brew*."[10] Despite the unconventional instrumentation and Miles's unorthodox recording methodology, the engineers handled it, and at times were already ahead of the curve. In fact, with the possible exception of the ring modulator, they were even responsible for inventing many of the studio effects such as the echo machines that were commonly used by a variety of artists and albums including *Bitches Brew*. "It was newer to the musicians than to the engineers,"[11] said Davis reissue producer Michael Cuscuna. For the *Brew* sessions, the engineers used a T-1, or "Teo-1" (designed specifically for Macero) tape delay to create the echo effects heard on the record.[12] "Teo-1 is a tape recorder, I think it was an old Ampex, which, instead of having a regular headstack—Erase, Record, Playback heads—it had an Erase, Record, and multiple playback heads on a long bar with thumb screws for each head," explained *Brew* reissue engineer Mark Wilder. "This allowed the heads to be moved up and down the bar to create the different delays."[13]

Macero's biggest duty for *Brew* was the laborious, painstaking handling of the recordings once Miles left the studio. With a stack of tapes and a razor blade,[14] Teo and his engineering staff shared the tedious task of going through all the tapes one by one to begin editing and mixing, which took over a month to do. "It wasn't with these ProTools [editing software] where you could put it through a computer and make a nice splice there," remarked Macero." You did it with a 16/30 [tape reel]. We would work hours to find the right splice and to find a right beat and to find the right accent. You had to find the right incoming sound, the right outgoing sound. It was very difficult."[15] This is where Teo's ability as a composer and arranger really came into play. It all started with Miles, who is noticeably dominant throughout *Brew*, as well as many of his other records. Similar to how Miles would set up live performances with his rhythm section and the soloing order, Macero would set up sequences "so when Miles would come in, it would be so great and so emotional, you just had to like it."[16]

Macero would pick apart the jams and find ways to cohesively glue it all together. The order of the parts could be reconfigured, or a chunk from an extended work could be used to form an entirely new composition (such as "John McLaughlin"), but no plug-ins from some other day exist. *Bitches Brew* contains no additional playing from preexisting or newly recorded work, only cutting and pasting from what was already there. "It was all ensemble, it was done at the same time," explained Lenny White. "They just took the bridge and put it as the introduction and put the B section where the C section is and created a new composition."[17] Once the post-production crew was through, all of the work from the three *Brew* sessions had some new twist or turn.

Aside from "Pharaoh's Dance," the title track saw the most extensive post-production work. The rubato section is two combined takes lasting approximately six minutes. The groove section starts with Harvey Brooks's bass line and Davis's finger snaps, followed by Bennie Maupin's bass clarinet, which was looped twice. Brooks's part is repeated, followed by three more loops of Maupin's clarinet, setting up the groove section. More edits follow at 12:45 and 13:30, and then the rubato section is edited in at 14:37. The groove section reappears, and more continuous play happens until another edit at 22:02. Finally, one last appearance of the rubato section returns (24:06) to cap the piece off.[18]

Over the years there has been a never-ending argument over Macero and Davis's ethics outside the studio. Some feel that splicing a record once it has been recorded is very anti-jazz, ruining the magic and spontaneity of a band working in the moment. Holland, who was present both in and out of the studio with Miles at the time, initially had his reservations about *Bitches Brew* because the album felt too controlled and removed from what he was used to doing live with Miles. "My only feeling about it is that we weren't documenting what the band was doing live and that was a big disappointment to me at the time because I always viewed the recording sessions as a documenting of what we were developing in the real world." Holland did, however, acknowledge that he was just a kid in those days and has become more enlightened about Davis's motives over the years. He realized that Miles never thought of *Brew* as being a live documentation. "Miles saw those recording sessions as something being explored within the studio context, a tool you can take advantage of."[19] Teo's take on these matters

```
Teo Macero
JACK GOLD           copies:  Clive Davis, Bruce Lundvall, Marvin Cohen
February 25, 1970


RE:  MILES DAVIS


According to our last conversation, I understood that I had
carte blanche to record Miles Davis any time, any place.

It seems that now the Sales Department is dictating recording
policy to me.  Is this the new procedure regarding Miles Davis?
If so, then let all arrangements be made by the Sales Department.
I will be happy to be in attendance.

I am not making a move regarding the recording of Miles at
Fillmore East until I hear from you directly.



TM:cc
```

Courtesy of Sony Music Entertainment

is simple: it was what Miles wanted. He compared it to a great writer or filmmaker, where there has to be an editing process to weed out mistakes or unwanted material. The way *Brew* was recorded was almost a stream-of-consciousness style, with the tapes constantly rolling. Miles directed much of the music with post-production already in mind: clump here, clump there, and we'll put it all together later.

This radical recording strategy made the overall sound very atmospheric and wide open. Miles and Teo would have everyone close together, but each player was close-miked, making them sound very distant from one another. When the record was mixed, Teo spread out the band to make the music sound grand and majestic. The end result was something that went beyond the stage.[20]

From strictly an executive standpoint, Macero also had the final say once everything was recorded and mixed.[21] Unlike the calculated pop world, where there is a rigorous review process determining what songs an artist should cut, what the album should consist of, and what the single should be, artists like Davis, Johnny Cash, Leonard Bernstein, or any other legendary figure did not have to go through any A&R loops to cut an album. When Miles Davis delivered an album, that was the album.[22] When Columbia went to work on *At Fillmore* the following year, Macero encountered a corporate snag, and got into a tiff with A&R chief Jack Gold over the recording procedure. The sales department was trying to dictate a new policy to him, but Macero would not hear of it. "I understood that I had carte blanche to record Miles Davis any time, any place," wrote Macero, who made sure to forward copies of his letter to Columbia top brass, Clive Davis, Bruce Lundvall, and Marvin Cohen. The mishap was cleared up when Macero pulled rank and threatened to walk out on all technical aspects of recording the album unless the sales department stayed out of the way.[23]

Being that it was so experimental, and somewhat anti-pop, an album like *Brew* could very well have never seen the light of day had it been recorded in more recent times, especially if it was from any other artist. "We had as producers almost complete control because the sales people would have to take whatever we gave them," explained Macero. "But nowadays, they tell you what they want."[24]

Artistically Vested

It has always been unclear just how much Miles was involved during post-production, ultimately questioning how much heart was in his own record. "He left a lot of work for Teo," said Tonkel, who recalled brief listening sessions between the two, going over what to use for the record. "Then Miles went on his way. . . . You hear little of the engineers and what they did."[25] Beginning in the seventies, many producers were just as big as the artists themselves. Producers such as Phil Ramone and Gary Katz were pictured alongside Billy Joel and Steely Dan respectively on their album covers. More recently, someone like Rick Rubin or Danger Mouse only has to list himself as a producer for a record to sell.[26] But in the fifties and sixties, engineers and producers were only the cogs in the wheel and were never properly recognized for their contributions. In many cases, engineers and producers were not even listed on album jackets. Laico remarked, "I laugh because when you work for a big corporation, your name means nothing." Moore remembered seeing his name on the album's first incarnation (although Laico's is missing), but noticed that it was suddenly dropped on later reissues. "They never paid attention to the person doing the editing, and that's [sarcastic chuckle] where the album is made," said Moore. "They conveniently dropped my name, those names from the earlier days. It's not the kind of thing that the Masterworks [classical] department would do, but the jazz or the pop people wouldn't have room to put all those names down, that kind of attitude."[27]

If Davis was out of the picture once the recordings were made, it would seem like *Bitches Brew* was a mercenary commercial venture, and that Teo should be given credit for being the man behind the curtain. Since its release, Macero has been resentful for both the working conditions of the material, and the lack of recognition he received for putting it all together.[28] He was even somewhat arrogant about the artistic control he was given to construct the compositions during their final phases: "I had carte blanche to work with the material. I could move anything around, and what I would do is record everything, right from beginning to end, mix it all down and then take all those tapes back to the editing room and listen to them and say, 'This is a good little piece here, this matches with that, put this here.'"[29]

Macero insisted that Davis was nowhere to be found once the sessions were over, stating that in all the years they worked together, Miles came to the editing room only four or five times. He felt that Miles always wanted to take credit for everything, which was one of the reasons why he did not like listing the other musicians on his records. "If you heard those raw tapes of the sessions you'd realize that all those effects, those echoes, the way the things were pieced together were done by me, not Miles."[30] Whatever he did with the tapes, Macero would try to run it by Miles, but would only get glib responses like "That's fine," or "That's OK." On several occasions Teo even bragged that the electric instruments, including the Fender Rhodes, were all his idea and that they came free through Columbia. Davis, however, not only requested but demanded these items, and was responsible for coughing up the money for them.

Contrary to Macero's take on things, Miles was quite vocal on how he wanted the parts arranged, and confided in Teo to follow the orders and add his own insight. Shortly after recording "Bitches Brew," for example, Miles took the tapes home to review what he and the band played and what he could do with it. He then sat down and typed Teo a letter detailing how he wanted the piece organized—which Teo carried out to the very last detail. He began with the overall structure, explaining how the rubato section should start and end the piece: "Take the last two takes, which are the same thing, and stick the first take on the beginning (the slow part in C minor with the C pedal). The second take, put on the end with the C pedal in the C minor and all the drum noise which ends the first side. Now we have the beginning and an ending. The first part of the tape is tuning up and the rest is where it starts. It begins with the conversation between you and me where you say, 'Just stomp that shit off.' That's where I want this whole side to start."

Miles Davis
312 West 77th Street
New York, New York

Job 53069
Part II
Recorded 8/19/69

Project 10735
Take One

Dear Teo;

Take the last two takes, which are the same thing, and stick the first take on the beginning (the slow part in C minor with the C pedal.) The second take--put on the end with the C pedal in the C minor and all the drum noise which ends the side. Now we have the beginning and an ending. The first part of the tape is tuning up and the rest is where it starts. It begins with the conversation between you and me where you say, "Just stomp the shit off." Thats where I want this whole side to start. Don't forget to overlap the C with the bass clarinet introduction--in other words, run it together. After you put on the introduction then you put the ending on and the rest runs straight through as is. It should be about 27 to 30 minutes.

The part before which you're going to use for the introduction and ending, there's a little section that really swings. It starts off with the bass clarinet and its really tight swing. Use this more than once when there's a lull in the feeling, but don't use it after the introduction. If you want to lead into the introduction with it thats okay.

Don't break any of the sections. Have them run together whether they are high in volume or low in volume.

This is one side that I want you to work on. If you are not sure you have the right take, phone me in California.

Extend the bass clarinet intorduction and let it play twice before the trumpet comes in--just repeat it over.

Sincerely,

Miles

Miles Davis

Courtesy of Sony Music Entertainment

Miles then instructed how the bass clarinet should merge into the rubato section, setting up the groove section: "Don't forget to overlap the C with the bass clarinet introduction—in other words, run it together. After you put on the introduction then you put the ending on, the rest runs straight through as is. It should be about twenty-seven to thirty minutes." Next, he described more ways to tinker with the introduction: "The part before which you're going to use for the introduction and ending, there's a little section that really swings. It starts off with the bass clarinet and it's really tight swing. Use this more that once when there's a lull in the feeling, but don't use it after the introduction. If you want to lead into the introduction with it, that's okay."

Miles did not want anything else messed with, so he told Macero not to break any of the sections. Realizing that there may have been some continuity issues when each section was recorded, he mentioned, "Have them run together whether they are high in volume or low in volume." After the assignment was given, Miles remembered a specific idea he had for looping the bass clarinet: "This is one side that I want you to work on. If you are not sure you have the right take, phone me in California. Extend the bass clarinet introduction and let it play twice before the trumpet comes in—just repeat it over."[31]

That September following the recording sessions, Miles also spent three days side by side with Moore in the editing room fine-tuning the master tapes. Miles's arrival took Moore by surprise not only because it was something Miles had never done before, but also because of what he wanted done with the tapes. "He had a specific thing that he wanted to do," recalled Moore. "What he wanted to do forced him to listen to everything and figure out what he wanted to take out and what he didn't want to take out." What Moore discovered was that Miles was taking out every bass solo played by Harvey Brooks. Moore speculated why Miles did not want these solos on the finished record—the most likely reason being that Brooks was not much of a soloist in Miles's eyes—but never questioned Miles's intentions in the editing room. The whole encounter struck Moore as odd, because the only other edit that Miles wanted was to correct a few off-key trumpet notes; but that request was not feasible since adjusting his pitch would affect the pitch of all the other instruments.[32]

In all fairness to Teo and his staff, they were the ones physically there to carry out the work. It is also likely that Miles was not as involved in his later projects. During the seventies when Davis was constantly touring, delving into debauchery, and working in and out of health problems, Teo was pretty much left alone to his devices, which certainly could have stirred up some animosity toward the trumpeter. It is, however, rare that any artist will work side by side with a producer or engineer during the editing and mixing of an album. Cuscuna feels that most musicians simply do not have the patience for it. "I've rarely had an artist sit next to me." Subsequently, there were days when Teo lightened up, and recognized Miles's input and authority, acknowledging that any idea he had was subject to Miles's approval.[33] But overall, Teo's resentment towards Miles stuck with the producer until the day he died. He often compared himself to Beatles producer George Martin, who Teo thought never got the recognition he deserved. "If he [Martin] hadn't been there, there wouldn't be no Beatles," Macero proclaimed to George Cole in 2001. Macero had a chance to peek into one of the Beatles sessions and was not impressed with what the band could deliver without their trusty producer. "I saw the four of them and they were really not players. It was the weakest kind of playing. I don't think the Beatles gave him credit. They should get down on their knees and thank George Martin. They don't give the producers the credit."[34]

Aftermarket

Over the years, there has been a lot of interest in *Bitches Brew*'s unreleased rehearsal material. When Columbia released *The Complete Bitches Brew Sessions* in 1998, critics and fans were not exactly thrilled with the limited amount of additional insight on the sessions. The unissued material, however, is in fact rehearsals and not the finished work as Miles saw it. When deciding on what to pull out from the vaults, there is always the matter of principles and artistic integrity. Considering the abundance of material put out by Davis in his lifetime, if he wanted it to be released, he would have done so. Davis decided to deliver the album as a finished product without the scraps, false starts, and incomplete takes deemed unsuitable. "These artists were very careful about what they wanted on their record," explained Macero. "That's why when they put these reissues out and all these outtakes and everything else on the great records, it's a mistake!"[35] "To me they are an invasion of an artist's privacy," remarked Cuscuna. "You should be putting a lot of thought and care before you override the decisions of the artists and producers. You should have a pretty good reason."[36] The unearthed tracks that found their way onto the 1998 compilation were not the leftover scraps from *Brew*, but completed takes of pieces recorded around the time of *Brew*'s creation that never found a home in Davis's lifetime.

The Columbia engineering staff had their hands full dusting off these counterculture-era tapes from the vaults. In preparation for *Brew*'s digital and analog re-release, they decided to get the mixes as close as could be to the original musical statement, which meant remixing the album from the original session eight-track, one-inch reels. This controversial move did not sit well with all listeners, including the original engineering/production staff (especially Macero), but was never considered a replacement for the original mix (both mixes are still in print). It was made to give, as Wilder explains, "a better picture of what when on in the studio and the evolution of this body of work." This was an arduous task, but it would eliminate a lot of tape hiss and achieve a better dynamic range. The team was looking to strip down some of the post-production work, or, in other words, "the layer of technology applied during the mix between the music and the listener, such as the reverbs, Teo-1, all the EQ and compression, and the dramatic mix moves, which there are many," as Wilder points out.[37] The last thing the crew wanted to do was over-compress the album. Teo loved compression and he loved brightening stuff, but with modern technology, a record can be remastered in a full-dynamic-range way without squashing or punching the sound.[38] Over the years, Teo has been blamed for overdoing it sometimes—and not just with Miles. His work on Monk's 1967 album *Underground*, for example, was lambasted not only for the massive editing job ripping out portions of each soloist's work, but for the super-compressed production, making the volume levels too hot.[39]

Hot levels were also a problem on *Bitches Brew*. To get the album to sound huge like a rock record, Macero started every microphone at maximum level. Any tweaking would not raise the volume, but push the signal into the saturation point, creating distortion. It also caused leakage into the microphones, making it difficult to isolate the instruments. "All the leakage was there because Teo overshot his thought," said Laico. But Macero did not care. He kept pushing the levels higher, making it almost unbearable to stay in the room and nearly impossible to record. As long as it was loud, Macero could live with some distortion, and so could the audience who buys it. "It was a large group and it caused me some puzzlement," said Laico. "He wanted everything top level from the first bar on and I didn't know if I could do it successfully."[40] With the utmost care, both Laico and Tonkel were able to control the room sound and fight the distortion. On the final playback, some distortion coming from the Fender Rhodes is audible, but it is most likely coming from a cranked amplifier and not the microphones.[41]

Leakage was also a concern in the editing room. When Moore sat down with the tapes he noticed McLaughlin's guitar coming into Davis's and Shorter's microphones because Miles wanted McLaughlin close to him in the studio. Since it was difficult to separate the tracks, Moore was limited, but still managed to get a mix he was happy with.[42]

Tonkel and Moore continued to work with Davis on future albums, but *Bitches Brew* would be the last time Laico and Davis would join forces. If Miles and Macero were going to continue recording electric music at ear-piercing volumes, he did not want any part of it. Laico was a product of a different generation. Similar to George Avakian, he loved recording Miles acoustic and could not make heads or tails of this electric business. "It's just the way I felt," said Laico. "I could not fake myself to say that I'm gonna try. I was in love with his trumpet sound."[43]

In the late nineties, Macero was initially slated to join the team to attack Davis's entire Columbia catalog, but there was a conflict of interest on how to go about doing it. While the rest of the team was looking to keep the mixes natural and true to their original context, Macero was looking to compress the records further, add some EQ, and punch it up just like he always did. Despite his being the one who made all these records in the first place, nobody agreed with his input, so they cut him out. "They wanted me to supervise it. I said, 'What does that mean?' They said nothing. They didn't want me to touch the tapes,"[44] ranted Macero on WCPN Radio. The snubbing left Macero bitter and spiteful about the whole project. He insisted that Davis never would have agreed to release any of the added material on *Brew* and would have been furious with the way the original album was remixed and remastered.[45] In the end, Teo walked out, and left *Bitches Brew* and the rest of his legacy with Miles Davis behind him.

6. Aftermath

If his recent musical pose has been one of narcissistic decadence—as even his cover art, especially on *Bitches Brew* and *Live Evil* indicates—then the price of eternal youth has been a loss of mastery. His sound is blanched, his ideas unfocused, his melodic patterns gnarled and sometimes ugly.[1]
—Gary Giddins

After a while, I felt like somebody had my hand tied down to a table and was slowly driving nails through it.[2]
—Stanley Crouch

To Stanley Crouch and people like that, they need to be reminded that it takes courage to leave all your security blanket behind and jump without a parachute.[3]
—Carlos Santana

The Pimp

Miles Davis was an international celebrity prior to *Bitches Brew*. Since his early days on 52nd Street with Bird and Diz, he had had a certain mystique and aura of "cool" that bewildered listeners. He was a Juilliard dropout, a junky, a hustler, a criminal beaten and busted by police. His personality was blunt and crass. He said very little but was outspoken. His onstage demeanor—the S-shaped figure, thin, trumpet pointed down. He was the bad boy, the "Prince of Darkness." There was also an aura surrounding his music. He was trend setting, an innovator in constant flux. He changed the face of music at least five times. As with Bob Dylan, you did not go to his show expecting a nostalgic, greatest-hits set. You wanted to know what he was going to do next.

As 1970 approached, the money started rolling in from *In a Silent Way*. Record sales were up, which led Miles to sniff out some money from the record company. He was still after the $20,000 he requested from Columbia and badgered Macero and his secretary Corinne Chertok for the cash:

112   Aftermath

```
Corinne Chartok (Teo Macero)
PETER GOLDSMITH
July 22, 1970


I submitted an arranging bill for $3,000.00 to be paid to
Miles Davis.

Talent Payment called to say that this amount would be
deducted from Miles' outstanding loans and interest to
CBS.

Is this the procedure from now on?  I must know so that
when Miles calls and asks where his money is I can say,
"_____ has decided that your advances are to be deducted
instead of sending checks to the union".

Please advise.  Of course, I can always transfer his calls
to you for reply.  If you've never had the pleasure of speaking
to Miles Davis on the phone, you're in for a big treat!!



love,
```

Courtesy of Sony Music Entertainment

Dear Corinne,
    Please tell Walter Dean that I have $20,000 due me and I'd like to have the check dated as of January 1, 1970.
    Sincerely yours,
    Miles Davis

By January 8, Miles decided to up the ante and make some further demands on his boss, Clive Davis "and gang":

Dear Clive,
    Now that we're starting off a new year and since we've been selling records, I should like to make some suggestions that would make for better working arrangements for all of us.

    1. Instead of making financial advances to me from time to time, establish a $75,000 per year guarantee, against the regular royalties to be paid quarterly. This would be automatic and eliminate many phone calls requesting money.

2. In order to avoid confusion in the approval of single releases, the producer and I will decide in this direction, if you and your gang agree.

The cost of producing our albums is not that high and I believe that with what has been happening, plus an additional push, we should have a hell of a year in 1970 and all of us can make more money.
The above is not unreasonable so let's make arrangements to set this up immediately.
Miles Davis[4]

He was right. *Bitches Brew* quickly became an international sensation, making Miles Davis one of the hottest names on the entire music scene. The response was remarkable. Sales in its first month were seventy thousand and rising. By year's end it would reach four hundred thousand units sold; eventually it went gold in 1976 and platinum in 2003. He was now being booked in huge houses that rock stars called home. The typical Davis gig had been in smoky clubs holding a couple hundred people, not auditoriums seating three thousand, amphitheaters seating over ten thousand, or festivals attended by six hundred thousand. Along with skyrocketing record sales and concert attendance, he was now applauded by both jazz and popular media. Even though Miles was really stretching out here, many critics recognized and celebrated his visionary capabilities and new direction. Shortly before *Brew*'s release, Miles graced the cover of *Rolling Stone* and was the subject of a huge editorial, followed by a glowing review of the record.[5] In the original *Down Beat* review in 1970, Jim Szantor gave the album a full five-star rating, stating that "You'll have to experience this for yourself—and I strongly advise that you do experience it."[6] Later that year, the National Academy of Recording Arts and Sciences awarded Davis the Grammy for Best Jazz Performance. Even his fellow pimping[7] community recognized *Bitches Brew* when it was awarded Record of the Year in the Best Big Band classification by *Playboy*.

At the same time, his commercial success and new direction were slammed. For over forty years, writers, fans, friends, mentors, protégés, and more conservative critics have argued that Miles "sold out," that he abandoned his former greatness for fame and fortune and watered down the true core of jazz. "I wasn't involved with that at all," lashed former Davis producer George Avakian. "Miles was out to make money at that time, let's put it that way."[8] Clark Terry, one of Davis's contemporaries and influences, candidly stated, "What they hear in it is less significant that what they don't

PLAYBOY

HUGH M. HEFNER
Editor-Publisher

April 29, 1971

Columbia Record Company
Mr. Jim Brown
Promotion Department
51 W. 52nd Street
New York, N.Y.

Dear Mr. Brown:

Congratulations on being recognized by the readers of *Playboy* Magazine who have named your record, Bitches Brew/Miles Davis, as the 1971 Record of the Year, in the Best Big-Band classification.

This is the 15th year *Playboy* has held its annual competition and each year's poll makes us even more delighted that we are able to help recognize outstanding contributions to music.

Please accept not only the acknowledgement of our readers but also my personal thanks for your artistry.

Sincerely,

Hugh M. Hefner
President

/md
Enclosure

THE PLAYBOY BUILDING · 919 N. MICHIGAN AVE. · CHICAGO 60611 · MICHIGAN 2-1000

Courtesy of Sony Music Entertainment

hear. What they don't hear because it's not there is the real balls of jazz, the chord progressions, the structures, and so forth."[9] His critics felt that there was an absence, an infidelity to the jazz tradition in his music.

For certain listeners, *Bitches Brew* and its proceeding efforts were also a watering down of the aesthetics of the African American tradition as a whole. Naysayers argued that by allowing popular tastes to dictate his art, Davis had failed to preserve that tradition at a time when African Americans were increasingly conscious of and committed to their cultural heritage. In other words, he stopped playing black music. The most outspoken was Stanley Crouch, who stated that Davis's new sound typified the failure of the "black male genius." He argued that Davis's search for fame and fortune distorted his self-expression in his music. No longer a role model for social uplift and artistic vision, Davis turned his back on the jazz tradition and allowed popular tastes to dictate his "presentation of self."[10]

Selling Miles

I have just completed listening to all four sides of GP-26 Bitches Brew [by] Miles Davis. This is a "breakthrough" album to understate the fact. We must find every way possible to expose people to this music.[11]
—Del Costello, April 2, 1970

They do what I tell them to do, man. They don't own me. I make my own records . . . I'd die before I let that shit happen to me.[12]
—Miles Davis, 1969

In the mid-sixties Miles had enjoyed his most critically acclaimed period. His quintet with Wayne Shorter, Tony Williams, Herbie Hancock, and Ron Carter is considered by many the greatest band of all time, not just for Davis or in jazz, but of any musical genre. His career, however, was in a financial and commercial tailspin. His music did not connect with the public ear entranced with rock and roll—the voice of the generation—making his mid-sixties records some of the worst-selling of his career. Even the 1998 Grammy award–winning box set of all of this material was one of the lowest sellers (about 18,000 units sold, compared to the *Bitches Brew* box which sold close to 40,000) of all his reissues. He was at his artistic height, but was leaving the public behind.[13]

Davis was now 43 and wanted to remain relevant. "Clive felt I wasn't making enough money for the company," an almost vulnerable Davis wrote.

NEWSLETTER
WESTERN REGION

LOS ANGELES
SAN FRANCISCO
SEATTLE
DENVER
HONOLULU

TO: WESTERN REGION SALES PERSONNEL

FROM: DEL COSTELLO

cc: New York Marketing, Clive Davis, Teo Macero

I have just completed listening to all four sides of GP-26 "Bitches Brew" Miles Davis. Rather than the usual request to listen to the album and see for yourself, read the liner notes by Ralph Gleason. He tells you what you have to sell. This album is a "breakthrough" album to understate the fact.

We must find every way possible to expose people to this music. GP-26 has the chart feel. It's todays music - just like Santana. Check the lineup....not only do you have some of the strongest musicians in the country on the two records, but check the make up of the personnel.... three drummers, two basses, etc.

How do we expose this GP? Underground and jazz stations, radio buys, underground newspaper ads, college newspaper ads, giveaway samples to key buyers and clerks to spread word of mouth exposure. We have a monster in our hands if we do all of the numbers we know to expose, promote, merchandise, and SELL this potential SMASH. I want everyone in the region to give this GP "your best shot". I want feedback. Tell us what you are doing to chart this one. This is not a jazz album - it's Santana, Blood Sweat & Tears, etc. GET THE MESSAGE. Sell it like you sold Blood Sweat & Tears and Santana. Promote it the same. Let's cook!

Regards,

Del

DC:bs

April 2, 1970

Courtesy of Sony Music Entertainment

"I wasn't prepared to be a memory."[14] So the shift went into high gear. He knew it was time to create something sublime and get on top again, but his detractors felt that what he did was not from the heart, but from pressure from Columbia bigwigs. Davis would argue that he was doing what he had always done, which was continue to reinvent and surprise himself, and it was not for Columbia, record sales, or young whites.[15] In a 1973 interview for Boston's *Real Paper*, a quite frank Davis explained how Columbia was marketing his music and talked about the misconceptions people had that he was being told what to do by the higher-ups: "I ain't like that, man, about no fucking market. Listen to what I say. Hendrix had no knowledge of modal music; he was just a natural musician. He wasn't studied, he wasn't into no market, and neither am I. Columbia tries to get me into that shit but I won't let them do it. They wanted to put some of my music on some kind of sample record of their black music, and I said fuck that shit. Leave my music alone."[16]

Despite plummeting sales in the mid-sixties and his at times difficult behavior,[17] the label still loved Miles and treated him like a white rock star. With this privilege, Davis was able to take advantage of the record company and create the music that he wanted to produce.[18] "He didn't compromise anything. All he did was what musicians do best, which is try to convince people that whatever they are doing is what the business people want," argued Bob Belden. "I don't think they wanted to make a rock album," said Lenny White. "They maybe wanted him to do something a little bit different, but not to make no rock album. That was Miles's own idea."[19] Of course Columbia wanted a return on their investment, but Miles was someone difficult to control. In his autobiography Davis is quite forthright about the lack of credit he and his musicians received and blamed most of the debate on discriminatory slander. "Some people have written that doing *Bitches Brew* was Clive Davis's or Teo Macero's idea. That's a lie, because they didn't have nothing to do with none of it. Again, it was white people trying to give some credit to other white people where it wasn't deserved."[20]

It was not so much that Columbia execs were the puppeteers looming over Davis; rather, it was how they handled his music *after* it had been recorded. As early as *Filles de Kilimanjaro* in 1969 (recorded in 1968), record executives felt that his music was not so far removed from the free-form psychedelic rock bands of the time and began positioning him in those markets. The advent of modern electric instrumentation in his bands only sweetened the deal. In an interoffice memo from April 1, 1969, Columbia Vice President of Merchandising Bruce Lundvall wrote to Director of Advertising and Creative Services Morris Baumstein: "What Miles is doing on records and in live appearances now will certainly be listened to with interest by serious rock buyers. Can we plan some small space ads that aim Miles at the rock audience?"[21] With *Bitches Brew*, his potential appeal became more obvious; Columbia thought they had something that could break through

Bruce Lundvall
MORRIS BAUMSTEIN   cc: Messrs. Farr, Salem, Macero
April 1, 1969

Once again, I feel we should place a few ads in the underground press for Miles Davis' Lp product. Bob Altshuler sent me the attached rave review, from Rolling Stone, on the new Miles album "Filles De Kilimanjaro." What Miles is doing on records and in his live appearances now will certainly be listened to with interest by serious Rock buyers. Can we plan some small space ads that aim Miles at the Rock audience?

BL/jb

Courtesy of Sony Music Entertainment

and promote as a "crossover" album from a very talented, highly marketable figure. Normally, an album with long, dissonant, instrumental tracks would spell commercial doom for any artist, but Columbia thought otherwise and rolled the dice. The label felt that the record was exciting and had a lot in common with successful acts on their label who mixed jazz with rock, such as Blood, Sweat, and Tears and Chicago. Columbia even placed Davis on tours where Blood, Sweat, and Tears were headlining. The idea is surprising, considering how much Davis hated those bands (and how much different from Davis's music those bands actually sounded). "Blood, Sweat, and Tears is embarrassing to me," remarked Davis. "They try to be hip, but they're not."[22] On April 2, 1970, Columbia Western Region Sales Manager Del Costello drafted a company newsletter championing *Bitches Brew*, stating that it felt just like the music of the day and had instant chart appeal. He listed his suggestions on how to market the album, which included underground and jazz radio stations and various newspaper ads. "We have a monster in our hands if we do all of the numbers we know to expose, promote, merchandise, and sell this potential smash." He explained that this was not a typical jazz album, but an album that could make some money. "Tell us what you are doing to chart this one. This is not a jazz album—it's Santana, Blood, Sweat, and Tears, etc. GET THE MESSAGE. Sell it like you sold Blood Sweat and Tears and Santana. Promote it the same. Let's cook."[23]

Columbia knew it was crucial that Davis reach a young audience. By connecting with these listeners, the commercial life of the artist (and the label's investment) would have the chance to grow. "Marketing music is

CBS MEMORANDUM

```
FROM:  Steve Popovich
  TO:  TEO MACERO
DATE:  April 7, 1970
  cc:  R. Alexenburg, J. Brown, L. Wills, D. Costello, C. Thagard
```

The following excerpt is taken from Lou Wills' weekly report for the week ending April 3, 1970:

BITCHES BREW - Miles Davis - just received this great album. Again Miles scores! This LP should greatly surpass "In A Silent Way". Miles has really outdone himself this time. Will have stations reactions next week. I am very sure they will feel the same way I do about this album.

SP:dn

Courtesy of Sony Music Entertainment

very different than marketing package goods like soap, cosmetics, food," said Baumstein. "The record company makes a big investment in an artist and you try to make the career last as long as possible so the investment ends up being a profitable investment."[24] It was also the young audience, of course, who were buying records and attending concerts.

The label started attacking underground, college, and rock radio. If they could get *Bitches Brew* played on these young demographic radio stations, Davis would reach a whole new audience and have the potential to generate massive sales. Again, based on the album's characteristics, this was not easy to do. The label closely monitored the album's progress and feedback from the stations. They realized the potential problems deejays might have with these enormous pieces,[25] so Columbia began making radio-friendly edits of the tracks and shipped them out to radio stations across the country. Cuscuna, who was a disc jockey for Metromedia in Philadelphia at the time, remembered getting the full record and being bewildered. Even for a free-form deejay, the music seemed bizarre and certainly unmarketable. "I was surprised. What the fuck am I supposed to do with this?"[26] With tons of rhythm and bass and no discernible hooks, *Brew* certainly did not have the commercial appeal of a typical pop hit. But somehow, listeners began tuning in.

Along with typical jazz media, Columbia approached rock publications like *Rolling Stone* for advertising and hired top graphic designers from their

120   Aftermath

A NOVEL BY MILES DAVIS

Bitches Brew is an incredible journey of pain, joy, sorrow, hate, passion, and love.
Bitches Brew is a new direction in music by Miles Davis.
Bitches Brew is a novel without words.

Bitches Brew is a specially priced 2-record set.
ON COLUMBIA RECORDS

Bitches Brew Promo Ad. Courtesy of Sony Music Entertainment

> BITCHES BREW
> MILES DAVIS
>
> Teo Macero
>
> I finally had a chance to hear it all. It's really wild — and great!
>
> CD 1/19

CLIVE J. DAVIS

Courtesy of Sony Music Entertainment

CBS RECORDS

A Division of Columbia Broadcasting System, Inc.
51 West 52 Street
New York, New York 10019
(212) 765-4321

Clive J. Davis, President

Dear Bill:

Historically, Miles Davis would not be of much interest to you for the Fillmore. However, I believe Miles is well on his way to really breaking out of his jazz bag. All the fantastic reviews in ROLLING STONE and Ralph Gleason's latest articles calling Miles' most recent albums the best he's heard anywhere in a decade have given him tremendous impetus. The "underground" is ready for Miles. His sales have measurably increased and I have finally softened him to play the Fillmore type emporium. I would appreciate it if you could express interest to him. In playing a role as "guest impresario" for Columbia, a bill with The Flock, Taj Mahal and Miles might be a real sleeper for you. No one of them would get that much bread as to make it hard to pay all; further, each appeals to that kind of music buff as to make it possible for all to be enjoyed. Creatively it would be a gigantic coup as each artist is felt to be a potential big artist and each has a growing fanatic following. Well, the rest is in your hands.

Santana, as you know, is unstoppable. Total sales with tape are now over 400,000 and going strong.

Warmest regards,

Clive

P.S. I saw Johnny Winter and Chicago Friday night at Fillmore. The evening was electrically exciting. Chicago was very good and Winter just keeps getting better all the time. The combination of him and his brother Edgar had the capacity house on their feet all night.

Mr. Bill Graham
Fillmore West
1545 Market Street
San Francisco, California

November 17, 1969/ob

bc: Teo Macero

Courtesy of Sony Music Entertainment

creative service departments to do the layouts, increasing the massive investment and risk the label was taking. Jazz publications paled in circulation compared to rock magazines like *Rolling Stone*, so in order to take out full-page ads, a large budget had to be established.[27] Since recent Davis sales could not justify the new marketing budget, the label had to dip deep into deficit spending. Despite it all, Columbia believed that this record would far exceed previous projected sales. They were right.

Perhaps the most pivotal marketing step came from the president of Columbia himself, Clive Davis. Clive had championed Miles ever since he first took office. When he heard *Brew*, he was ecstatic. "I finally had a chance to hear it all," he wrote in a personal note to Macero. "It's really wild—and great!"[28] Clive knew that if Miles was to reach a young audience with this exciting new music, he was going to have to play in front of them. On November 17, 1969, Clive wrote a letter to Bill Graham proposing some dates for the Fillmore East and West. "Historically, Miles Davis would not be of much interest to you for the Fillmore. However, I believe Miles is well on his way to really breaking out of his jazz bag." He told Graham that Davis was doing something that would connect with the Fillmore rock crowds and be able to fill the seats. "The 'underground' is ready for Miles. His sales have measurably increased and I have softened him to play the Fillmore type emporium."[29] Miles was reluctant, but eventually warmed to the idea. He had a close relationship with Clive and acknowledged all the times Clive bent over backwards for him. So when the boss approached him to do the Fillmore gigs, he was happy to return the favor.[30] Touring would be everything. They could book him with established rock artists and launch a new fan base. The marketing execs could promote the album in every record store. They could set up posters in each city and have local deejays play the record. The more he toured, the greater the exposure.

The Package

A fresh, unique packaging design was also critical for selling the goods. For starters, Miles had to come up with a name. During the sessions, Miles was snidely calling the project *Listen to This*, and he probably would have kept if it were not for his new wife, Betty. Miles went over other possible names with her and came up with *Witches Brew*, but Betty, being the edgy, over-the-top rocker that she was, suggested *Bitches Brew*, and it stuck. On November 14, 1969, Davis told Columbia the new name and then sought out an artist to capture the music's essence. He knew exactly where to look.[31]

CBS MEMORANDUM

FROM: Teo Macero
TO: JOHN BERG, JOE AGRESTI, PHYLLIS MASON
DATE: November 14, 1969

RE: MILES DAVIS   CS 9961   XSM 151732/3   PROJECT # 03802

Miles just called and said he wants this album to be titled:

"BITCHES BREW"

Please advise.

cc

Courtesy of Sony Music Entertainment

Miles went back to the trendy, no-name boutique run by Colette Mimram and Stella Douglas for some help. He complained that his latest records were not selling enough, and based on what she saw with his previous record covers, Douglas could see why. Douglas suggested that he would sell more records if he could find an image that not only captured the music's essence, but also the consciousness of its surroundings as well.[32] Douglas introduced Miles to the European surrealist painter Mati Klarwein, who was part of the East Village glitterati scene at the time, and the two immediately hit it off. Like Miles, the artist was cutting edge, and never dwelled on the past. "He [Klarwein] said he had a case of 'nowstalgia,'" said Klarwein's daughter Serafine.[33] According to Klarwein's wife Caterine Milinaire, Davis asked Mati to come up with a fresh concept for the record cover.[34] After hearing the music, Mati came up with a concept "steeped in African beauty and widened by Eastern mysticism." The piece signifies the communion of races with its barrage of interracial imagery including an iconic hand gesture (sketched from photographs taken by Caterine), a Tibetan sign for protection from negative energies, which is showcased in black and white to symbolize the current racial problems in America.[35] Klarwein painted the original, which is approximately the same size as the album jacket, using the Mishe technique, a Dutch style that uses many layers of oil paint so the piece has enough depth for light to go in and bounce back out. Because of its complicated process, the piece took months to create.[36] Miles was thrilled. He told Klarwein that this is what he wanted and had the artist handle the legwork to turn it into his new album cover.[37]

Klarwein handed it off to Columbia's art director John Berg to shape the idea for the LP format. Berg was a friend of Davis and a master designer, handling all of the label's iconic covers over the years, including Dylan's *Blonde on Blonde* and Bruce Springsteen's *Born to Run*. He immediately saw the piece's realism and the sensitivity to the times that it portrayed. Berg went to work handling all the layouts and creating the title's distinguished Novel Gothic typography, which all took less than a week to do. He also served as the liaison between the artist and A&R department for getting approval for all covers, but just like the music inside, any executive handling for Davis's new album was overridden. "He had demands. He wanted such and such an artist, a certain kind of style, and he would get his way because he was Miles Davis," said Berg.[38] Regardless, the record company was thrilled with the image because, according to Lundvall, "It had the visual appeal of a rock and roll album."[39]

The iconic liner notes were penned by Ralph Gleason, a prolific jazz and rock writer, who gained notoriety with his work in *Down Beat* and *Rolling Stone*. Gleason was a big fan of Miles and was called in by his friend Macero to write the piece. "electric music is the music of this culture and in the breaking away (not breaking down) from previously assumed forms a new kind of music is emerging. the whole society is like that. the old forms are inadequate,"[40] proclaims Gleason in his eerily prophetic notes. He encourages a musical society without labels or limitations, foretelling the response of many Davis fans. Gleason emphasizes his point by defying the boundaries of grammar and abandoning all upper-case letters.

On the Road

Davis premiered at New York's Fillmore East on March 6–7, 1970, opening for Neil Young with Crazy Horse and Steve Miller, followed by a four-night stint at San Francisco's Fillmore West opening for the Grateful Dead, beginning April 9. "That was an eye opening experience for me,"[41] recalled Davis, who stood before a crowd of five thousand young, white hippies who barely knew who he was. The band sounded like they had something to prove at these early shows, demonstrating intense virtuosity and command throughout. Miles was no amateur, and the audience relished the experience. The shows provided a loud, but balanced sound of sheer power and at least a contact high for all in attendance.[42]

Graham also set up Davis for another four-night stand at the Fillmore East June 17–20, sharing the bill with Laura Nyro,[43] a popular singer who was influenced by Miles and even approached him to sit in on one of her studio sessions in 1969. Miles did show up, but told Nyro, "I can't play on this. You did it already," which she accepted as a high compliment. Nyro responded by giving Miles a box of red roses at one of his Fillmore East gigs.[44]

Davis had respect for most of the bands he was paired with except Miller. "Steve Miller didn't have shit going for him. I'm pissed because I got to open for this non-playing motherfucker." In return, Miles would purposely show up late for the shows so Miller would be forced to perform before him. This did not sit well with Graham. "I see that Bill is madder than a motherfucker because he's not waiting for me inside like he normally does, he's standing *outside* the Fillmore."[45] The two were already on bad terms when Graham refused to pay Davis's typical $5,000-per-concert wage and only offered him union scale ($1,500). The animosity increased when Graham lowballed Davis for the West shows. "They're gonna make a lot of money for those four nights," bellowed Davis. "What are they gonna do, give me a set of clothes, a watermelon?"[46]

Despite various financial disagreements, Davis toured relentlessly with various personnel up until he called it quits in 1975, making *Bitches Brew* seem like it was supported by a five-year tour. He continued to perform at large venues and festivals, including the massive Isle of Wight Festival in England on August 29, 1970, where he performed before an estimated crowd of six hundred thousand people.

The live shows also got their share of trashings from the media. His long pieces, which would take up entire sets, were called shallow, monotonous, and disjointed. He got hammered for his use of electric trumpet, the wah-wah pedal, and his improvisational style. In his *New York Times* review of Davis's 1972 Philharmonic Hall performance in New York, an unconvinced John Wilson wrote, "It was very much like Mr. Davis's other appearances in the last year or two—a continuous, unbroken stream of what is essentially mood-setting music."[47] Wilson took note of Davis's "sputtery" improvisational style on multiple occasions (Fillmore East 1970, Avery Fisher Hall 1971, Philharmonic 1972). He argued that the wah-wah pedal marked a serious regression in Davis's playing, creating limitations in his tonal range, and making his playing sound more like something you might hear in a typical rock or blues act.[48] Gary Giddins was not any easier on the trumpeter. "What I miss most of all is the sound of Miles Davis, which I think is so disguised by amplification that it just doesn't have the heart that I associate with him."[49]

Others felt that the amplified trumpet with all the bells and whistles actually enhanced and expanded Davis's trumpet style and tone. Similar to what Hendrix achieved with the similar effects on his guitar, Davis was able to reinvent the blues sound and expand the possibilities of the trumpet. He got more of a vocal effect and was able to command his dynamics and timbre in funky, innovative ways. He was also able to produce (especially with the wah-wah) more slurred tones, which is essentially the language of the blues. *New York Times* writer John Rockwell took note of this in his review of the 1974 Carnegie Hall show. "Mr. Davis's coloristic explorations with an amplified trumpet, using the mute purely to affect timbre, for instance, rather than to quiet volume, were intriguing."[50] Dan Morgenstern also argued that despite the sometimes distorted output of the electric instruments in concert, Davis still sounded like he always did. "It's amazing how much Miles is on there. Sometimes you don't recognize him because the sound is so distorted, but he's all over the place."[51] Much as with Hendrix, the bluesy phrasing and subtleties of Davis's playing remained, but were drenched in modern effects, creating a very postmodern performance.

Finding an Audience

Miles's audience isn't where it used to be, but then either is his music.
—Columbia ad, 1969

My own suspicion is that Davis is as infatuated with his sudden status as superstar to young blacks as he is concerned with his need to sell lots of records to maintain his fast lifestyle.[52]
—Gary Giddins, 1976

Miles always had a unique relationship with his audience. Throughout the fifties and sixties, he would take a solo and walk off stage, taking the spotlight away from him and placing it onto his bandmates. During the late sixties and early seventies, he never left the stage, becoming more hands-on as a leader, but still deflected attention away from himself. He never announced any of his pieces, acknowledged applause, or played encores. When he was through with his set, he walked off the stage with his eyes straight ahead.[53] He was so engrossed with the band sound that he would turn his back to the audience, which of course, caused an uproar. "Nobody asks a symphony orchestra conductor why he turns his back on the audience,"[54] snarled Davis. He would also insist that it enabled him to get a better sound because he thought that certain notes came out better on particular parts of the stage.[55] In every case the focus was on the music and not Miles Davis, the icon. "They come to listen to the music, not to look at me," explained Davis in 1972. "If they wanted to see me, I'd put on a topless act."[56]

Miles sought a reconnection with young African American listeners. He had to. The jazz clubs were filled with mostly white listeners, and young blacks were into the new sounds of Motown, funk, soul, and rock because it was more relevant to their lives than what most jazz artists were churning out. *Bitches Brew* worked because it tapped into these resources and made a statement about the modern African American experience and what it was like to be young, angry, and disillusioned. Miles was thrilled when blacks started listening again. On January 8, 1970, while *In a Silent Way* was taking off, he wrote to Clive Davis, "Incidentally, Bob Altschuler has been doing a fine job publicity wise, because the blacks are starting to buy more records too. Right on."[57] Over the years, Miles tried to keep this going and chipped in on the publicity side as best he could. For instance, in 1972 Davis purchased $2,000 worth of tickets to his Philharmonic Hall performance and handed them out to young fans who could not afford them.[58]

Bitches Brew touched upon the complexity of the African American experience and drew upon both the past and present. Along with the hip funk/soul stylings of Sly Stone and James Brown and the complex, cacophonous textures of Hendrix, Davis dove into the simplicity of the blues and the ruggedness of his musical roots. "I was trying to play music I grew up on, that roadhouse, honky-tonk thing that people used to dance to on Friday and Saturday nights,"[59] remarked Davis. It certainly was not a carbon copy of boozy, honky-tonk jamming, but more of a continuation.

As *Brew* caught on like wildfire, everybody got into it regardless of race. When Cuscuna heard Davis at Philadelphia's Electric Factory in the early 1970s, he recalled that the audience was "a mixture, but mostly white."[60] Quincy Troupe remembered a Davis performance in Los Angeles in the early 1970s where not only blacks and whites were in attendance, but also Hispanics and Asians.[61] He even reached the transmundane. In a review of the Philharmonic performance in 1972, *New York Sunday News* columnist Hugh Wyatt recalled an audience of about three thousand racially mixed twentysomethings, most of whom were "hard rock freaks."[62]

And there were many of every kind to go around. Most of the post–*Bitches Brew* concerts were sold-out events. Despite the negativity in the press, saxophonist Azar Lawrence was floored by the response the band got the night he performed with Davis at Carnegie Hall in 1974. "Sure it did [receive criticism]. Nonetheless, great numbers of people flocked to it. He had no problem filling up the auditorium. It was packed that night. Those who had criticized, I think their numbers were a small percentage compared to those who were enjoying it."[63] *Down Beat* columnist Bert Stratton was part of an enthusiastic crowd in Ann Arbor shortly after *Brew*'s release. The four-thousand-seat auditorium was practically filled to hear Davis's band. "Miles's performance received an overwhelming reception: far out, freaky, heavy, and every other catch phrase was thrown around. A standing ovation was assured."[64] As Lawrence pointed out, the music was not for everyone. The ones who loved it, loved it. There were people who could see his vision, and those who misunderstood it.

Hate Mail

The greatest example of self-violation in the history of art.[65]
—Stanley Crouch

It was just an extension which went into the commercial popular language of that time, instead of continuing in the surroundings in which it began.[66]
—George Avakian

It was the veteran fans who seemed to bring the brunt of the scrutiny. When *Bitches Brew* came out, it did not match the old stuff. Like a devotee yelling for "Satisfaction" at a Rolling Stones show, the new material just was not cutting it for them. At the same time, Miles was driving new fans in by the hordes. So Miles found himself with a divided audience: post–*Bitches Brew* and pre–*Bitches Brew*. The newbies enjoyed it on its own merit, whereas the vets had Davis's past to judge it against.

For more conservative listeners, things got even uglier when Davis took his show on the road. A month before the *Bitches Brew* sessions, Davis performed at the Newport Jazz Festival along with an unusual array of rock and jazz groups. The set, previewing some of the upcoming *Brew* material, was a success, but it also raised a brow with longtime fan and Newport founder George Wein. "I'll tell you exactly what I told Miles: 'you know, Miles, I used to say there was no way I could get on the stand and play with you. But now, I think anybody could get on the stand and play with you.'"[67] As Davis continued to tour and record after *Brew*, Macero received several pieces of off-color mail demanding refunds for 1970's live recording, *At Fillmore*. "I just purchased what turned out to be my last Miles Davis record," wrote a veteran fan from Michigan. "I don't know how long you fools can fool the public into buying such trash." "The closest comparison I could draw is that they sounded like four sides of a band warming up,"[68] wrote an irate listener who felt duped that the album jacket did not warn him of what the record would entail.[69] Many concertgoers were also outraged. "We walk out to play. He [Davis] plays the first note, they start throwing stuff on stage. A roll of toilet paper went by my head," explained James Mtume about a 1971 show in which Davis instructed the young percussionist to "play through it."[70] During a 1971 performance in Belgrade, audience members began yelling, booing, and walking out. "For Miles and everyone in the band, there was no difference in listening to James Brown or to John Coltrane," recalled Gary Bartz, who was Davis's saxophonist that night. "But just like racism segregated people, different types of music were segregated as well."[71] "Most of the folks I watched with couldn't make heads or tails of it—strange how the recent Miles can appear to be the ultimate reduction to his old fans yet unfathomable to many non-jazz folks,"[72] wrote Bob Blumenthal in his 1972 review of the Philharmonic date. "[Philharmonic] was the first time I realized the *divide* that Miles was creating," said Mtume. "The old jazz fans were confused; some of them were actually *angry*."[73] His debut at the Montreux Jazz Festival in 1973 did not fare much better, with Davis's first set ending with a hail of jeers from the Swiss audience. Davis's backers, however, applauded his second set, once again showing an audience broken apart.[74]

"Now that I'm getting my shit together, Miles is gonna have to change. As far as he's gone now, it sounds like a bunch of noise,"[75] Freddie Hubbard, an artist who was also attacked for his own electric efforts in the seventies, told Leonard Feather in 1972. Miles was getting it from all ends, including members of his inner circle. In 1975 Davis brought in Sonny Fortune to his

January 25, 1971

Dear Mr. Rothenberg,

I am sorry you are not pleased with our latest Miles Davis album.

You must understand that there are many Miles Davis record buyers who believe in his "New Directions" in music and who welcome his new sound as witness the great reviews the album has received.

Since we cannot refund your money, we are sending you under separate cover some of our latest Columbia albums which we hope you will enjoy.

Sincerely yours,

Teo Macero

Mr. Robert S. Rothenberg
159-43 82nd Street
Howard Beach, New York 11414

(Mailed Charlie Byrd latest album, Paul Robeson, Kostelanetz Whales First Class February 11, 1971. cc)

Courtesy of Sony Music Entertainment

new working band, but the saxophonist immediately had his reservations. Fortune grew up admiring Davis as a pioneer in the music industry and was thrilled to get the call to come work for him, but when he joined the band, Fortune discovered that this was not the same Miles that he and his peers grew up with. Despite the financial gains and notoriety, Fortune felt out of place and quit Davis's band that same year, never to return again. "By the time I got to the band it was a different Miles that I knew. It was a brand new Miles to people like me. Some ways this Miles was a Miles for those of us who knew Miles before this Miles. We weren't as sure about it as Miles was."[76]

There is no question that Davis had an exceptional career before *Brew*, including the 1960s quintet, but to recreate a group like that would be asking for the impossible. "Following up a band that has Wayne Shorter, Ron Carter, Tony Williams, and Herbie Hancock is like trying to form a band that's going to be as good as the Beatles, if not heavier musically,"[77] argued Davis alum Adam Holzman. Even more out of the question would be to ask Miles to work in a vacuum and no longer innovate just to please others. He had *never* turned backwards, so why would he start now?

"Then jazz becomes lost in the miasma of modern classicism. It lost its balls,"[78] wrote a dyspeptic Ralph Gleason. Davis was not only being punished by his very own work, but by other people's work as well. He was written off because his new music lacked certain characteristics, prominent in *other* key jazz artists' work, that are essential to the aesthetics of jazz. This new wave of criticism, spearheaded by Crouch, Amiri Baraka, Martin Williams, and Wynton Marsalis in the eighties and nineties, knowingly or unknowingly attempted to reduce jazz to a standard formula, canonizing an entire art form whose sole premise is self-expression. This school of thought suggests some form of absence in the music; it is missing what Duke Ellington, Louis Armstrong, and many others before Davis had already accomplished. This criticism was something Davis could not shake for the rest of his life.

But Miles was ever the chameleon. He had always been revered as a musician in perpetual motion, a constant innovator. The *Bitches Brew* faithful understood that every performance was part of an ever-evolving greater whole. He worked in a continuum, not a vacuum, which made him difficult to define. Unlike many groups who have tried to duplicate Davis's success, he never wanted to stick with a working formula that would immortalize his sound. He wanted to be identified as indefinable. As Davis's music was changing month to month, he kept finding new places further and further away.[79] As soon as his listeners caught up with him, he was already onto something new. As with any great improviser, there is a constant transformation, a new meaning. There is unfamiliarity to both the listener and the player.

The Transgression of Miles Davis

I have to change. It's like a curse.[80]
—Miles Davis

In 1965 Bob Dylan strapped on an electric guitar, formed a rock band, and released "Like a Rolling Stone," creating gigantic waves in the folk community. When he had found a larger audience, Dylan was lauded for turning his back on the tradition he helped create. Four years later Miles was up against this very same wall, and had difficulty shaking these connotations for the remainder of his career. Was Miles Davis a sellout? With the inclusion of electric instruments and beats that were associated with the popular British and American rock acts, purists argued that Davis's music was a cheapening of the highest level of black art and culture and lacked a social consciousness of preserving the jazz tradition and maintaining cultural values.[81] In order raise social consciousness, an artist must free himself from the dictates of the market, but with Miles's rock beats, funky clothes, and red Ferraris, his detractors felt he flew the coop. Because of Davis's skyrocketing success, critics such as Crouch coarsely proclaimed that Davis "represented an unmitigated failure of the black male genius."[82] He felt that Davis's embrace of funk and rock represented dollar signs and a deviation from the pillars built by giants such as Armstrong and Ellington.[83] In other words, he was only into Hendrix, Stone, Brown, and the like because they made money as black musicians. Crouch argued that, by incorporating external influences that reflected current commercial tastes, Davis "turned his back on the inherent heroism of the jazz tradition and neglected his duty as role model and agent in social uplift by letting popular tastes dictate his aesthetic and social vision and presentation of self."[84]

Miles was by no means a culturally devoid artist. After all, Davis himself was trying to bring back black kids to a genre labeled "dead." Part of the reason why blacks were running away from their heritage music was because a good portion of it became so engrossed with itself that it became indigestible. The avant-garde jazz movement, which continued to gain wind as the sixties progressed, had its followers, but in its attempt to keep everything socially conscious and pure, the music was often too abstract and self-indulgent, which alienated much of its potential audience. "You have some kind of form. You start somewhere," explained Davis. "I mean, otherwise we'd all be living outdoors."[85] There were times when Miles, Sly, JB, and Jimi approached the outer limits, but they all found a way of creating music that was accessible to their generation.

Miles simply had his own way of doing things. He had nothing against traditional forms, but they were something he had already worked with ad nauseam. Similar to conventional harmony, traditional forms were too restrictive and tired. In Miles's eyes, it was not a dead writing style but rather a style that needed to be revised. Traditional forms were a crutch that interrupted his creative process. He made it clear that he had no intention of revisiting or reusing what had already been used in the exact same fashion.

His music offered both preservation and innovation, something that was neglected in much of the music being produced around him. "You're not losing anything with what we're doing now; you're gaining everything you lost, because you've heard all the other shit over and over again."[86] So much of jazz has been formulaic over the years, and many artists work from a premeditated pattern. Davis never had any intentions of becoming stagnant.

Moving On

I haven't heard myself play in the 1940s and 50s . . . in forty years.[87]
—Miles Davis, 1986

All in all, Miles despised the critics. To him they were all just outsiders. "I don't pay attention to these white critics about my music. Be like somebody from Europe coming criticizing Chinese music. They don't know about that. I've lived what I've played."[88] Davis was an African American living through and narrating the African American experience through his own eyes. He was not trying to sell the experiences of someone else. Azar Lawrence put it simply, "We were all African Americans. That *was* the African American experience. The forefront of how we define black music in America is called jazz. The African American experience is only defined by those experiences of the African Americans who were doing it."[89]

Bitches Brew illustrates the ever-expanding aesthetics of the jazz tradition. With a constant flow of self-expression attached to previous forms, jazz grew from work songs, to country blues, to Dixieland, to swing, to bebop, to the outer limits. The entire history of jazz chronicles the ever-changing experiences of the African American. It illustrates not the ability to withstand change, but how to react creatively to new situations. For the ever-changing jazz scene (with Davis responsible for much of the change), Miles never relied on anyone's past—even his own. "He said to me, 'Keith, you know why I don't play ballads anymore? Because I love playing ballads so much.' That's the sign of an artist," remembered Jarrett. "He has to be conscious enough to see that even what he loves has to move."[90] Davis never even listened to his previous recordings. When asked if he listened to his 1960s quintet or his efforts with Gil Evans, he blurted, "I don't listen to them. They sound funny to me."[91] Realistically, how long could Miles keep reliving the past anyway? "This is 1972 and you got 747s and satellites flying all around," Davis explained to reporter Cliff Smith. "How long do they want me to play 'Body and Soul'?"[92] By 1973 Miles had dropped all of the *Bitches Brew* pieces from his live repertoire, never to be played again. He was using an array of different musicians and tinkering with new ideas. Miles Davis never suffered from a loss of identity; he remained an artist in constant formation.

7. Beyond *Brew*

Bitches Brew was at the core of what we were trying to do with *OK Computer*.[1]
—Thom Yorke of Radiohead

The Money

Here I am playing and don't have nothing to show for it. Going into debt and yet the clubs are crowded, lines wrapped around the block! So I just said to myself, fuck it, if they don't pay me what I want, I'm not making it anymore.[2]
—Miles Davis, on touring in 1956

In 1969 Miles Davis owed Columbia Records a whole lot of money. His lifestyle, with its Ferraris, Manhattan brownstones, and fast women was not a pennywise one, and all-time-low record sales were not the best means of support. So the ever-profligate Miles had to resort to loans, advances against royalties, and some crafty moves in order to take care of himself. On October 23, 1969, Teo Macero sent a memo to Clive Davis in regard to Miles's financial predicament: "I mentioned to Miles that he is presently in the hole for $90,000 in paid advances and an outstanding loan of $30,000. Of course, Miles laughs at all of this. I am rather bewildered but he says a deal is a deal and he is requesting more money for the additional record." Columbia had already given Davis a $10,000 check for his work on *Bitches Brew* on September 8, but Miles was not happy with this. Since *Brew* was going to be a double album,[3] and he had recorded two and a half albums worth of material, Miles sought another $20,000. Clive wrote back to Macero: "[Administrative Vice President] Walter Dean will speak to you. I feel Miles has to be realistic about the loans. Also, we don't sell anymore if it's a two record set, perhaps less in view of the higher price. We should be fair, but Miles must be realistic." Miles got his money. On November 11, Dean cut him a check for $20,000 and put an additional $5,000 toward his outstanding loans. Columbia certainly had faith in *Brew* since the payout was justified as an "advance album payment."

CBS MEMORANDUM

```
Accept          Regr
Appropriate action
Background?     Status?
Fyi             Note & Return
No need to return
Phone CJD       Comment
Reply Direct    File
Suggest reply
To discuss
Copy to CJD     URGENT
```

FROM: Teo Macero
TO: CLIVE DAVIS   cc: Walter Dean
DATE: October 23, 1969

RE: MILES DAVIS

We made payment to Miles recently of $10,000. for his new album which will be released in January. However, this will be a two record set and actually he has recorded enough material for 2½ albums.

My dilemma is as follows: He has requested another $10,000. but would like $20,000. Walter suggested $5,000.

I mentioned to Miles that he is presently in the hole for $90,000. in paid advances and an outstanding loan of $30,000. Of course, Miles laughs at all of this. I am rather bewildered but he says a deal is a deal and he is requesting more money for the additional record.

Please give the above your kind and sincere attention.

TM:cc

[Handwritten annotations in margin:] After Dean will speak to you. I feel Miles has to be realistic about the loans. Also, we don't sell anymore if it's a 2 record set, perhaps less in view of the higher price. We should be fair but Miles must be realistic.

Courtesy of Sony Music Entertainment

In December Miles was shaking down Columbia for yet another $20,000. So Dean, obviously bewildered himself, had to go to the archives on this one and do the math. He wrote to Miles of his findings: "I asked the accounting department to review the number of albums recorded by you in 1969 and the payments made to you to make sure that we paid you all the money that was now due you. To my surprise, I found that not only did we not owe you any money but that you were overpaid. During 1969, we gave you $62,500

CBS MEMORANDUM

FROM: Teo Macero
TO: WALTER DEAN
DATE: December 9, 1969

RE: MILES DAVIS

As per your conversation with Miles Davis, please will you prepare a check for $20,000.00, advance album payment, less the following charges:

1. $8,000.00 to be applied against his outstanding loan to Columbia Records

2. $2,185.43 to be applied against his account for equipment he purchased.

Thank you for your cooperation.

cc

Courtesy of Sony Music Entertainment

in advances." Dean went on to list the five advances Davis had already received, the paid recordings that were scrapped ("The Ghetto Walk," "Early Minor," and other material that was eventually released some thirty-plus years later), and the $5,400 Columbia shelled out for the music equipment Miles wanted for *Brew*. "Therefore, according to our records, you are not entitled to any additional advances at this time," Dean concluded. This is what provoked Miles to write the previously mentioned haughty letter to

CBS RECORDS

A Division of Columbia Broadcasting System, Inc.
51 West 52 Street
New York, New York 10019
(212) 765-4321

Walter L. Dean
Administrative Vice President

December 31, 1969

Mr. Miles Davis
312 West 77th Street
New York, N. Y.

Dear Miles:

As I mentioned to you on the telephone yesterday, I had asked the Accounting Department to review the number of albums recorded by you in 1969 and the payments made to you to make sure that we paid you all the money that was now due you. To my surprise, I found that not only did we not owe you any money but that you were overpaid. During 1969, we gave you $62,500 in advances, as follows:

February 26	$10,000
April 17	7,500
July 7	10,000
September 18	10,000
November 11	25,000

The February 26 payment covered "IN A SILENT WAY" which was completed on February 18. The April 17 payment was for three-quarters of an album recorded February 20 including the selections "THE GHETTO WALK" and "EARLY". This album has apparently never been completed. The July 7 payment was an advance against an album to be subsequently recorded. However, when the next album was recorded on August 19, 20 and 21 the July 7 advance was overlooked and the September 18 advance was given to you. This album, which has not yet been released, contains the selections "JOE", "SANCTUARY" and two untitled selections. The $25,000 advance of November 11 ($5,000 of which was charged against your outstanding loans) was based on information that you had recorded a new double album for which we were giving you $15,000 and a single album for which we were giving you the additional $10,000. Our records indicate that two selections were recorded on November 19 and two selections were recorded on November 28. All of these are untitled.

(cont'd...)

Mr. Miles Davis   -2-   December 31, 1969

Assuming that these recordings were in fact enough for a double album and a single album, there is an overpayment of $10,000 arising from the July 7 payment for which no product was received. If less than three records result from the last two sessions, then the overpayment will be greater than $10,000.

In addition, as you know, we have outstanding bills of approximately $5,400 for musical instruments purchased for you. Therefore, according to our records, you are not entitled to any additional advances at this time.

With kindest regards.

Sincerely,

WLD:dlv

(b) cc: Messrs. Davis, Goldman, Macero and Cohn (M.)

Courtesy of Sony Music Entertainment

Clive Davis "and gang" for the $75,000 annual salary with all the bells and whistles on January 8, 1970.[4]

Needless to say, both Columbia and Miles made their money as soon as *Bitches Brew* took off. Especially high sales figures for a double album and the touring revenue Davis would be getting from large, packed venues added up to no small change.[5] By 1971 Miles was getting an unprecedented amount of money for touring. George Wein paid Miles $130,000 for a twenty-six-date summer tour alone. He also paid him $70,000 for one Avery Fisher Hall performance in 1975.[6] In the early sixties, Davis would typically earn $2,500–3,500 for most concerts, $3,500 for a major festival, and $3,500–4,500 for a week in a club.[7] Now the ante was raised. Davis knew this album's potential,[8] and made sure he was not getting shortchanged when it came to compensation as he had so many times throughout his career.[9]

```
                        MILES DAVIS
                   312 W. 77TH STREET
                      NEW YORK CITY
                     January 6, 1970
```

Mr. Clive Davis & Gang
Columbia Records
51 W. 52nd Street
New York, New York

Dear Clive;

    Now that we're starting off a new year and since we've been selling records, I should like to make some suggestions that would make for better working arrangements for all of us.

    1. Instead of making financial advances to me from time to time, establish a $75000. per year guarantee, against the regular royalties, to be paid quarterly. This would be automatic and eliminate many phone calls requesting money.

    2. In order to avoid confusion in the approval of single releases, the producer and I will decide in this direction, if you and your gang agree.

    The cost of producing our albums is not that high and I believe that with what has been happening, plus an additional push, we should have a hell of a year in 1970 and all of us can make some more money.

    The above is not unreasonable so lets make arrangements to set this up immediately.

    Incidently, Bob Altschuler has been doing a fine job publicity wise, because the Blacks are starting to buy more records too.

    Write On.

                                               MILES DAVIS

Courtesy of Sony Music Entertainment

Post-*Brew* Sessions

There truly is no rest for the wicked. The year and a half following the *Bitches Brew* sessions was a whirlwind of hard touring and recording. From November 1969 through June 1970, Davis was booked sixteen times in Studio B, the majority of those dates being in the first half of 1970. In between some studio time in the fall of 1969, Miles launched a ten-date stint in Europe to get the ball rolling. As the hectic session work ramped up in early 1970, Davis made his Fillmore East debut March 6–7, followed by more studio work, his premiere at the Fillmore West April 9–12, a quick gig at Berkeley's

MEMORANDUM

FROM: Roselind Blanch
TO: Walter Dean   cc: Marvin Cohn, Eugene Friedman, Teo Macero, Anthony Rubino
DATE: December 29, 1969

This is to summarize my discussion with you concerning purchases made for Miles Davis and also to list out those purchases which have been made. As we agreed at our meeting, I am telling Miles Davis that all future purchases of any nature are to be put through Marvin Cohn's office. As a matter of fact, this has already come up and I forwarded Miles' request to Marvin.

Here is a summary of Miles Davis' purchases:

One Knaga Tape Recorder	$1,200.00
Recording Equipment	1,052.58
Electric Pianos And Other Fender Equipment	1,451.65
Six Fiber Board Cases	254.04
Microphones And Speakers	1,369.76

All of the above except the last item have been memoed through accounting to be billed to Miles Davis. The last item will be memoed before the year end.

Thank you.

Courtesy of Sony Music Entertainment

Greek Theatre, five more days in the studio, and a four-night residency at the Fillmore East June 17–20 before a summer, fall, and winter U.S. tour. That summer, he played Madison Square Garden, the *Dick Cavett Show*, and the gigantic Isle of Wight Festival—a far cry from the previous summer's club tour. He had found his Woodstock. Everything was happening.

Davis booked two studio dates, November 19 and 28, to tie up some loose ends and afterthoughts from the *Brew* sessions. The November 19 crew was large and featured a mix of new and familiar faces. Harvey Brooks, Bennie Maupin, John McLaughlin, and Chick Corea stuck around, but Miles created a new percussion section featuring the Panamanian-American drummer Billy Cobham, Brazilian percussionist Airto Moreira, and the Indian tabla and tamboura master Bihari Sharma. Herbie Hancock joined Corea in the keyboard section, Ron Carter teamed with Brooks on bass duties, Steve Grossman replaced Wayne Shorter on soprano saxophone, and Khalil Balakrishna was added to play sitar.

The music has the *Brew* essence, but the multicultural instrumentation adds a new level of exoticism. Davis recorded his original piece "Yaphet," which has a loose samba feel mixed with Indian instrumentation, electric keyboards, group improvisation, and Miles's reverb-laden trumpet gliding on top. "Great Expectations," a Davis and Joe Zawinul collaborative effort, is a bizarre yet effective blend of funk, ambient, and world music (the sitar really steals the show). Zawinul's "Orange Lady," which had been tinkered around with on day one of the *Brew* sessions, finally saw the light of day. It is comprised of three sections including a curious Part C: a blend of samba, Indian, and jazz textures that creates a unique groove. This spacious, ambient piece recalls "In a Silent Way" or "Sanctuary" with its slow, hazy tempo and melancholic melody.

"Orange Lady" eventually found its way onto Davis's 1974 album *Big Fun* as part of "Great Expectations." The track was originally released without Zawinul's permission and credit, but Zawinul's publishing company, Gopam, caught wind of this. According to Gopam's Laurie Goldstein, this was all too common an occurrence on both Miles's live and studio recordings at the time. "Joe used to call me constantly. He would do sessions with Miles and things would turn up on records. He would incorporate them into his own 'tunes.' I loved Miles and so did Joe, but you always had to keep your ears and your eyes open. He did it more than once. It got to the point where every time Miles released something, you better check it." Goldstein quickly wrote to Davis to ensure licensing of "Orange Lady" and hired an attorney to draft an agreement. Once again, Miles was taking credit for other people's work, but this time he was not getting away with it. "You had a two step process because you were dealing with someone who is as knowledgeable and experienced as Miles, but you also had Teo, and Teo should have known better as well,"[10] said Goldstein.

The remaining piece from the day, "Corrado," is Davis's version of a three-chord rocker. Similar to *Brew*'s title track, the piece features cacophonous interplay blended with Davis's echo-drenched trumpet. Miles is once again in excellent form, powerfully and effortlessly blowing for nine-plus minutes over a drudging, chaotic groove. McLaughlin is also on top of his game, contributing a grinding, wah-wah infused solo, which almost resembles a demented version of Santo and Johnny's "Sleepwalk."

Davis assembled the same group for the November 28 session but also added Larry Young to thicken up the keyboard section, Jack DeJohnette to pair with Cobham in the percussion department, and swapped Carter with Dave Holland for bass detail.

"Trevere," a short tune by Davis standards (just shy of six minutes), feels more like a part of a larger piece rather than a sole composition. A swelling, dissonant piece with frantic, yet somehow controlled keyboard and percussion work, it is juxtaposed by Miles's light, melodic, muted trumpet. Davis's "The Big Green Serpent" is similar in nature to "Trevere"—short, building, and also coming off more like an idea as opposed to a complete composition. The band also recorded two takes of Davis's "The Little Blue Frog," a straightforward, loose jam based on a bass riff by Brooks, who haphazardly titled the piece. Surprisingly, this nonchalant jam, accompanied by an edited version of "Great Expectations," was chosen as a single by Columbia.

Davis continued to play at small clubs such as the Cellar Door, Village Gate, and Colonial Tavern for the remainder of 1969 with scaled down road groups before getting back in the studio in late January 1970. The January 27 session at Studio B had a similar lineup to *Bitches Brew*, except it is missing Brooks and Young, has a rhythm section of DeJohnette joined with Moreira and Cobham, and has Balakrishna on sitar. Two tracks were recorded: Davis's massive twenty-one-minute jam "Lonely Fire"[11] and the oddly chosen cover of David Crosby's "Guinevere," which comes off more like a hypnotic meditation than a formal recitation of the Crosby, Stills and Nash classic (it spans over twenty-one minutes).

Despite grumblings between Davis and Zawinul over the rights and arrangements of the compositions, leading to the keyboardist's departure, Miles continued to play Zawinul's music and seemed to be constantly searching for his sound. Along with "Orange Lady," Miles worked on three more Zawinul-penned tracks on January 28 and February 6, 1970. The January 28 band, with the same cast as the day before minus Balakrishna, spent some time on Zawinul's slow groove "Double Image," along with a haunting reading, slow to the point of being almost still, of Shorter's "Feio." On February 6 Davis used the January 28 lineup sans Maupin to record more Zawinul music: a second, shorter version of "Double Image," the aforementioned "Take It or Leave It," and the nineteen-minute, slow and lonely "Recollections," another piece reminiscent of "In a Silent Way."

These were some revealing days for the trumpeter. They show Miles being creative, risk-taking, and generally happy. Some of the chances taken were successful, while others needed a little more refining. The end result was Miles forging most of these efforts, for the majority of them would not be released during his lifetime.[12]

Jack Johnson

I'm Jack Johnson, heavyweight champion of the world. I'm black. They never let me forget it. I'm black all right. I'll never let them forget it!
—Jack Johnson, as read by Brock Peters

On February 18, 1970, Davis began work on *A Tribute to Jack Johnson*, an album that would serve as a soundtrack for Bill Cayton's documentary on the legendary boxer.[13] Released on February 14, 1971, the album was the big studio followup to *Bitches Brew*, even though Columbia never gave it much attention. Around the time of its release, the record company unveiled *At Fillmore*, commemorating Davis's run at the Fillmore East from June 17–20, 1970. Columbia dedicated much more time and effort to the live release, treating the *Jack Johnson* album more like an afterthought. Without the marketing push, the album would peak at only 159 on the Billboard 200 chart, a disappointment considering *Bitches Brew* had peaked at thirty-five. "They kept repeating Fillmore, Fillmore, Fillmore overtly as a selling point. Whereas *Jack Johnson*—a far superior album that would've connected much better with this audience they were actually going after—was completely ignored,"[14] recalled session and Lou Reed guitarist Robert Quine. Davis insisted that Columbia did not want an album so close to white rock music coming from a black musician, but that reasoning is hard to believe.[15] Despite its snubbing by the record company, the album was universally praised. Even Columbia finally came around to appreciating the work by revisiting the album and its surrounding sessions for the *Complete Jack Johnson Sessions* box set in 2003.

The massive Jack Johnson (1878–1946) was the working-class son of two ex-slaves living in Galveston, Texas. After a formal education lasting some six years, Johnson dropped out of school for pastures greener than what the South during the late nineteenth and early twentieth centuries could offer a black man. Recognizing his talents at an early age, Johnson took up illegal prize fighting (which led to some jail time in 1901) before hitting the boxing circuit legitimately, leading to a heavyweight championship in 1908. By defeating James Jeffries in the "Fight of the Century" in 1910, Johnson earned $65,000 and bona fide celebrity status.

Johnson had a "flamboyance that no black man should have."[16] He was cocky, decadent, confident, courageous. An infamous womanizer, Johnson was married three times—each time to a white woman. In 1912 he was arrested for "transporting women across state lines for immoral purposes." He gorged on high fashion, the finest champagne, fancy cars . . . all the best that money could buy. He even died flamboyantly in a high-speed automobile accident at the age of sixty-eight. Johnson lived the life he chose and let nothing stop him. "Johnson portrayed freedom—it rang just as loud as the bell proclaiming him champion,"[17] wrote Davis in his personally penned liner notes for the record.

Miles was ecstatic when he was approached to write the film score. He obsessively researched Johnson's life and all things boxing. "He would discuss boxing with an intensity you couldn't imagine,"[18] said Cayton. He spent hours in the studio working on new material for the film. Johnson became a hero for Miles and a role model for what a black man could and should achieve in this world.

Davis was into boxing all his life. By the late 1950s, he began taking it more seriously and would train rigorously at various times. It even helped him kick his heroin habit in the early fifties. He was influenced by the way professional fighters such as Sugar Ray Robinson would seek perfection from the sport and restrain themselves from distractions and vices. "When he [Robinson] started training, he wouldn't make it with chicks. He disciplined himself and all that! Man, now that's a motherfucker—and Jack Johnson too!"[19] When asked why he idolized fighters so much, Miles responded, "because they don't miss—like Joe Louis didn't miss, and Jack Johnson was twenty years ahead of his time. Fighters just turn me on and make me want to do something."[20]

Davis's love of boxing illuminates his streetwise scruff and self-defense against a world that in his eyes was always on his tail. Boxing was a shield, and its power emancipated the trumpeter. But boxing offered more: a grace and refinement that elevated him above the riffraff trying to hold him down.

And Miles found music in boxing. Any Miles solo has the graceful, elegant, weaving, jabbing, relentless, blow-raining sound of a fighter. "I had that boxer's movement in mind, the shuffling movement boxers use. They're almost like dance steps, or like the sound of a train. When you think of a big heavyweight coming at you it's like a train," wrote Davis in reference to *Jack Johnson*. There's always movement, whether on stage or in the ring, and no time to let your guard down. "I play from my legs. You ever notice?

That's to keep from breaking my embouchure. . . . If you drop your hands, you'll break your embouchure and break the flow,"[21] he told *Rolling Stone*'s Don DeMicheal in 1969. On stage, his band would often land blows, throwing the trumpeter off guard, but Miles would keep his balance and counterpunch, as Davis once described answering a fast 4/4 beat with a series of triplets. And if he wasn't playing, he was still on stage surveying every move around him. "When you box, you gotta watch a guy," explained Davis. "You understand? You gotta watch him, anticipate him . . . you gotta say if he jabs, I'm gonna stop it with my left hand. All this stuff has to be like this [snaps fingers]."[22]

Throughout the sessions Miles sounds inspired and fresh. It certainly helped that Miles was thrilled with the work of his sidemen. After a take of "Duran," for example, Miles is overheard telling McLaughlin, "That's some raunchy shit, John," in a gleeful tone. It was all too easy; Miles instructed very little, let the musicians do what they did best, which made them feel comfortable, and which, in turn, made Miles comfortable. "It was nice to play with him without having him speak to you verbally," said Cobham. "Because you learn so much from what he said through his instrument."[23] As always, Miles had a way of flexing muscle and getting everything he needed without pointless instruction. "What happened with all the musicians who played with Miles in the studio was strictly Miles's doing," explained McLaughlin. "Let's make that perfectly clear. Miles's records were always quite carefully directed by him, orchestrated in a way that was not quite obvious. Because he had that thing, that ability to be able to make musicians play in a way that they would not normally think of."[24]

After nearly two months of recording, one day something really clicked. On April 7 Miles went into the studio with a stripped-down, rock-style band: bass, guitar, drums, sax. There was also Hancock on a Farfisa organ, but that was a total fluke. In fact, Hancock was not even scheduled to play that day. He popped in with a bag of groceries in one arm and a copy of his latest record to hand to Miles. Miles took one look at Hancock and the Farfisa sitting in the corner and ordered him to play. Hancock told Miles he could not stay, but Miles would not take no for an answer, so Hancock climbed behind this completely foreign organ (he did not even know how to turn it on) and tried to acquaint himself with the instrument. The session began serendipitously. While Davis, Macero, and the engineers were setting up, McLaughlin began noodling a shuffle riff to pass the time. This got the group revved up and had Miles running out of the control room with the red record light illuminated behind him. The end result was "Right Off."

"Right Off" feels different from the *Bitches Brew* tracks and pretty much anything else Miles had done before. It has the clean, straightforward Buddy Miles beats, ostinato bass patterns, dominating, heavy rock guitar work, and minimal group interaction coming from a tight-knit group. Although there are post-production plug-ins and edits, the production quality still feels very raw. Macero even gave the recording a good amount of reverb, but it still sounds like an informal rock group jam session.

Even though he was not in the room when McLaughlin started the riff, Davis is credited as sole composer. The questionable authorship of "Right Off" recalls the "Directions in Music" stance Miles took that got him into a little trouble on *Bitches Brew*. Since the fifties, there has been a debate as to what Davis took credit for writing and what he actually composed. Little was formally contested until Miles tried to snag "Sanctuary" from Shorter, and when Zawinul called him out with some of the discrepancies in his pieces. In the eighties, Davis was taken to the mat for co-composer rights on some of the tunes he and John Scofield worked on. "Right Off," however, falls into the cracks of the debate, and was never contested by McLaughlin. The guitarist tossed it off, saying it was no big deal, just an old-school bandleader thing. Being that it was Miles's band, his date, and his concept, Miles should get the credit.[25]

"Yesternow," recorded that same day, benefits from the same production style and band play, but begins in a much more subdued way. The opening section feels more like atmospheric soundtrack music with its dark undertones and grinding rhythms, along with a centered bass ostinato keeping it all together. Despite the challenges faced by improvising over something so slow, McLaughlin and Davis pull off robust solos. As they reach the ten-minute mark, Grossman lays some tasteful saxophone work before a dream-induced slice of "Shhh/Peaceful" material is dubbed in, followed by inserted excerpts of various takes of "Willie Nelson." The piece winds down with a surreal Miles solo that Macero edited in from one of the November 1969 sessions, dubbed with some dark Macero orchestral work, and Brock Peters's Jack Johnson quote to close it off.

Even though Davis had the tracks he wanted for his album, the studio work for *Jack Johnson* persisted into May.[26] Although the material feels loose, Miles was infatuated with getting the project just right. Hours of studio time, endless boxing research, and deep thought had Miles both enthusiastic and apprehensive. "The question in my mind after I got to this was, well is this music black enough, does it have a black rhythm, can you make the rhythm of the train a black thing, would Jack Johnson dance to that," said Davis. "Because Jack Johnson liked to party, like to have a good time and dance."[27]

In Davis's quest for validation and perfection, he always kept the boxer's mentality in mind throughout. He even took to naming most of the pieces after famed fighters ("Ali,"[28] "Konda," "Duran," "Sugar Ray," "Johnny Bratton," "Archie Moore"). He was pretty consistent with his instrumentation—lean and tight—as well as what he wanted it to produce—slick funk and hard rock—making *Jack Johnson* and the surrounding sessions the closest Miles ever came to making a rock record. Aside from the moody, slow sections that coincided with some of the film's footage, everything was a foot-stomping seventies funk jam that would indeed make Johnson proud.

Live Evil

Fan: "Miles, why don't you play like you used to play?" Miles: "How did I used to play?"[29]
—from John McLaughlin

At the tail end of the *Jack Johnson* sessions, Davis began tinkering with some new ideas using a larger group. He had a triple-decker keyboard section consisting of Corea, Hancock, and Keith Jarrett along with three percussionists: DeJohnette, Moreira, and newbie Hermeto Pascoal. He brought Carter back into the fold, and kept Grossman on soprano saxophone. Three of the tracks they recorded on June 3–4, "Nem Um Talvez," "Selim," and "Little Church," were combined with live material from a string of gigs recorded at Washington's Cellar Door on December 16–19, 1970, to form the double album *Live-Evil*. The mixing of live and studio material fit a certain motif Miles was thinking about during the album's creation: one of opposites clashing and merging together. Even some of the titles—"Sivad," "Selim," *Live-Evil*—promoted this idea. "That reversal was the concept of the album: good and bad, light and dark, funky and abstract, birth and death,"[30] explained Davis. Once again, Miles sought out Mati Klarwein for the album cover.[31] At first, the two took part in intimate listening sessions of the new material, trying to put what was on tape onto canvas. Klarwein came up with a psychedelic/surrealistic portrait of Betty Davis, but Miles did not like it. So he went back to Klarwein's studio and found two paintings that best represented his opposites theme.[32]

Initially, Miles was looking for *Live-Evil* to be an extension of *Bitches Brew*, but the album took on a life of its own, especially with the addition of the Cellar Door material. The studio work, with the large ensemble, has the dense, dissonant, almost mortifying sensation of *Bitches Brew* at its darkest, but the live material found Miles and company stretching out further and exploring new directions. For the Cellar Door he was back with a new smaller group featuring saxophonist Gary Bartz, Michael Henderson, Jarrett, DeJohnette, Moreira, and McLaughlin, who showed up for the last night. With the tighter ensemble, the music has the same punch as *Jack Johnson*, with its stripped-down, loose, rock-ready feel, but is much more interactive and experimental. The band also had the same organic energy as on *Bitches Brew*, but with a few more twists. Part of it was the heavy funk backbone provided by DeJohnette and Henderson.

Michael Henderson was only 19 years old when Miles grabbed him from Stevie Wonder's group. Even though he already had experience with some of the biggest names in modern music, Henderson was starstruck when Miles, escorted by his young wife Betty, rolled into Wonder's dressing room to meet his future bassist at Harlem's Apollo Theatre. "I noticed that everyone had turned around and was looking at him," said Henderson. "They were looking at him with their jaws dropped. Betty comes in and she had on this see-through blouse with no bra." Henderson got a call about a month later, but had reservations about leaving Wonder for Miles's band. He asked a friend for advice, and the response was fairly obvious. "If Miles is calling you, get your bass and run; run to wherever he wants you to be." Miles cleared up things on the business side with Wonder ("I'm taking your fucking bass player") and set up Henderson for the *Jack Johnson* rehearsals.[33]

With his funk and R&B background, Henderson made a major impact on the band. His solid groove foundation not only kept the band in check, but made the music feel exciting and fresh. Despite having no jazz experience whatsoever, Henderson kept true to himself and Miles loved him for it. He treated the young bassist like a son, and encouraged everything he brought to the band. Henderson joined the touring group on October 1,[34] and Miles knew he would get heat for the drastic turn his music was taking, especially with the addition of this young funk/Motown-style bassist. "They would say that it was my fault that there was a raw funk on this album [*Live-Evil*]," said Henderson. "I was the blame and the reason for this new expression that Miles was laying down."[35] Sadly enough, Henderson's role as a foundation player was misunderstood. Since he was the anchor of the entire ensemble, critics argued that his playing was uninventive. This was something Henderson could not shake throughout his tenure with Davis. In 1976 he was trashed by Gary Giddins in a *Village Voice* review of Davis's live album *Agharta*. Giddins found his playing detached from everyone else and too lethargic. "He has been with Davis longer than anyone else in the present band, but his contribution becomes increasingly nebulous."[36] But all this heat had no effect on Miles whatsoever. "I want you to know that Miles told me if I ever played any of his old music he would fire me," explained the bassist. Miles and his band knew that this was not just some third-rate funk act. "Miles never wanted just a funk band when I knew him. He wanted a band that could be many things,"[37] wrote Jarrett in response to some less-than-warm words from future Miles bassist Marcus Miller. This was a highly complex, interactive band with players just too good to be anything less.

With his new working band in place, Miles dropped all of the *Bitches Brew* material except for "Sanctuary" and the title track (and those two would be history by 1972), in many ways marking the end of an era and the dawning of a new one. "The Cellar Door was really the end result of the whole *Bitches Brew* direction; it's the last small group format before Miles moved on to his more wild, psychedelic phase, when he began using multiple guitarists and percussionists, and playing organ,"[38] wrote keyboardist Adam Holzman in 2005. Jarrett argued that DeJohnette's departure on May 7, 1971, marked the true end of the era. After DeJohnette left, Jarrett felt that Miles no longer had players "who could surprise him." Whether this is particularly an affront to replacement drummer Al Foster is for anyone to judge. "Miles pleaded with Jack to stay, at least through the European tour. He offered him more money," said Jarrett. "Hell, I even pleaded with Jack. Miles was losing his core of players whose grasp of jazz's improvising past motivated and pushed Miles to higher and higher ground."[39]

The Fall

From 1975 until early 1980 I didn't pick up my horn; for over four years, didn't pick it up once. I would walk by and look at it, then think about trying to play. But after a while I didn't even do that.[40]
—Miles Davis

After DeJohnette's departure, Davis's relentless touring continued. As Jarrett explained, Davis was using a variety of different players, some staying longer than others, and exploring concepts deeply drenched in psychedelia and dark funk. Even though he was quickly phasing songs from the smash seller out of his repertoire, *Bitches Brew* was now in the grasp of the public, and Davis was hitting the big venues almost exclusively. Clubs? No. It was now theatres, amphitheaters, halls, playhouses, and auditoriums. He toured across the United States, Europe, Japan, and Brazil. He was not in the studio as much as he had been in 1970, but he still managed to record several notable and experimental works including *Get Up With It* and *On the Corner* in 1972 in between a hectic touring schedule. The money was pouring in. The first half of the 1970s was Davis's commercial peak.

So what happened? It is clear that Davis's addictive personality worked for him when it came to positive things such as his creativity, but it also got the best of him when it came to drugs and alcohol. His first brush with drug dependency was his well-documented heroin habit in the early fifties. After setting himself straight for a time, he moved on to cocaine and alcohol in the mid-sixties, which came with disastrous consequences, including the crumbling of his marriage with Francis Taylor. "It became so violent. I feared for my life," said Taylor. "Whatever the demons were, they were too deep and he never wanted help."[41] He managed to stave off the wolves when Mabry came into his life, but once she left, Miles was up to his old tricks again.

Davis's relentless health problems did not help either. His physical ailments began with bad hips dating back to the early sixties. As a result of sickle cell anemia, Miles suffered from crippling arthritis and would have several hip operations throughout his life to alleviate the pain. In October 1972 the already shaky Miles crashed his Lamborghini, breaking both his ankles. Needless to say, he was hobbled and depended on prescription painkillers to aid in his recovery. Drinking and cocaine crept back into his life to complement the codeine, morphine, Percodan, Seconal, and whatever else he could get his hands on, leading to bleeding ulcers and a heart attack in 1974.

During this period Miles also ran into more trouble with the law. In February 1973 Davis was arrested on drug and gun charges at his Manhattan brownstone. Accompanied by a 23-year-old white prostitute named Jody Fisher, the 46-year-old Davis locked himself out of his apartment and began banging on the door. Fearing a break-in, a neighbor called the police, who found a ".25-caliber automatic and three envelopes containing cocaine in the nearly empty apartment."[42]

In January 1975 Davis stumbled through a tour of Japan with pneumonia, bleeding ulcers, hip and leg problems, and a serious drug and alcohol problem. In March he was hospitalized for the ulcers, followed by another hospital stay for nodes in his larynx in April. As his body deteriorated, Davis was cancelling shows regularly. "Miles did slow down at the end, and he missed a lot of gigs," explained Davis discographer Peter Losin, who had second-row tickets to see him at the Riverside Theatre in Milwaukee on March 28, 1975, but Davis canceled the show after collapsing onstage in St. Louis a few days earlier.[43] He underwent another hip operation that year, intensifying his chemical dependency, and forcing the cancellation of an eleven-city U.S. tour and a stint in Japan.

Did all of this affect his music? Yes. The heavy weight of pain, over-touring, and drug addiction slowly broke Davis's spirit. "I must say that the music was rather confusing and chaotic at times," said seventies sideman Dave Liebman. "There were a lot of drugs around. It can't be denied... pills and cocaine and there was a lot of it. This affected everything."[44] At times the music was still gripping, tight, and venomous, such as his Carnegie Hall performance in 1974 (*Dark Magus*), but other times it sounded sloppy and uninspired. Whatever was left from the *Bitches Brew* era seemed to vanish into thin air. "When I left that band, there was nothing left to say, basically. It was time to just go and do some structured things. What else could I do?"[45] said Henderson, who stayed until the very end in 1975.

Davis's last commercial album before retirement, *Agharta*, which documents his Tokyo show on February 1, 1975,[46] was slammed in the media. "One wonders what Sly Stone, who played a decisive role in Davis's original decision to plug in, must think of this band," wrote *New York Times* columnist Robert Palmer. Palmer, who championed *Bitches Brew*, could not find one kind word for this performance. He hangs the entire band's playing ("disembodied," "whines," "noisy," "disjointed," "turgid") and Davis's asleep-at-the-switch leadership ("directionless," "sloppy"). "Davis began having more trouble with his health. Whatever the reasons, the music has sunk to a shockingly banal level, which the faultless Japanese engineering of *Agharta* renders with pitiless clarity," concluded Palmer.[47] Giddins, in his *Village Voice* piece, "Miles Davis Plays Dorian Gray," found some bright moments in the set, most particularly Sonny Fortune's sax work, but dismissed most everything else. "What bothers me about this music is its lack of will. Miles doesn't exploit the backbeat, he succumbs to it, and the worst consequence is not the ensuing monotony—which theoretically a soloist could turn to his advantage—but how much harder it becomes for Davis to assert his identity against the din.... *Agharta* isn't just a bad record, it is a sad one."[48]

The end of the line was at Central Park on September 5, 1975. In the middle of the show, Miles stopped. "He was crying in pain," said Davis friend and photographer Teppei Inokuchi, who was backstage that day. "Then he went into a limousine and disappeared."[49]

So Miles hung it up. "It was just that I took so much medicine I didn't feel like playing the trumpet, didn't feel like listening to music. Didn't want to hear it, smell it, nothing about it."[50] At this point, he wasn't about to rely on his past either. He was too vain to churn out any old tripe just because he could. He also had too much pride for audiences to "take pity on him" on stage in this condition. So Miles retreated to his brownstone on West 77th Street, which became his "Hotel Splendour 1980"[51] for nearly five years. At one point he did not leave the house for six months. He would sit there with a massive projection-screen television, one bulb burned out, never turned off, watching old boxing videos, inhaling vast amounts of coke, taking pills and heroin, and drinking cognac and Heineken.[52] Miles was also back to his old womanizing ways, fancying scores of faceless women. Occasionally friends would stop by to visit, but usually he would avoid any contact. According to Davis even Mick Jagger knocked on the door at one point, but he would not let him in.[53] The faces that flashed by were mostly hangers-on and drug dealers. "People take advantage of you when you're fucked up. There are no friends when you're using,"[54] said Davis. Wein recalled one particular visit that he could never forget. "I went over there one time and it was really terrible. He'd been beaten up; he'd actually been hurt. Some guys had come in and beaten him up because I think he owed them money and he was sitting in the bathroom and he had a pistol in his pocket. It was a macabre scene."[55] Davis's psyche was spinning. Lydia DeJohnette remembered one visit in which she found the man who never looked back in some sort of nostalgic time warp. She noticed all kinds of awards and memorabilia hanging on his walls that were never there before. He was even talking about the old times and old friends.[56]

"Bored is the word. So bored you can't realize what boredom is,"[57] explained Davis. During this period, Miles was actually convinced to record some new music. Several people in his life tried to pick him back up again, get him off the drugs, and lift him from the pit of self-pity he was lying in. Eleana Steinberg, a friend of Davis, put him in touch with Julie and Larry Coryell for a studio project on March 30, 1976, and another on March 2, 1978.[58] Despite getting out of the house, Miles did not play trumpet at either of these rehearsals, just organ. Sounding completely uninterested throughout, the trumpeter was not ready for any kind of work, so the sessions were halted and the recordings were shelved.

Davis's motivation to get out of this funk finally came from a need for money (he still had no intention of dying poor), the will to be innovative and stay on top, and the help of his ex-wife Cicely Tyson. Tyson would come by, clean the place up, throw out the girls, help Miles curb the drinking and drugs, and gradually get him back in shape. With Tyson's help, Miles started thinking more clearly, and began thinking about music again.

In 1981 Miles did return and continued to play until his death in 1991, but not without more baggage. The loss of practice and embouchure, advancing age, and the pummeling his body took were setbacks he had trouble overcoming. Many of his projects featured some of the best young artists of the eighties and nineties and were innovative, including his final album, *Doo-Bop*, which fused jazz with hip-hop, but his chops, "puttery" at times, were not as demanding as they once were. Still, Miles pushed to the best of his ability, continued to seek out and guide fresh talent, and worked hard until the day he died.

Sons of *Bitches Brew*

Of all the turbulence *Bitches Brew* and its surrounding era withstood, plenty of accolades came out of it. Many Davis alumni, particularly those from *Brew*, became stars in their own right. Davis was right to send off McLaughlin, for he started the Mahavishnu Orchestra, one of the most successful jazz fusion groups of the seventies, and has retained an acclaimed legacy for his musicianship. Ditto for Shorter and Zawinul, who teamed up to form Weather Report, another dominating fusion act. Maupin joined Hancock's band to record *Head Hunters*, jazz's first platinum album. Chick Corea and Lenny White worked together as members of Return to Forever, who carried a great following throughout the seventies and still possess star status. Harvey Brooks went back to being a studio musician for rock and pop acts, becoming one of the most in-demand bassists in the seventies and eighties. Holland and DeJohnette have constantly toured and recorded for the past forty-plus years. Putting *Bitches Brew* or any other Miles Davis album on a résumé at the very least guaranteed a solid career in the music business. Some Davis graduates have even kept the album's legacy going. In 2011 Maupin, Al Foster, and other alums formed Bitches Brew Beyond, commemorating the wild, funky sounds that resonated in 1969.

Bitches Brew may not have been the first jazz fusion record[59] and its sound never duplicated, but its innovations and success made it an institution, propelling the jazz fusion movement of the seventies, various funk and crossover idioms of the seventies and eighties, and to some degree smooth jazz, whose popularity went well into the 1990s. While many veteran and upcoming acts stayed the course and continued to make great straight-ahead jazz in the seventies and beyond, there were also numerous players who flooded the new scene with rock beats, funk and R&B-infused grooves, and a barrage of electric instruments.

The problem was not that jazz players were following Miles, but that they looked toward Miles for all the wrong reasons. Many acts in the seventies saw *Bitches Brew* and other modern Davis works as formulas, and their results were just the same as their motivations. Record labels such as Creed Taylor's CTI tried to exploit certain acts and get them into the new wave of jazz fusion, with artists such as Art Farmer, Milt Jackson, Freddie Hubbard, Grover Washington Jr., Bob James, and George Benson making highly produced, pop-tinged records with varying results. After Clive Davis resigned in 1973, Columbia even tried to capitalize on the jazz fusion wave and constructed an overcrowded roster of crossover acts including Janne Schaffer, Rodney Franklin, and Dexter Wansel.[60] Clive's cutting-edge business instincts were now replaced by target markets, demographics, and accountants. Even if the musicians had talent and vision, many of the records were made with enormous budgets, sometimes sapping the spontaneity and feeling from the performances. A typical jazz album at the time could cost anywhere between twelve to forty thousand dollars to make. Hancock's *Head Hunters* cost one hundred thousand dollars.[61] Other jazz artists, similar to some of the seventies progressive rock groups that punk bands rebelled against, made music so complex and self-absorbed it lost many listeners. About Return to Forever's 1973 virtuosic album *Hymn of the Seventh Galaxy*, Stuart Nicholson wrote, "Yet for all its superficial gloss, the mechanical splendor of these workouts was emotionally distancing."[62] The bottom line is that a good portion of the seventies jazz fusion sounds uninspired, somewhat dated, and non-resonant. "I don't think the music really came from a deep source," said Liebman. "Even though the guys tried, it was an attempt to be popular. They were playing with full intensity and they weren't thinking that when they were playing that way but the kind of milieu that it was in was coming into the popular. It was like, we can sell records and that was always underneath it all."[63]

Radiohead

As the years pass, the ghosts of *Bitches Brew* still linger throughout modern music. In 2003, nearly a quarter century after its release, the record received platinum certification from the Recording Industry Association of America, signifying one million sales, and illustrating a whole new wave of listeners. When all the bands that ceased to capitalize on its success and the sons of *Brew* moved on to other projects, there were many musicians who did not try to be Miles or look for a winning formula, but rather sought his essence. What is remarkable is the variety of music that Miles has his thumbprint on and what these musicians actually got out of him and his album.

It could be argued that *Bitches Brew* and other Davis albums of the period helped lay the foundation for rap and hip-hop. Since the eighties, beats, bass lines, and other instrumental segments from these records have been looped and sampled countless times by hip-hop artists, providing an early structure for the genre. The bass line for "Bitches Brew," for example, was used in songs by Mobb Deep, the Roots, House of Pain, and Heavy D & the Boyz, to name a few.[64] These artists were clearly inspired by Davis's staccato-laced, woven diction and rhythm-driven music, which have become key characteristics of rap and hip-hop.

The virtuosity of the performances and complexity of the arrangements Davis (as well as other fusion acts) offered were also a primary influence on progressive metal acts such as the Mars Volta, who modeled *Bitches Brew*'s enormity and aggression for their 2005 album, *Frances the Mute*.[65] Others:

- "A record such as *Bitches Brew* had simply never been made before, not by Miles Davis, not by any group. In depth, composition, instrumentation and delivery, *Bitches Brew* is visionary, unmatched and still amazes to the present day."[66]—Henry Rollins, Black Flag
- "I can hardly stand to listen to anything except *Bitches Brew*. . . . I think because I am searching for something . . . but I can't find it as long as I'm thinking about it. *Bitches Brew* sounds like that."[67]—Wayne Coyne, Flaming Lips
- "Miles Davis to me was a jazz giant, although my interest in Miles came late in my musical discoveries, and *Bitches Brew* being my first album by him. Miles Davis's music and career taught me to musically pursue a creative evolution within one's genre and beyond, and it works."[68]—Dave Lombardo, Slayer
- "I know some teenagers who discover *Bitches Brew* and it allows them to expand their imagination. Miles Davis was able to create something that even Jimi Hendrix and I were like, 'wow, he's coming into our arena, but we can't go into his.'"[69]—Carlos Santana

- "He created atmospheres with his talent. Rooms change when his songs unfold."[70]—Brandon Boyd, Incubus
- "I listen to Miles all the time. The art on the *Bitches Brew* album cover is what first drew me to it. The music is incredible. The album itself is timeless."[71]—Nas

"*Bitches Brew* by Miles Davis has this incredibly dense and terrifying sound. That's the sound I was trying to get. The only other place I'd heard it was on an Ennio Morricone record. I'd never heard it in pop music," stated Radiohead's Thom Yorke in 1999 when describing *Brew*'s influence on the band when making their breakthrough album, *OK Computer*. "I didn't hear it there. It wasn't there. It wasn't like we were being snobs or anything, it was just like, this is saying the same stuff we want to say."[72] On the surface, *OK Computer* and *Bitches Brew* sound nothing alike. There are no twenty-minute jams, group improvisation, extended solos, or multi-layered instrumentation setups on *OK Computer*. As Yorke explained, the similarities are at the heart.

OK Computer was Radiohead's breakthrough album in 1997. Following two mildly successful records by the group, *OK* would go on to sell over seven million copies worldwide, catapulting the band into the global arena and dazzling the critics, many of whom called it one of the greatest recordings ever made. As Miles had done on *Bitches Brew*, Radiohead were able to tap into the youth culture and embrace the temperament of the times. Their songs dealt with universal themes such as isolation and alienation ("Let Down," "Climbing Up the Walls"), political and artistic compromise ("Electioneering"), devastation, disillusionment, and finality ("No Surprises"), paranoia and phobias ("Airbag," "Lucky"), the bored and mundane ("Subterranean Homesick Alien"), artificiality and consumerism ("Fitter Happier"), and capitalism ("Karma Police," "Paranoid Android").[73]

Brew and *OK* pair well when it comes to overall mood. Yorke described his album as something that sounds shocking at first listen, but has a consistency and atmosphere that reasons with the chaos and puts what is disturbing in perspective. *OK Computer* is not a "concept" record in a conventional sense, but it feels like an album and not a group of isolated singles. In fact, the band took two weeks just to formulate the track list. Like *Brew*, it was organized chaos. The band loved the atmosphere and pandemonium that bellowed from *Brew*—the big, gritty sound of the multiple pianos, drummers, basses, and tried to capture that essence on their record. "That's why

Bitches Brew is so good, beyond just Miles's trumpet playing," said Jonny Greenwood. "We love how he got together that sense of chaos."[74]

The band has candidly spoken about how *Brew*'s frenzied, absorbing, big, yet claustrophobic feel specifically inspired "Subterranean Homesick Alien." The Fender Rhodes, echo effects, and general psychedelia where obvious nods, but there is more lurking beneath the surface. "'Subterranean Homesick Alien' was born out of listening to *Bitches Brew* endlessly every time I drove my car. The first time I heard it I thought it was the most nauseating chaos. I felt sick listening to it. Then gradually there's something incredibly beautiful—you're never quite sure where you are in it," explained Yorke. "It seems to be swimming around you. It has that sound of a huge empty space, like a cathedral. It wasn't jazz and it didn't sound like rock and roll. It was building something up and watching it fall apart. That's the beauty of it . . . I completely missed it, but then again, I didn't."[75]

Both Davis and Radiohead created something that was anything but commercial, but at the same time had mass appeal. They both left behind works that were deemed credible and successful for something that crossed over into uncharted territory. Also like Davis, Radiohead would continue to challenge themselves and produce albums that further broke away from their predecessors. With the success of *OK Computer*, they took advantage of the privileges they had and did whatever they wanted. Despite the parallels between these artists, Greenwood went on to say that he felt uncomfortable citing Davis as an influence "because what he did is so much greater and different than anything we do. We've taken and stolen from him shamelessly, not just musically, but in terms of his attitude of moving things forward."[76]

Legend of the Cool

If you understood everything I said, you'd be me.[77]
—Miles Davis

Cool is forever. "Miles Davis is being inducted into the Rock and Roll Hall of Fame tonight. Not as an 'early influence,'" wrote *New York Times* columnist Ben Ratliff in 2006. "Davis is being recognized as a rock star."[78] Even more recently, when Green Day's Billie Joe Armstrong inducted Guns N' Roses into the Hall in 2012, he cited guitarist Izzy Stradlin as the "Miles Davis of rock and roll," not only because of the way he effortlessly weaved on stage with his bandmate Slash, but because of his hip, enigmatic nature. Since leaving Guns N' Roses in 1991, Stradlin has spent little time on the road and has given very few interviews. A private and somewhat reclusive person, Stradlin also opted out of his Hall of Fame induction that night. It is not that much of a stretch to see the connection—listen to *Bitches Brew*, followed by any rock record. But the music is only part of it. The young rockers have been idolizing Miles Davis, the man, year after year. He was *the* rock star. The only question is, would he have shown up to the ceremony? "What's a rock 'n' roll band?" Davis hissed at a journalist in 1970. "The only rock I know is the rock of cocaine."[79]

Miles Davis always saw the complexities in himself in a simple way. He never had a reason to stop and self-assess, for there was nothing there that was not who he was. "If I analyze myself, I won't be able to do anything. 'Why am I this or that?' I might as well go to an analyst,"[80] he told *Newsweek*'s Hubert Saal in 1970. Behind Davis's perplexing psyche was a core of authenticity and honesty—sometimes a brutal honesty—that at times rubbed people the wrong way and had others scratching their heads. "People sometimes think I'm difficult, because I always say what's on my mind, and they can't always see what I see,"[81] he explained to Chris Albertson. But as Miles later clarified, he called it as he saw it and had no regrets about it. How he acted or what he created may have been at times disagreeable, but it was always sincere and dished out because he felt it had to be.

Being honest with himself meant that by no means was he willing to put on a disguise or some song and dance just to get attention. For all the grinning and clowning that Louis Armstrong and Dizzy Gillespie did to draw in the masses, Miles was able to grab the public eye simply by defying it. "I don't know who's out there," said Davis about his new young audiences in 1972. "It doesn't make any difference because I'm a musician, not a showman. I'm no Uncle Tom."[82] And for all the pride he took in himself, he didn't consider himself an egomaniac. He argued that only vain people repeat themselves because that is what they are most comfortable doing.[83] Miles was never willing to deliver a retro package or rely on past glories in order to be reminded of how great he was. When Quincy Troupe asked Miles where his trophies and awards were during a visit to his Malibu home, to his surprise, he found them dumped in a closet. "You're only as good as what you're playing today," he told Troupe. "So I can't be thinking of no awards when I need to have my head into my music."[84]

But behind the suave, sinister persona and powerful creative force was a very withdrawn man, haunted by the demons circling his life and the social conditions determined to weigh him down. "I don't think I'm accepted. Black music isn't accepted," explained Davis in 1972. "You have to be white, have long hair and blue eyes and a nice looking face. They don't care what you play. They don't want to educate the people. But it doesn't bother me because I never expect anything."[85] "Basically Miles is very shy; that's the whole thing," said longtime friend Dizzy Gillespie, who felt that Miles was putting up a front to cover up his insecurities. Teo Macero noted that honest flattery made Miles uncomfortable, defensive, and cold. "Unless you have something to say to him, he's not going to listen. I mean, if you just go up and say, 'Yeah Miles, you're great' and pat him on the back, he doesn't want to hear that."[86] Troupe recalled setting up a live studio interview in 1988 with a spooked-out Miles. He made several attempts at loosening him up, but nothing was working, for the trumpeter had no interest in talking about himself. "Suffice to say the man was terrified."[87]

Miles Davis created *Bitches Brew* because he had to. He needed to be innovative and self-expressive—and was quite passionate about it. "Miles knew what he wanted . . . in general. But he wasn't that specific about what it was, but he knew it when he heard it," noted Harvey Brooks while working with him during *Brew*. "And he knew what it wasn't, which is really, primarily, what it is."[88] But what makes Miles Davis a charismatic, timeless figure is not only his originality, but his incredible will to achieve at any cost. Underneath the shyness, the darkness, and the tough skin that life gave him were a layer of warmth, beauty, and romanticism that could not be hidden in his playing. Whatever the method, it had to come out.

8. Miles in 3-D: Images of *Bitches Brew*

The Camera Lies

There is no such thing as inaccuracy in a photograph. All photographs are accurate. None of them is the truth.[1]
—Richard Avedon

Richard Avedon's words are absolutely right.[2]
—Jan Persson

"The camera never lies" is uttered by people whether they are watching the news, a documentary, reality television, flipping through a magazine, or absorbing any other kind of media. Of course, this phrase is a misleading one, for not every picture tells a story. Photographers and filmmakers are notorious for distorting the truth through image, creating the illusion of presence. It is even arguable whether a simple portrait can capture who a person really is.

In 1986 Miles Davis did a photo shoot with the legendary Irving Penn for his album *Tutu*. It was not the easiest session for Penn, for Davis walked in with a hairdresser and an attitude that befuddled the photographer and his crew. "I tried to talk to him when he walked in, but he completely ignored me,"[3] said Penn. Davis saw right through the photographer, knowing that he would be asked to take his shirt and bling off, exposing all of what the flesh could unveil about the trumpeter. It's as if Penn wanted the "gotcha shot" handed to him on a silver platter. Despite the rough start, Miles managed to tolerate Penn, keep his shirt on, and make the best of the session. Many of Penn's stylized black-and-white shots that day were instantly applauded,[4] by many who felt that they witnessed an intimate moment of a legendary figure toward the end of his life—the stark frontal portrait that dons the album cover, the close-cropped shots of Miles's cracked, sixty-year-old hands depicting an articulate man, a thinker, with plenty of battle scars from a life hard-fought. But Miles hated the shots. "I'm not this ugly," he complained. "Miles is a good looking guy and Irving couldn't capture it," explained Davis photographer and friend Teppei Inokuchi. "The expression is wrong. The whole thing is a disaster."[5]

A person looking at a photograph of themselves sees things that others do not, and conversely, the camera sees things the person cannot perceive. It can often be a shocking experience. "That may sound strange because people look at the mirror all the time, but you're not seeing yourself as others see you," said freelance and ex-Columbia photographer Fred Lombardi. "A photograph does things that a mirror doesn't show." Aside from photographing Davis in the sixties and seventies, Lombardi conducted numerous corporate portrait sessions with many angered faces in the aftermath. He did not use any strange lighting or staging, nor was he trying to capture these people's souls, just a straightforward surface shot. "With the people I had who hated the photographs, all I did was tell them the truth. That's what the fuck you look like!"[6] But was it the truth? If the camera can catch something that the subject cannot see, maybe what Penn shot was really who Miles was, but Miles could not see it, or face it.

If Penn's shots seem intimate and revealing, it could be by chance or from decades of experience because Penn never really knew Miles. After all, the session was just one of many big assignments for the photographer. "Irving Penn was a very stylized portrait photographer and a hell of a photographic artist," said photographer Tad Hershorn. "But what he might get in one shoot is gonna reflect how he was able to interact with Miles Davis."[7] Penn argued that portrait photography looks for something profound about the inside of the subject despite the limitations of the medium that can only capture the exterior. But how was Penn going to capture the truth if he did not know his subject?

Penn is famous for his portraits and fashion photography such as his *Vogue* covers that date back to the 1940s. By the 1980s Penn was used to capturing the soulless images of models who were told how to pose and act. The models and their incredibly versatile faces are there to act out a role, becoming whatever the designer or photographer wants.[8] So Miles showed up to Penn's session, but was asked to make poses, act and look a certain way, and basically not be himself.

Is there any truth in photography? This writing will make no claim to answer a question that cannot be answered, but will demonstrate the power of the lens and the visual narrative it can portray, a perspective different from that of someone in a theatre seat or with a set of headphones. Throughout his life, Davis was photographed countless times in countless scenarios by countless photographers. Each shot depicts a different perspective of the man, and each one telling, whether it is the truth or a lie. The very least a photograph can do is document an event, and although the *Bitches Brew* sessions were never shot, the surrounding period certainly was. Many of the shots taken and the stories behind them reveal a side of Miles Davis that parallels his music and persona in a way that can only be told through the camera lens.

Working with Miles

Being that he was neither a musician, producer, executive, family member, or female acquaintance, the photographer had a unique relationship with Miles Davis. Even as an outsider Miles never seemed threatened by a photographer; maybe it was his ego, but more likely because none of them were in competition with him. Regardless, most photographers approached Miles with caution, knowing well his reputation for being difficult with most people who came near him. "All I remember is that people warned me," explained *Rolling Stone* photographer Baron Wolman. "They said, 'you know, you're gonna have trouble with Miles. He doesn't like white people.'"[9] "Don't get the impression that this was a down-to-earth guy. He was a character,"[10] said Lombardi when asked about his Davis encounters. "Miles is very scary, he's tough to approach. I was just watching from the distance,"[11] remembered Inokuchi when shooting Davis at the Newport Jazz Festival in 1969. But once they got to know him, they discovered a whole other side of the man. It turned out that Miles was very warm, sincere, and generous about welcoming these people into his life and revealing himself to the masses.

Danish photographer Jan Persson experienced some initial awkwardness when Miles told him to "get off" while shooting him on stage in 1960, but Persson and Miles would eventually hit it off, forming a professional relationship that lasted some twenty-five years. He was on top of every European tour and even shot Davis in the studio for the *Aura* sessions in 1985. Miles loved his work and always requested copies of his shots. "Of course I knew his reputation, but he always accepted the conditions we as photographers have," said Persson.[12]

Lombardi's encounters with Davis were brief, but always left an impression. His first face-to-face assignment was set up with Don Hunstein at Miles's home, but the trumpeter was not in any condition to be photographed that day, telling them, "Not today man," in a hazed, but sincere manner. Lombardi was not offended, but impressed by Davis's gentlemanly behavior and taken by his strong presence. "Even on a brief encounter, something came through if you were sensitive to it. Even the way he looked at me." Lombardi had another run-in with Davis and his wife Betty at the Isle of Wight in 1970 and was surprised by their openness and casual guise. The two were just hanging out, sitting on the grass backstage when Lombardi passed by and asked to take a couple pictures, which they were more than happy to do. Later that day, Lombardi noticed Miles, draped in his red leather jacket, waiting in line by himself at a concessions stand. No one paid him much mind, just another face in the crowd. "He was not assertive in any way like 'I'm Miles Davis,'" said Lombardi. "He was like a shy kid. I could remember that pretty clearly. It was so evident." Regardless of his bravado, Davis would not have made many waves with the concession crowd anyway. "If he would have tried to beat the line by being a celebrity, the person wouldn't have known who he was," said Lombardi. "That's the case with ninety-nine percent of jazz musicians. They would know Jimi Hendrix but they wouldn't know Miles Davis from a hole in the wall. Today, most people wouldn't recognize Duke Ellington if he was on the A train."[13]

Despite the initial jitters, Inokuchi eventually bonded with Davis and maintained both a professional and personal relationship that lasted decades. Since Inokuchi was the same age as Miles's son Junior (as well as friends), Miles treated Inokuchi like a son. "He would talk to me about sex, drugs, and rock and roll just like Duke Ellington and Charlie Parker did to him."[14] He told Inokuchi he could shoot him whenever he was on stage at the Village Gate and to bring his camera whenever he came over. For a while, the two were inseparable, hanging out at the brownstone, drinking Heinekens together, and cruising all over the city in Miles's Ferrari.

When Wolman was shooting Miles and Betty at the brownstone for *Rolling Stone*, the three instantly hit it off. Betty was a no-brainer; the two had already worked together on a fashion shoot for one of her solo albums along with a photo session for *Rags*, and he had Betty in her comfort zone. "Betty and I didn't have any problems because she was doing what she liked to do, and that was pose,"[15] said Wolman. Because of his reputation, Wolman approached Miles with respect and sincerity. He would constantly talk to Miles while taking the shots, making it a comfortable, nonchalant experience. He was genuinely interested in their lives, humor, and their appearance, which struck a chord with Miles. He kidded Wolman that he looked a little out of shape and drove him down to Gleason's gym to hang out, get some shots, and maybe do a little sparring. Along with getting the experience of hanging out with such a unique figure, Wolman, like many of the other photographers, got the shots. "You can tell by the pictures that he opened up to me. There was no defiance."[16]

Unveiling Miles

What do we expect to see in a Miles Davis photograph? By 1970 Davis's notorious reputation and controversial new music crushed any expectations of seeing an ordinary man, but rather the "angry black man." Miles was a criminal, a short-fused wife beater, a controversial musician who turned his back to his audience. On top of that, he was a star, a black star, giving him the perception of looking "different."

How the audience perceives the visual image of Miles Davis has a lot to do with how they identify his music. Looking at Miles or even an album cover like *Bitches Brew* confirms (or de-confirms) the audience's expectations of what they are about to hear, or whether or not they would be willing to listen to it. For covers such as *Bitches Brew* or *On the Corner*, Miles hired artists who exemplified the black consciousness and catered to a young, hip, enlightened black fan base, giving record buyers the sense that this was black music inside the wrapper. His physical appearance circa 1970 only heightened this awareness. Miles's trendy regalia urged the music's modernity, but also bewildered listeners who wondered if Miles was doing black or white. Whether it was his exoticism, black authenticity, white mainstream dabbling, or notoriety, it worked, for the music reached the masses, especially curious white listeners.

Despite the difficult, complex demeanor of the man, these photographers came to find out that, yes, Miles Davis was an extraordinary figure, but he was also a regular guy—and this is how he was captured. He went to work, hung out with friends and women, and maintained a somewhat domestic home life. Miles had real feelings and always wore his heart on his sleeve. Miles loved Betty, his music, and embraced a sense of accomplishment as a black man living the American dream. He did not take shit, defied his naysayers, and led his life on his own terms both on and off the stage. Having that Ferrari or ferocious prowess in the ring and on stage was empowerment and he loved to show it off whenever he could. "The back story to him was getting in the car with him and going to the gym. . . . That's not the back story. *That's* the story,"[17] said Wolman, who asked Miles to pull over and take as many shots as he could of him leaning next to his exotic, expensive automobile. It wasn't that the photographers were in awe of driving around with Miles in a Ferrari; they knew that this was a big part of who he was. The car symbolized his adversity over a harsh existence: Yes, the black man can get there, too. There is hardly a shot of him with that car where he is not smiling.

Some of the most revealing shots of Miles Davis are not the ones capturing him as a musician, celebrity, or in some pretty pose, but the ones that capture him as a human being. Many of the photographers who shot Miles took the time to get to know him and his music in order to capture his essence in the shots. Inokuchi took to the extreme trying to find out who Miles was by not only being around his every move, but trying to duplicate his lifestyle as well. "Find out how the artist lives, find out what he eats, his clothes. That I did—because Miles smoked Marlboro cigarettes I smoked Marlboro cigarettes, he drinks Heineken beer, I drink Heineken beer."[18] The intimate, even mundane moments not only capture Miles's humanity but create a gateway into Miles's psyche and creative process. When Lombardi was shooting Miles at Avery Fisher Hall in 1972, he was looking for small instances—a smile, a laugh, a glance at the crowd, even his back turned to the audience—something that captured the heart of Miles and what he was experiencing. No matter how prepped he was, there was no predicting when that moment would take place, if at all. While on stage, Persson was looking for Miles's attitude and ambience, comparing the experience to improvising where a moment could spring from anywhere. "It is not only the music showing which way the images are taken. It can be the circumstances, the light, funny hats, sunglasses, and so on."[19]

The Shots

It was a little easier being a celebrity during the *Bitches Brew* era. There was less of a need for the paparazzi because gaining access to many famous people was fairly easy and there was not as much demand to glorify or debase these people. It is difficult to imagine any celebrity sitting on the grass at a concert or waiting in line at a concessions stand as Lombardi witnessed at the Isle of Wight. When Hershorn shot Davis in Dallas in 1969, had he known, he could have easily walked right up the stairs to the stage to get the shots he wanted without any press pass or hassle like he encountered at the same venue twenty-one years later. In those days, there was not as much of a boundary between performer and audience. "Photographers were right in front, running all over the place,"[20] said Lombardi about New York's concert heyday, be it the Fillmore East, the Beacon Theatre, the Palladium, or even Madison Square Garden. By the mid-seventies all of this had started to change, with the advent of press boxes, bodyguards, entourages, and heightened venue security to accommodate star power and inflated egos. These photographers, however, were there for the last gasp and were able to capture Davis more intimately and without so many agendas.

Even the corporate world did not have the same connotations that it does today. Columbia Records was founded in 1888 and quickly evolved into a major corporation, but retained much of its mom-and-pop sensibilities, taking chances on new acts, and running with forward-thinking producers and other creative people behind the scenes. Columbia is now owned by Sony Music Entertainment,[21] a much larger corporation with fatal bottom lines and low-risk decision making. Yes, Columbia was out to make money, but was also willing to take chances and do things on the fly. "Anyway it could happen, it could happen. I had cats bringing in canaries. Whatever works, it works. If it was valid, I would do it,"[22] said John Berg when describing the corporate methodology of the sixties. Berg stressed that it was not about style or delivering a brand; it was about ideas. He recalled a situation where he had to immediately whip up an album cover for *Santana's Greatest Hits* for an overdue deadline, which he finished in two minutes. "There was a meeting of seventy-five suits in a conference room. I grabbed this thing off the wall, some sort of portfolio by Joel Baldwin and that was it."[23] As a result, we have the iconic records that have transcended generations and changed lives. Columbia also knew what they were doing was important and made sure session photographers were on hand for whatever Bob Dylan, Miles Davis, Johnny Cash, or any other artist was going to do that day.

In the sixties being a photographer was not a glamorous profession. Session photographers were there to do jobs and were paid as staff employees. This, or course, has left some bitterness because the shots have become immortal, but many photographers are left without the rights to their shots[24] and measly royalties. But at the time, these photographers did not think much of it. "People say you're so lucky to hang around all these people, but at the time it was a job I was trying to do well,"[25] said Wolman who photographed every musician whose face donned the pages of *Rolling Stone* in its earliest years. The photographers were there because they loved the music and knew their subjects. Like Miles, their work was honest.

Baron Wolman

"There's one photo that's pretty revealing. His relationship with women, as you know, was difficult," said Wolman while flipping through his online gallery. The shot shows a warmth and peacefulness in Davis that is rarely captured. It was taken at Miles's home two months after *Bitches Brew* and one month into Betty and Miles's marriage. Baron described Betty as an outgoing, friendly person whose joy rubbed off on Miles, bringing out this gentle, tender side of him. "I think he's gentle up to a point [chuckles]," said Wolman who points out another shot from the wall featuring a more irritated Miles. "That's a little bit who he was too. 'Alright, give me a break. I don't give a shit about her. She's a woman.'"[26]

Jan Persson

Browsing with Wolman the shots at Miles's home, I could not help but notice a bizarre, circular couch upholstered in some velvet-type fabric that could not be taken out of any other decade than the one Miles was sitting in. "Look at that couch," I told Wolman. "Yeah I know. Look at the fringe pants,"[27] Wolman chuckled back. Davis's change in appearance at the time was something almost every photographer emphasized in their shots. Fashion reflected the massive changes in music and society as a whole. Davis's manifestation not only illustrates Betty's youthful influence on him, but his willingness to embrace change and stay ahead of the curve. And Miles was no dummy. Miles knew that staying on top meant looking the part. The dignified, now middle-aged Negro in the Brooks Brothers suit would only project the image of a has-been. "He's obviously into cooperating and doing the best he can for the photograph. He's happy to be photographed," said Lombardi. "He was aware of his visual image. He took pains to appear cool, to look like someone who had it together. He was vain and he knew what it meant to his career."[28]

While most would look foolish being engulfed in young culture like this in their forties, Miles looks fresh and iconic, the one everyone else had to keep up with—just like his music. Over forty years later, people look at him as a fashion icon just the same or even more so than a music star half his age. "I had seen his musical development parallel his clothing style. You can see how he changed clothing style when he changed his music in another direction," said Persson about his shots of Miles in November 1969. Persson is most recognized for his stage photography and unique ability to tell the visual narrative of jazz. "Jan Persson's work is never sentimental, anecdotal, or indiscreet, but it is always revealing; a rare instance of one art illuminating another," said Dan Morgenstern.[29] By the time he started shooting Miles in the sixties, Persson had already developed his style and knew the importance of what he was capturing. He realized that being on stage or in the studio encapsulates Miles not only for the music he was making but for how he acted and responded to his musicians and to his audience. Miles felt most comfortable in these settings because it was an environment he had control over.

All of Persson's shots from the Copenhagen gig illustrate the photographer's keen sense of imagery—the dense blacks, the vibrant colors, the contrast in lighting, the almost three dimensional textures, the necessity of detail. Persson even illuminates Davis's motion—the jabbing, sharp body cuts, contorting, seeking, like the omnipresent boxer. "The short version is some typical attitude and expression," stated Persson when I asked him what he wanted to capture that night. "And that means all connected to the person Miles Davis."[30] One shot even echoes the famed "Think Different" shot used by Apple in their 1997 ad campaign showing a contemplative Miles huddled over a music stand. The starched, Brooks Brothers look transformed into 1960s Technicolor, forever immortalizing Miles as one of the "crazy ones."

Teppei Inokuchi

"I had a great opportunity compared to other people. Every night without paying money at the Village Gate. Every night the place was packed and I just observed,"[31] said Inokuchi, rehashing his teenage years roaming around New York. In 1964 Inokuchi heard Davis for the first time in his native Japan and immediately decided to move to New York. He enrolled at New York University and spent his nights roaming the city in search of Davis in action. Soon, the school kicked him out, his parents cut him off, and he was left to make his way on his own. Without many options, he decided to seek employment at the Village Gate mopping floors. It was not great, but it gave him the opportunity to embrace the city's jazz scene and eventually to befriend his hero Miles Davis.

"I knew which angle he was good looking," said Inokuchi while shooting Davis at the Village Gate. The club was a dark place and Miles was a dark man, so capturing him was tricky. Miles hated flash photography while he was on stage and would be outraged by photographers distracting him with it. One time Miles got so irritated he stopped the show and refused to go back on, causing a blowout with the management. From there on out, it would be difficult to shoot Miles in the club, but he trusted Inokuchi to make it happen. Inokuchi realized that it was not the lighting, but getting the right angle to get the best shots. "It's the position I'm in and waiting for the moment. Then I click the shutter. Every night the music is different, but I know when the moment comes, it's automatic."[32]

Of the thousands of times Inokuchi captured Miles, there was one opportunity where he blew it. In 1969 Miles asked the young photographer to take some shots of him working out at Gleason's Gym; but unfortunately, Inokuchi brought the wrong equipment and was horrified when he saw the blurry shots. "Every day at Village Gate and at his place, he lived like Howard Hughes. Inside it's very dark, but the gym is bright." Most of the shots were garbage and now Inokuchi had to face Miles. "It was a disaster. Miles is waiting and I cannot face him, he would have killed me."[33] Luckily, Miles went easy on him, knowing that he was young, like many of his musicians. He decided to keep him around, but also decided to ask Wolman to take the gyms shots instead of giving Inokuchi a second chance. Fortunately for Wolman, he was able to capture a top-condition Davis in all his glory. "The one of him boxing is fucking amazing,"[34] proclaimed Wolman, who suggested I include it here.

Sitting in Inokuchi's SoHo loft, a place he has occupied since 1970, riding out the neighborhood's dark years and now (to his landlord's chagrin) rubbing elbows with New York's glitterati, the photographer presents a slideshow covering Miles from the late sixties up to the time of his death in 1991. Inokuchi certainly had Davis's trust, for Miles is covered candidly including shots around the time of his 1981 comeback where he is in his brownstone rehearsing, drinking, smoking, fancying various women, and even conversing with drug dealers out of his yellow Ferrari.

For my purposes, the Newport Jazz Festival shots from July 5, 1969 were the most essential. "I sat and waited so long just to get the right shot, the fingers hitting the valves,"[35] recalled Inokuchi, who felt it was all about the body language. He managed to get two fine shots that afternoon—a closeup detailing Miles's fingers on his custom trumpet, and the famous S-shaped silhouette that was immortalized by David Gahr the following year while Davis was playing at Tanglewood, Massachusetts. Inokuchi was satisfied with the day's work not only for capturing the trumpeter's demeanor, but also because he had a background of blue skies as opposed to the dark surroundings typically surrounding Davis.

Tad Hershorn

Hershorn was only 15 years old when he shot Davis at the Dallas Memorial Auditorium on July 18, 1969. Being that this was his first rolls of film covering a major jazz artist, he had his doubts on what he could accomplish, but he had the wisdom and inspiration from his father, who was a professional photographer, to get good shots. Despite the lack of experience, his inability to get the right angles that night, as well as arriving a bit late, Hershorn was still able to capture the *Bitches Brew* live band from an audience member's point of view. "I was taking a documentary approach and thought that way," said Hershorn. Even though Hershorn did not have the means to capture the more intimate moments of Davis as he would with him and many other jazz figures later in his career, he still had an opportunity in the Lone Star State to capture Davis's controversial turn as it unfolded that summer. This was Miles's new band with a sound and a look that was anything but the norm for a typical jazz festival in the sixties. "It really has as much to do with the photograph as what it actually documents," said Hershorn. "You want to see who they are. You want to try to get those moments that capture their humanity for good or ill. Good photographers will document what is happening, but they're getting beneath the surface just like a great musician takes you into his interior vision."[36] Even if the shots are not as artistic as Hershorn wanted them to be, they illustrate the essence of a man in transition, of moving away from his past as far as he could and creating the moment he was living in.

With No End (An Epilogue)

Growing up, I never liked jazz. Even when I began taking music seriously, my heroes were still Kiss and the like. It was not until my high school years, when I stumbled across a worn copy of *Bitches Brew* at the local library, that I began to take notice of jazz. My curiosity came from both boredom with my music collection at home and the wild album cover that was in my grasp. It felt like holding *Kiss Alive!* in my 5-year-old hands long before. If you are reading this, it is easy to see the rest of the story.

Why did I like the record so much? Well, for the same reason everyone else liked it. If you were coming from rock, you still had the pounding beats, the heavy guitar, the danger and the darkness. But of course, you had much more substance. Reminiscent of Bob Dylan getting bored of his rock record collection, you could listen to this album over and over again and find more of what Miles had to say. *Bitches Brew* became the gateway drug into jazz. Your next step might be a Return to Forever album, *Live-Evil*, and then jazz, in all its incarnations, sort of took over your life.

As a musician, I approached *Bitches Brew* the same way Eddie Van Halen handled Cream records: I stayed home, with some beer, and transcribed Miles's solos lick by lick. Similar to Eddie learning guitar via Eric Clapton, I would learn Miles Davis by studying what he played. This would be the heart of this project, with everything else taking shape around it.

Where Are They Now?

A writer will encounter many challenges when gathering information for a book, and this one was no different. The most difficult was trying to reach out to anyone affiliated with *Bitches Brew* and its surrounding period. Of course, so many people were helpful and made this book possible, but there were others who were simply unreachable for a variety of reasons. Because of the album's age, the most obvious explanation is the death of those involved which, of course, includes Miles, but that was hardly frustrating. There are some who are in poor health, and that, too, is something

I had to come to terms with from the beginning. There were also some who, through the casualties of stardom, refuse any contact from the living world and have moved on from Miles. There are Davis family members who have been screwed over by Miles, left out of wills, and cannot speak for legal reasons or out of bitterness. There are past cohorts who have turned out broke and resentful after the high times, including one former band member who wanted $2,500 for an interview. Some have an eerie tunnel-vision memory of these past events and spew out their stock stories to whatever you ask them, even if it has nothing to do with the question. There were some with no recollection of this time period at all ("If you remember the sixties, you weren't there"), and there were the ones who simply gave no interest to any inquiry.

My worst encounters were the Davis affiliates who cast halos over their own heads. I can understand that being asked about someone else's life and not your own for the past forty-plus years can turn anyone sour, but I think there is more to it. Call me naïve, but I have come to find that many people, especially highly recognized figures, will only do something for someone else if there is either something in it for them or a price to pay for their objections. Here are some beauties:

- "He feels he doesn't have the focus to comment on Miles's relationships."
- "Thanks again for your request, but at this point I have no product to promote."
- "I'm certain that whatever you're doing can be done without my help. You're certainly not the first writer to contact me in need of input."
- "Send me your questions and I'll let you know if I care to respond."
- "As a general rule, _____ does not give interviews. However, if you have specific questions, I'd be happy to present them to _____ for his consideration."

In truth, these conundrums and frustrations only enhanced my understanding of the man and allowed me to keep my focus on the music. It also made me search deeper to get the surrounding story. Even after all these years, there are still many people out there who knew Miles in some capacity and were involved with the album, and are not nursing any side effects and have another piece of the puzzle.

Oral history, however, is tough. As you can see, much of what people tell you has to be taken with an appreciation of its subjective nature not only for the aforementioned reasons but also because people can conjure up a memory of something even if it is not true. They like to remember things in a certain light. There are also people who explain occurrences in a slanted way to stay clear of bad quotes. Of course, all a researcher needs to know is "check your work."

Perhaps the saddest lesson I learned speaking to many people who were there was how they can succumb to bitterness even in the aftermath of something so extraordinary. The little guys, the cogs, the people so integral in the process, the ones who were not stuck behind a desk pushing pencils but carrying out crucial jobs many can only think of as a dream, were left behind, squashed by whoever was on top. Decades later, Miles Davis and *Bitches Brew* surpass legacy, and many subsidiaries reap overwhelming profits while the cogs have little or nothing to show for it. Even many of their names have been eroded away with time. Some who have felt shortchanged—yes, they were paid for services rendered, but shouldn't creating a legacy be worth a little more recognition?—came off defensive toward me, waiting to be screwed again. Some were shocked to hear someone reaching out to them at all. I often wonder what many of these people have done to get by all these years.

Luckily the music and Miles Davis's legacy still exist, but part of the history has vanished. Columbia Studio B and its many ghosts are long gone. Gone also are the radical late sixties, its liberal nature, its experimental spirit, a time when a jazz album of this magnitude, or for that matter any jazz album, could capture the world's ear.

Final Thoughts

At the end of writing a book, an author can begin to feel self-conscious. He will ask himself if he really knows his subject or, in the case of fiction, his characters. So I asked myself, "Do I really know who Miles Davis was?" I had no personal affiliation with Miles, except for his music, which I believe Miles would have thought to be the strongest relationship to have with him. What I have come away with is yes, this is an interesting story, but this is *really* interesting music. As I thought back to the *Bitches Brew* years when Miles hated his critics and doing interviews, I got it. If you really want to know him, you have to "listen to this."

Notes

Beginnings

1. Murphy, Frederick D. "Miles Davis: The Monster of Modern Music." *Encore: American and Worldwide News*. 21 July 1975, 39. The full quote: "I don't play rock. Rock is a white word. And I don't like the word jazz because jazz is a nigger word the white folks dropped on us. We just play black."

2. Troupe, Quincy. Interview by the author. 11 December 2000.

3. Davis, Miles, and Quincy Troupe. *Miles: The Autobiography*. New York: Simon and Schuster, 1989, 297.

4. Ibid., 298.

5. Ibid., 59.

6. Lerner, Murray. *Miles Electric—A Different Kind of Blue*. Film, Eagle Rock, 2004.

7. Douglas, Stella. Interview by the author. September 2012.

8. Roby, Steven. Interview with Stella Douglas. October 2007. steveroby.wordpress.com/2012/05/15/interview-with-stella-douglas-october-2007-by-steven-roby/

9. The two remained friends for some time after, but in the late seventies Davis closed himself off from almost everyone and Mabry became a recluse for a good thirty years. Several attempts to contact her for this writing were unsuccessful. The *Observer*'s Neil Spencer, who has seen the high casualty count of high flyers firsthand, told me, "Being held up as being the sassiest woman on the planet . . . that's going to leave some collateral damage unless you are especially strong." In 2010 her record company reissued many of her old solo albums and forced her to promote them. Spencer, one of the two or three people she spoke with, described her as "damaged and shy." Hardly a revealing interview, but she did deny the accusations of an affair with Hendrix, stating that the two broke up "because of his violent temper."

Chapter 1

1. Shelton, Robert. *No Direction Home: The Life and Music of Bob Dylan*. New York: William Morrow, 1986, 211.

2. Guralnick, Peter. *Last Train to Memphis: The Rise of Elvis Presley*. New York: Little, Brown, 1994, 173.

3. Ibid., 500.

4. Ibid., 175.

5. Ibid., 289.

6. Marcus, Greil. *Like a Rolling Stone: Bob Dylan at the Crossroads*. New York: Public Affairs, 2005, 158.

7. Crowe, Cameron. Liner notes to *Biograph*. Columbia, 1985.

8. Cott, Jonathan. *Bob Dylan: The Essential Interviews*. New York: Wenner Books, 2006, 90.

9. Marcus, 158.

10. Wein, George. *Myself Among Others: A Life in Music*. New York: De Capo, 2004, 284.

11. Lewis, Miles Marshall. *There's a Riot Goin' On*. New York: Continuum, 2006, 70.

12. Hopkins, Jerry. *Elvis: The Final Years*. New York: Berkley, 1986, 164.

13. Liner notes to *Jimi Hendrix: Woodstock*. MCA, 1994.

14. Shapiro, Harry. *Jimi Hendrix: Electric Gypsy*. New York: St. Martin's, 1990, 385.

15. Hendrix, Jimi. Interview on the *Dick Cavett Show*. 9 September 1969.

16. Interview with Vernon Reid. Studio360.org.

17. Pennebaker, D. A. *Jimi Plays Monterey*. Film, Criterion Collection, 2002.

18. Troupe, Quincy. *Miles and Me*. Berkeley: University of California Press, 2000, 57.

19. Carr, Ian. *Miles Davis: The Definitive Biography*. New York: Thunder's Mouth, 1998, 194.

20. Szwed, John. *So What: The Life of Miles Davis*. New York: Simon and Schuster, 2002, 301.

21. Benchley, Peter. "New Sounds from Miles Davis." *Reporter Dispatch* 22 July 1970.

22. Davis and Troupe, 318.

23. Ibid., 26.

24. Ibid., 129.

25. Edwards, Madera. *Electric Miles: Interpreting the Music of Miles Davis in a Black Power Context*. Unpublished, 2002.

26. Guralnick, 179.

Chapter 2

1. DeMicheal, Don. *"Miles Davis: The Rolling Stone* Interview." *Rolling Stone*. 13 December 1969, 26.

2. Liebman, David. Liner notes to Miles Davis, *Dark Magus* (CD reissue), Columbia/Legacy, 1997.

3. Saal, Hubert. "Miles of Music." *Newsweek*, 23 March 1970. Reprinted in Maher Jr., Paul, and Michael K. Dorr. *Miles on Miles*. Chicago: Lawrence Hill, 2009, 69.

4. Feather, Leonard. *From Satchmo to Miles*. New York: Stein and Day, 1972. Reprinted in Gary Carner, *The Miles Davis Companion: Four Decades of Commentary*.

5. DeMicheal, Don. "And in This Corner, the Sidewalk Kid . . ." *Down Beat*. 11 December 1969. Reprinted in *The Miles Davis Reader*. New York: Hal Leonard, 2007, 91.

6. Davis and Troupe, 289.

7. Budds, Michael. *Jazz in the Sixties*. Iowa City: University of Iowa Press, 1990, 94–95.

8. Almost every studio track on *Live-Evil* and *Big Fun* has different instrumentation, some stranger than others.

9. Lerner, *Miles Electric*.

10. Ibid.

11. Dibb, Mike. *The Miles Davis Story*. Film, Sony, 2002.

12. Belden, Bob. Liner notes to *The Complete Studio Recordings of the Miles Davis Quintet 1965–June 1968*. Columbia, 1998.

13. Silvert, Conrad. "Herbie Hancock: Revamping the Present, Creating the Future." *Down Beat*. 8 September 1997.

14. Lerner, *Miles Electric*.

15. Belden, liner notes to "Quintet."

16. Belden, Bob. Interview with the author. 19 June 2000.

17. Cross, Charles R. *Room Full of Mirrors: A Biography of Jimi Hendrix*. New York: Hyperion, 2006, 286.

18. Shapiro, *Electric Gypsy*, 348.

19. Davis and Troupe, 323.

20. Gaumont, Dominique. "Comment J'ai Rencontre Miles." *Jazz Hot* 388, September 1981.

21. Zawinul, Joe. Interview in *Jazz Times*. April 1992.

22. Macero, Teo. Taken from original session sheets and memorandums in the Teo Macero Collection, New York Public Library.

23. Davis and Troupe, 296.

24. Ibid.

25. Zawinul, Joe. Liner notes to *Zawinul*, Atlantic 1971.

26. The first instance of the name in print came from a *Village Voice* piece called "The Lost Quintet" by Peter Keepnews, August 1986.

27. Davis and Troupe, 297.

28. Lerner, *Miles Electric*.

29. Ibid.

30. Davis and Troupe, 291.

31. Ted Panken. Interview with Jack DeJohnette. 18 April 2009. jazz.com/features-and-interviews/2009/6/15/in-conversation-with-jack-dejohnette

32. Mattingly, Rick. "Jack DeJohnette: Stretching into Infinite Time." *Drum!* February/March 1999, 57.

33. Ibid.

34. Ibid.

35. Tompkins, Les. "Talking to Les Tompkins." *Crescendo*, 1969. Reprinted in Maher and Dohr, 65.

36. Ibid., 64.

37. Lerner, *Miles Electric*.

38. Tompkins, 66.

39. Lerner, *Miles Electric*.

40. Keepnews, Peter. "The Lost Quintet." Reprinted in Bill Kirchner, *The Miles Davis Reader*, 187.

41. Haid, Mike. Interview with Chick Corea. *Fuse*. Fall 1998.

42. "Jazz for What It Is." *This World*. 13 August 1972.

43. Holzman, Adam. Interview by the author. 19 March 2008.

44. Troupe, Quincy. Interview by the author. 11 December 2000.

45. Davis and Troupe, 83.

46. Lerner, *Miles Electric*.

47. Davis and Troupe, 406.

48. Macero Collection.

Chapter 3

1. DeMicheal, "*Rolling Stone* Interview," 22.

2. Gray, Christopher. "STREETSCAPES: CBS Studio on 52d; At One Time, the 'Last Word in Broadcasting Design.'" *New York Times*, 7 August 1988. nytimes.com/1988/08/07/realestate/streetscapes-cbs-studio-on-52d-at-one-time-the-last-word-in-broadcasting-design.html.

3. Cuscuna, Michael. Interview by the author. 27 October 2011.

4. Macero, original session sheets and memorandums New York Public Library.

5. Suchow, Rick. Interview with Harvey Brooks. ricksuchow.com/press-group-307.html/.

6. Interview with Don Alias. September 1999. digitalinterviews.com/digitalinterviews/views/alias.shtml.

7. Cohodas, Nadine. *Princess Noire: The Tumultuous Reign of Nina Simone*. Chapel Hill: University of North Carolina Press, 2012, 259.

8. Weiss, David. "Don Alias: Percussive Color of the Brew." *Drum!* February/March 1999, 64.

9. Ted Panken. Interview with Jack DeJohnette. 18 April 2009. jazz.com/features-and-interviews/2009/6/15/in-conversation-with-jack-dejohnette.

10. Cole, George. Interview with Bennie Maupin. thelastmiles.com/interviews-bennie-maupin.php.

11. Carr, Ian. *Miles Davis*. New York: William Morrow, 1982, 285.

12. Davis has been quoted saying this numerous times.

13. Morgenstern, Dan. Interview by the author. December 2011.

It is believed that Miles invited Betty Mabry to the sessions, but there is no confirmation on this. I asked Frank Laico if she was present on August 20, and he said she was not. In fact, he never recalled seeing any of Davis's wives at any of the sessions he worked on.

The shot of Davis and Macero on the inner jacket of *Bitches Brew* was taken in January 1970 by Don Hunstein.

14. Moon, Tom. *1000 Recordings to Hear Before You Die: A Listener's Life List*. New York: Workman, 2008. 1000recordings.com/music/bitches-brew/.

15. Cole, Maupin interview.

16. Pond, Steven. *Head Hunters: The Making of Jazz's First Platinum Album*. Ann Arbor: University of Michigan Press, 2005, 134.

17. Ouellette, Dan. "*Bitches Brew*: The Making of the Most Revolutionary Jazz Album in History." *Down Beat*. December 1999, 34.

18. Haid, Interview with Chick Corea.

19. Cobham, Billy. Interview by the author. 15 January 2009.

20. Pond, 135.

21. Terrell, Tom. "Street Time." *Wax Poetics*. October/November 2007, 151.

22. Ouellette, 34.

23. Tate, Greg. Liner notes to *Bitches Brew: The 40th Anniversary Collector's Edition*. Columbia, 2010.

24. Cole, Maupin interview.

25. Cobham interview.

26. Tingen, Paul. *Miles Beyond: The Electric Explorations of Miles Davis, 1967–1991*. New York: Billboard Books, 2001, 65.

27. Pond, 135.

28. Davis, Tony. "Lenny White: The Making of a Legend." *Drum!* February/March 1999, 59.

29. White, Lenny. Interview by the author. 22 February 2006.

30. Carr, 263.

31. Ibid.

32. White interview.

33. Roy, Badal. Interview by the author. 12 December 1999.

34. Terrell, 148.

35. Tompkins, Les. "Talking to Les Tompkins." *Crescendo*. 1969. Reprinted in Maher and Dorr, 64.

36. Szwed, 265.

37. Davis and Troupe, 300.

38. DeMicheal, "*Rolling Stone* Interview," 25.

39. Roy interview, 1999.

40. Belden, Bob. Liner notes to *The Complete Bitches Brew Sessions*. Columbia/Legacy, 1998.

41. Terrell, 154.

42. Ibid.

43. Roy, Badal. Interview by the author. 4 April 2000.

44. Terrell, 144.

45. Dibb, *The Miles Davis Story*.

46. Ouellette, 37.

47. Ibid.

48. Pond, 135.

Chapter 4

1. Milkowski, Bill. Interview with Wayne Shorter. 12 June 2005. abstractlogix.com/interview_view.php?idno=75.
2. Feather, *From Satchmo to Miles*, 108.
3. Davis and Troupe, 299.
4. Porter, Lewis. Class notes taken in Graduate Topics: Miles Davis. Rutgers University. 4 April 2008.
5. Porter, Lewis. Interview by the author. 4 April 2008.
6. Tingen, 66.
7. White interview.
8. Mattingly, 57.
9. Litweiler, John. *The Freedom Principle: Jazz after 1958*. New York: William Morrow, 1984, 227.
10. Pareles, Jon. "Miles Davis in a Playful Mood at Avery Fisher Hall." *New York Times*. 27 June 1988. query.nytimes.com/gst/fullpage.html?res=940DE0DB1030F934A15755C0A96E948260.
11. Lawrence, Azar. Interview by the author. 17 September 2008.
12. Cobham, Billy. Interview by the author. 15 January 2009.
13. Lawrence interview.
14. Ibid.
15. Terrell, Tom. "Street Time." *Wax Poetics*. October/November 2007, 148.
16. All studio banter is from the original master tapes of *Bitches Brew*.
17. Cole, Maupin interview.
18. Richie, Nora. Interview with Bennie Maupin. revivalist.okayplayer.com/2010/12/03/bennie-maupin-the-stories-of-bitches-brew/.
19. Cole, Maupin interview.
20. I asked Lewis Porter about this chord configuration and it reminded him of John Coltrane. "The chords are each a major third apart as in *Giant Steps*, outlining an augmented triad and giving an effect of no tonal center."
21. Dibb, *The Miles Davis Story*.
22. Belden, *Complete Bitches Brew Sessions*.
23. Interview with John McLaughlin. 27 November 2010. cabbagerabbit.com/2010/11/27/john-mclaughlin-interview/.
24. [*Sic*]. Miles heard a tape of McLaughlin, Williams, and Larry Young playing at Club Baron. Since Williams's drums were already set up for the gig that night, Lifetime did some rehearsing at the club during the day.
25. Davis and Troupe, 296.
26. Lerner, *Miles Electric*.
27. Milkowski, Bill. John McLaughlin: Interview (#23). 16 April 2004. abstractlogix.com/interview_view.php?idno=23.

28. Mercer, Michelle. *Footprints: The Life and Work of Wayne Shorter*. New York: Tarcher, 2007, 133.

29. Brodacki, Krystian. "The Original Batman: Wayne Shorter Remembers Miles Davis." *Jazz Forum* 1/1992 (vol. 132), 24.

30. "Adventures on the Golden Mean: An Interview with Wayne Shorter." *SGI Quarterly*. January 2012. sgiquarterly.org/feature2012Jan-5.html.

31. Brodacki, 24.

32. Carr, 261.

33. Belden, *Bitches*.

34. Alias, Don. Interview from digitalinterviews.com. September 1999.

35. Zawinul, Joe. interviews.org/inner/zawinul.

36. Ibid.

37. Ibid.

38. Ibid.

39. Glasser, Brian. *In a Silent Way: A Portrait of Joe Zawinul*. London: As Long As It's Hot; 2nd rev. ed., 2009, 112.

40. Panken, Interview with Jack DeJohnette.

41. Liebman, David. Liner notes from *Dark Magus*. Columbia/Legacy, 1997.

Chapter 5

1. DiGirolamo, Olana. *Play That, Teo*. Film, Play That Teo Productions, 2010.

2. Cuscuna, Michael. Interview by the author. 12 November 2004.

3. Artists House Interview. "Producer and Arranger Teo Macero on His Early Career in the Music Business." April 2004. artistshousemusic.org/videos/producer+and+arranger+teo+macero+on+his+early+career+in+the+music+business.

4. Belden, Bob. "Teo Macero 10/30/1925—2/19/2008." jazztimes.com/articles/21278-teo-macero.

5. Lee, Iara. Interview with Teo Macero. *Modulations*. (Film, September 1997. furious.com/perfect/teomacero.html.

6. Both "Nefertiti" and "Gingerbread Boy" and their studio banter can be found on Miles Davis, *The Complete Columbia Studio Sessions, 1965–68*. Columbia/Sony, 1998.

7. Cole, George. *The Last Miles: The Music of Miles Davis 1980–1991*. Ann Arbor: University of Michigan Press, 2007, 23.

8. Moore, Ray. Interview by the author. 19 October 2012.

9. Laico, Frank. Interview by the author. 19 August 2012.

10. Macero, Teo. "Teo Macero on Creating 'Bitches Brew' with Miles Davis." Artist's House interview. July 2004. artistshousemusic.org/videos/teo+macero+on+creating+bitches+brew+with+miles+davis.

11. Cuscuna, interview.

12. It is uncertain if the T-1 was invented specifically for *Bitches Brew*. Wilder noted that it was the first time he had heard it used on a Davis album, but neither he, Cuscuna, nor Belden could recall it being used on another artist's record prior to *Brew*.

13. Wilder, Mark. Interview with the author. 14 May 2014.

14. Since Macero was relegated to supervising the mixing and editing sessions, Ray Moore was the one who physically cut the tape with the razor blades.

15. Cole, *The Last Miles*, 24.

16. Ibid.

17. White, Interview.

18. Ibid.

19. Prasad, Anil. "Dave Holland: Fundamental Truths." 2000. innerviews.org.

20. Engelbrecht, Michael. Interview with Brian Eno for his radio program and the German magazine *jazzthetik*, 24 March 1996. music.hyperreal.org/artists/brian_eno/interviews/me_intr4.html#Madly.

21. Lundvall, Bruce. Interview by the author. 21 December 2011. "Let's be perfectly clear. Macero was the one to sign off on the project and hand it over to A&R. But it's not at all likely he could veto a record Miles approved of."

22. Cuscuna, Interview.

23. From Teo Macero Collection, New York Public Library.

24. Cole, *The Last Miles*, 22.

25. Ibid., 24.

26. Rubin is notorious for charging an exorbitant amount of money for his services in exchange for being a ghost in the studio. For example, he was called in to produce Metallica's *Death Magnetic* album in 2008, but according to the band's singer James Hetfield, he was hardly a force in the studio. "Rick Rubin's producing . . . whenever he's there," he told VH1 before its release.

27. Moore, interview.

28. Lewis, Joel. "Running the Voodoo Down." *The Wire*. December 1994, 24.

29. Ibid.

30. Ibid.

31. Macero Collection, submitted by Ryan Mahoney.

32. Moore, interview.

33. Macero, Teo. Transcript from the Miles Davis Conference, May 10–11, 1996, Washington University, St. Louis.

34. Cole, *The Last Miles*, 23.

35. Jackson, Bobby. Jazz Tracks interview with Teo Macero. WCPN Radio. 3 June 2001.

36. Cuscuna, interview.

37. Wilder, Mark. Interview with the author. 14 May 2014.

38. Ibid.

39. Kaplan, Fred. "Lost in Production: A Reissue of Thelonious Monk's Underground Reveals the Great Album It Should Always Have Been." 11 September 2003. slate.com.

40. Laico, Interview.

41. Not to beat up on Rick Rubin, but coincidentally, *Death Magnetic* was also criticized for its high volume levels. Because the album was so highly compressed, distortion is clearly audible on the finished product.

42. The album was mixed in both the two-track stereo and four-track quadraphonic formats. Even though it was released, the quadraphonic mix never panned out. "I never heard it work," said Moore. "If I didn't hear it work in the studio, how the hell is anybody on the outside gonna hear it?" Moore did mention that a reel-to-reel tape version exists where the quadraphonic mix functions properly. Moore, interview.

43. Ibid.

44. Jackson, Macero interview.

45. Merlin, Enrico. "Slow Brew." *Audiomedia*. May 1999. web.archive.org/web/20051001114409/audiomedia.com/archive/features/uk-0599/uk-0599-brew/uk-0599-brew.htm.

Chapter 6

1. Giddins, Gary. "Miles Davis Plays Dorian Gray." *Village Voice*. 8 March 1976, 71.

2. Lerner, *Miles Electric*.

3. Ibid.

4. Macero, Teo Macero Collection.

5. Winner, Langdon. Music review, *Bitches Brew*. *Rolling Stone*. 28 May 1970. rollingstone.com/music/albumreviews/bitches-brew-19700528.

6. Szantor, Jim. Music review, *Bitches Brew* by Miles Davis. *Down Beat*. 11 June 1970, 21.

7. I am not stating that Davis was a pimp in the literal sense, but figuratively.

8. Avakian, George. Interview by the author. 9 October 2004.

9. Feather, *From Satchmo to Miles*, 132.

10. Porter, Eric. "It's About That Time: The Response to Miles Davis's Electric Turn." *Miles Davis and American Culture*. Gerald Early, ed. St. Louis: Missouri Historical Society Press, 2001, 143.

11. Macero Collection.

12. DiMicheal, "*Rolling Stone* Interview," 26.

13. Cuscuna, Interview.

14. Davis and Troupe, 298.

15. Tingen, 298.

16. Davis, Stephen. "Miles Davis: An Exclusive Interview." *Real Paper*. 21 March 1973, 12.

17. When asked by Stephen Davis in the *Real Paper* interview if he was satisfied with Columbia, Davis replied, "Uh, uh man, by no means. I ain't satisfied. They don't do anything for you unless you're white or Jewish . . . by now I don't even talk to them anymore." At the time, Davis was particularly upset with how Columbia was handling the cover art for *On the Corner*. They were not happy with the Corky McCoy artwork Davis had chosen, but Davis countered, "And I *told* them how to merchandise nigger music man. Put

Chinese on the covers, put brothers and sisters on 'em, whatever they gonna call us next, that's what you put on the covers to sell us."

18. Belden, Interview.
19. White, Interview.
20. Davis and Troupe, 298.
21. Macero Collection.
22. DiMicheal, "*Rolling Stone* Interview," 23.
23. Macero Collection.
24. Baumstein, Morris. Interview by the author. 23 December 2011.
25. This was also a common occurrence the following year with *At Fillmore*. On February 26, 1971, Macero received a letter from Brown University explaining the difficulties deejays were having cueing the long live tracks.
26. Cuscuna, interview.
27. The first ad in *Rolling Stone*, declaring *Bitches Brew* "A Novel by Miles Davis," was in the 14 May 1970 issue, 51.
28. Macero Collection.
29. Ibid.
30. Carr, 279.
31. Macero Collection.
32. Douglas, Interview.
33. Klarwein, Serafine. Interview by the author. 9 August 2012.
34. Klarwein, Caterine. Interview by the author. 30 May 2013.
35. Klarwein, Serafine. *Bitches Brew: The 40th Anniversary Collector's Edition*. Columbia, 2010.
36. The original was stolen and the Klarwein family believes it is somewhere in Morocco.
37. There is speculation from both Berg and Douglas that *Bitches Brew* was not commissioned. Their consensus is that the piece had already existed and was chosen by Miles from Klarwein's downtown studio. "If you remember the sixties, you weren't there, so the saying goes. I should remind Douglas and Co," Caterine told me in 2013. "Since I was living with Mati at the time while he painted *Bitches Brew* [the two later split up], I remember that it was commissioned. It was not a painting Mati had done previously." Despite disagreement among the involved parties, it is, however, odd that the original *Bitches Brew* painting was the size of a gate-fold record cover. One other oddity is the price of the painting. Douglas insisted that Davis paid $1,000 for the piece (an honest price tag considering Gregg Allman paid Klarwein $1,500 to create the *Laid Back* cover in 1973), but it is not likely that Miles would shell out any money that he thought Columbia might provide. At the time of the album's release, Columbia paid for the rights to use it and Klarwein kept the original (although no records at Columbia exist for this transaction). In a 1993 interview Klarwein mentioned that Davis approached him in the 1980s still looking for the piece, but he told him that he sold it some twenty years ago. The two also collaborated the following year for *Zonked*, a piece intended for *Live-Evil*, but which was never used by Davis.

38. Berg, John. Interview by the author. 5 September 2012.

39. Lundvall, Bruce. Interview by the author. 22 December 2011.

40. Gleason, Ralph. Liner notes to *Bitches Brew*. Columbia, 1970.

41. Davis and Troupe, 300.

42. Morgenstern, Dan. Interview by the author. December 2011.

43. Losin, Peter. Interview by the author. 2 January 2012.

44. Kort, Michelle. *Soul Picnic: The Music and Passion of Laura Nyro*. New York: St. Martin's Griffin, 2003, 77.

45. Davis and Troupe, 300.

46. Carr, 279, 282.

47. Wilson, John. "Miles Davis and Group Play Philharmonic Hall." *New York Times*. 1 October 1972, 66.

48. Wilson, John. "Bartz Takes Stage with Miles Davis." *New York Times*. 28 November 1971.

49. Watrous, Peter. "Electro Analysis: Miles Davis Live, Plugged In, and Reconsidered." *Jazziz*. December 1997, 64.

50. Rockwell, John. "To Davis and Fans, a Concert Is Just Part of the Whole Story." *New York Times*. 15 September 1974, 56.

51. Watrous, 64.

52. Giddins, 71.

53. Benchley, "New Sounds from Miles Davis."

54. Zwerin, Mike. "Son of Miles: The Price of Silence." 1998. culturekiosque.com/jazz/miles/rhemiles2.htm.

55. Franckling, Ken. "Miles Davis—Life Size." Jazz Journalists Association Library, 1986.

56. Smith, Cliff. "Trumpeter Outlaws Word 'Jazz.'" *Courier News*. 7 April 1972.

57. Macero Collection.

58. Wein, 466.

59. Davis and Troupe, 316.

60. Cuscuna, Interview.

61. Troupe, Interview.

62. Wyatt, Hugh. "Miles Davis Back with New Sound." *New York Sunday News*. 1 October 1972.

63. Lawrence, Interview.

64. Stratton, Bert. "Caught in the Act: Miles Ahead in Rock Country." *Down Beat*. 14 May 1970. Reprinted in Frank Alkyer, *The Miles Davis Reader*. New York: Hal Leonard, 2007, 253.

65. Crouch, Stanley. "On the Corner: The Sellout of Miles Davis." *Reading Jazz*. Robert Gottlieb, ed. New York: Pantheon, 1996, 898.

66. Avakian, interview.

67. Azzerad, Michael. Interview with George Wein. 11 November 2010. milesdavis.com/us/bblive.

68. Macero Collection.

69. Macero kept these letters and personally responded to them. He could not issue refunds, but sent these listeners several copies of more traditional jazz records as a courtesy.

70. Lerner, *Miles Electric*.

71. Tingen, Paul. "The Cellar Door Recordings." 2005. Miles-beyond.com/cellardoor.

72. Blumenthal, Bob. "Music: Sons of 'Bitches.'" *Boston Phoenix*. 24 June 1973, 6.

73. Mtume, James. Liner notes to *The Complete On the Corner Sessions*. Columbia/Sony, 2007, 25.

74. Liebmann, Nick. Liner notes to *Miles Davis: The Complete Miles Davis at Montreux*, Columbia, 2002, 8.

75. Feather, Leonard. *The Pleasures of Jazz: Leading Performers on Their Lives, Their Music, Their Contemporaries*. New York: Horizon Press, 1974, 45.

76. Fortune, Sonny. Interview by the author. 15 September 2008.

77. Holzman, Adam. Interview by the author. 19 March 2008.

78. Gleason, Ralph. "Miles Davis: The *Rolling Stone* Interview." *Rolling Stone*, 13 December 1969, 22.

79. Morgenstern, Dan. "Miles in Motion." *Down Beat*. 3 September 1970, 16–17.

80. West, Hollie. "Black Tune." *Washington Post*. 13 March 1969, L1, L9.

81. Baraka, Amiri. *The Music: Reflections on Jazz and Blues*. New York: William Morrow, 1987, 268–76.

82. Crouch, Stanley. "Play the Right Thing." *New Republic*. 12 February 1990, 30–37.

83. Porter, "It's About That Time."

84. Ibid., 143.

85. Tompkins, "Talking to Les Tompkins," 61.

86. Feather, *The Pleasures of Jazz*, 102.

87. Lerner, *Miles Electric*.

88. Baraka, Amiri. "Homage to Miles Davis." *New York Times*. 16 June 1985.

89. Lawrence, interview.

90. Dibb, *The Miles Davis Story*.

91. Feather, *The Pleasures of Jazz*, 101.

92. Smith, Cliff. "Trumpeter Outlaws Word 'Jazz.'" *Courier News*. 7 April 1972.

Chapter 7

1. Sutcliffe, Phil. "An Interview with Thom Yorke." Q, October 1999. Reprinted in Rock's Backpages Library. rocksbackpages.com/Library/Article/radiohead-an-interview-with-thom-yorke.

2. Davis and Troupe, 213.

3. *Bitches Brew* was initially slated to be a single LP.

4. Macero, Teo Macero Collection.

5. In his autobiography, Davis claims he was making an annual salary of $300–400,000 in the seventies.

6. Wein, *Myself Among Others*, 464.

7. Hentoff, Nat. *The Jazz Life*. New York: Da Capo, 1978, 54.

8. Only a year before, Miles requested an advance of only $5,000 and would receive a total of $10,000 for *Filles de Kilimanjaro*. It was no secret what kind of money the rock stars were getting, which raised the ante.

9. Meanwhile, Davis's studio and road musicians were paid union scale and nothing else. Miles was not into bonuses or anything out of pocket.

10. Goldstein, Laurie. Interview by the author. 3 July 2012.

11. A sample of "Lonely Fire" is used throughout the Notorious B.I.G.'s "Suicidal Thoughts," from his album *Ready to Die* (1994).

12. "Great Expectations" and "Lonely Fire" were released on *Big Fun* (1974), "Guinevere" on *Circle in the Round* (1979), and the short version of "Double Image" found a spot on *Live-Evil* (1971). Everything else was finally released on *The Complete Bitches Brew Sessions* (1998).

13. Cayton also used other Davis material for the film, including excerpts from *Bitches Brew*.

14. Milkowski, Bill. Liner notes to Miles Davis, *The Complete Jack Johnson Sessions*, Columbia/Sony 2003.

15. Davis and Troupe, 315.

16. Dibb, *The Miles Davis Story*.

17. Davis, Miles. Liner notes to *A Tribute to Jack Johnson*. Columbia, 1971.

18. Chang, Dean. "Miles's Blow by Blow." *New York Daily News*, 17 March 1996.

19. Hall, Gregg. "Miles: Today's Most Influential Contemporary Musician." *Down Beat*. 18 July 1974. Reprinted in Alkyer, Frank. *The Miles Davis Reader*. New York: Hal Leonard, 2007, 105.

20. Ibid., 105.

21. DeMicheal, "The *Rolling Stone* Interview," 26.

22. DeMicheal, "And in This Corner, the Sidewalk Kid," 91.

23. Chambers, Jack. *Milestones 2: The Music and Times of Miles Davis Since 1960*. Toronto: University of Toronto Press, 1985, 204.

24. Milkowski, *Jack Johnson* liner notes, 72.

25. Milkowski, Bill. Interview by the author. 12 July 2012.

26. *The Complete Jack Johnson Sessions* covers music recorded from February 18 to June 4, 1970. Some of the later material found its way on *Live-Evil* ("Nem Um Talvez" and "Selim" from June 3). On May 21 Davis recorded "Konda," the last piece named after a boxer. Until 2003, the bulk of the recordings where either unreleased or unissued in full.

27. Davis and Troupe, 315.

28. "Ali" is almost a direct reading of Buddy Miles's "Who Knows" from Jimi Hendrix's *Band of Gypsys* album, recorded at the Fillmore East January 1, 1970.

29. Lerner, *Miles Electric*.

30. Davis and Troupe, 317.

31. The piece they collaborated on (*Zonked*) was never purchased by Davis and was shelved until the Last Poets licensed it for their 1993 album *Holy Terror*.

32. Klarwein, Serafine, Interview.

33. Henderson, Michael. Liner notes to Miles Davis, *The Cellar Door Sessions 1970*. Columbia/Sony, 2005.

34. Henderson's first gig was on the *Tonight Show*, 1 October 1970. The Fillmore West was October 16–18, then Cellar Door in December. Dave Holland's last gig was the Isle of Wight festival, 29 August 1970.

35. Ibid.

36. Giddins, "Miles Davis Plays Dorian Gray," 71.

37. Jarrett, Keith. Liner notes to Miles Davis, *The Cellar Door Sessions 1970*. Columbia/Sony, 2005.

38. Holzman, Adam. Liner notes to Miles Davis, *The Cellar Door Sessions 1970*. Columbia/Sony, 2005.

39. Jarrett, *Cellar Door*.

40. Davis and Troupe, 333.

41. Dibb, *Miles Davis Story*.

42. "Miles Davis Arrested Here on Drug and Gun Charges." *New York Times*, 25 February 1973.

I spoke with Teppei Inokuchi about this incident and he gave a different account of what happened. According to Inokuchi, Miles was giving him a ride home when he spotted Fisher on 14th Street. Before dropping him off, Davis asked him for a small gun and bag of cocaine that Inokuchi was holding for him. He was wary of holding the contraband himself because the night before he went after another girl at his place with a butcher knife and knew the police were after him. Sure enough, the cops were at his place waiting for him when Miles and Fisher arrived at his home. Miles went to jail and was released on $50,000 bond the next day.

43. Losin, Peter. Interview by the author. 1 May 2012.

44. Ibid.

45. Terrell, Tom. "Street Time." *Wax Poetics*, October/November 2007, 148.

46. *Agharta* was released along with *Pangaea*, which also chronicles the concert (afternoon and evening sets).

47. Palmer, Robert. "A Jazz Giant Explores Rock." *New York Times*, 4 April 1976.

48. Giddins, "Miles Davis Plays Dorian Gray," 71–72.

49. Inokuchi, Teppei. Interview by the author. 28 August 2012.

50. Chambers, 284.

51. Hijuelos, Oscar. *The Mambo Kings Play Songs of Love* (1989). While the outcome may not have been as fatal as the Mambo King's, the circumstances were just as grim.

52. Ibid., 331.

53. This occurrence with Jagger is most likely from an earlier time. In Al Aronowitz's piece "A National Treasure" (*Blacklisted Journalist*, 26 May 1970; reprinted in Maher and Dorr, *Miles on Miles*, 73), he describes taking Jagger to meet Miles, and Miles not letting him in the front door. It is doubtful that Jagger attempted to come back during this period.

54. Szwed, 349.

55. Ibid., 346.

56. Carr, *The Definitive Biography*, 330.

57. Chambers, 284.

58. Peter Losin also lists a rehearsal Davis did for a TDK commercial on 26 December 1976, with Davis on organ along with Cosey, Henderson, and Foster.

59. *Jazz fusion* is a broad term and is used here not to label Davis's, or any other artist's, style but to easily reference the music in this context. This is especially important in the case of Davis, who never wanted his music labeled.

60. Nicholson, Stuart. *Jazz Rock: A History*. New York: Schirmer, 1998, 208.

61. Pond, *Head Hunters*, 2005.

62. Nicholson, 201.

63. Liebman, interview. Jazz fusion, funk, and various crossover artists from the seventies were very influential on rap and hip-hop. Bob James's "Nautilus" and "Take Me to the Mardi Gras" (CTI, 1974, 1975), for example, have been sampled in dozens of hip-hop tunes. Gopam manager Laurie Goldstein explained to me how busy her office is with rappers' inquiries for music rights, especially Hubbard's seventies work. "A *lot* of Freddie. They love Freddie."

64. whosampled.com

65. Schafer, Joseph. "Deconstructing: The Rise, Demise, and Legacy of The Mars Volta." 7 February 2013. stereogum.com/1254741/deconstructing-the-rise-demise-and-legacy-of-the-mars-volta/top-stories/.

66. "*Bitches Brew*: 40 Years of Inspiration." *Revivalist* 21 December 2010. revivalist.okayplayer.com/2010/12/21/bitches-brew-40-years-of-inspiration/. Rollins was part of the United States Postal Service Forever stamp ceremony in 2012. The image chosen for the stamp was Davis's iconic S-shaped silhouette captured by photographer David Gahr in 1970.

67. Ibid.

68. Ibid.

69. Ibid.

70. Ibid.

71. Promotional material. PR Newswire. 24 May 2010. prnewswire.com/news-releases/bitches-brew-by-miles-davis-celebrates-40-years-94752209.html.

72. DiMartino, Dave. "Give Radiohead Your Computer." Yahoo Music 5 February 1999. web.archive.org/web/20070814183856/music.yahoo.com/read/interview/12048024.

73. Sutherland, Mark. "Return of the Mac." *Melody Maker* 31 May 1997. greenplastic.com/coldstorage/articles/melodymaker053197.html.

74. Varga, George. "Radiohead's Jazz Frequencies." *JazzTimes*, November 2001. jazztimes.com/articles/20174-radiohead-s-jazz-frequencies.

75. Sutcliffe, "An Interview with Thom Yorke."

76. Radiohead too sampled Miles. "Miles Runs the Voodoo Down" can be heard looped throughout "Kinetic" (2001).

192   Notes

77. Saal, "Miles of Music," 70.

78. Ratliff, Ben. "A Jazz Legend Enshrined as a Rock Star?" *New York Times*, 13 March 2006, E1, E7.

79. Ibid.

80. Saal, 70.

81. Albertson, Chris. "The Unmasking of Miles." *Saturday Review* 27 November 1971. Reprinted Kirchner, *A Miles Davis Reader*, 192.

82. Smith, "Trumpeter Outlaws Word 'Jazz.'"

83. Saal, "Miles of Music," 70.

84. Troupe, *Miles and Me*, 26.

85. Smith, "Trumpeter Outlaws Word 'Jazz.'"

86. Hall, Gregg. "Teo . . . The Man behind the Scene." *Down Beat*, July 1974, 15.

87. Troupe, *Miles and Me*, 79.

88. Brooks, Harvey. "A View from the Bottom." 20 February 2008. youtube.com/watch?v=vda7n18pjvI&feature=related.

Chapter 8

1. Wilson, Laura, John Rohrbach, and Richard Avedon. *In the American West*. New York: Harry N. Abrams, 1996. richardavedon.com/#p=-1&a=-1&at=-1.

2. Persson, Jan. Interview by the author. 10 September 2012.

3. Fielden, J. "The Stranger Behind the Camera." *Vogue*, November 2004. vogue.com/vogue-daily/article/vd-remembering-irving-penn-the-stranger-behind-the-camera/#1.

4. At auctions, prints have fetched thousands of dollars.

5. Inokuchi, Teppei. Interview by the author. 29 August 2012.

6. Lombardi, Fred. Interview by the author. 7 September 2012.

7. Hershorn, Tad. Interview by the author. 2 September 2012.

8. Hunstein, DeeAnne. Interview by the author. 4 September 2012.

9. Wolman, Baron. Interview by the author. 25 August 2012.

10. Lombardi, Fred. Interview by the author. 23 April 2013.

11. Inokuchi, interview, 2012.

12. Persson, interview.

13. Lombardi, interview, 2013.

14. Inokuchi, interview, 2012.

15. Betty being a spotlight grabber before a camera during this period only thickens the plot about her ongoing reclusiveness. Wolman himself tried to reach out to her in light of her album's recent reissues and got nowhere either. Neither he nor any of his contemporaries could make heads or tails of it, speculating that she either became obese or is fighting some other health issue.

16. Wolman, interview, 2012.

17. Ibid.

18. Inokuchi, interview, 2012.

19. Persson, interview.

20. Lombardi, interview, 2012.

21. Sony purchased Columbia Records in 1988. On a few occasions during interviews, I have mistakenly said Sony instead of Columbia to employees and affiliates of the sixties and was quickly corrected that at the time it was *Columbia*, not Sony.

22. Berg, Interview.

23. Ibid.

24. Piracy is also a big problem. When Wolman and I were sifting though Google Images for his shots, he continuously and woefully pointed about shot after shot that was published without permission.

25. Wolman, interview, 2012.

26. Ibid.

27. Ibid.

28. Lombardi, interview, 2013.

29. Morgenstern, Dan. Preface from *Jan Persson: Jazz Portraits*, København: Tiderne Skifter, 1996.

30. Persson, interview.

31. Inokuchi, interview, 2012.

32. Ibid.

33. Ibid.

34. Wolman, Baron. Interview by the author, 3 May 2013.

35. Inokuchi, Teppei. Interview by the author, 26 April 2013.

36. Hershorn, interview.

Music Credits

"Bitches Brew"
By Miles Davis
©1969 JAZZ HORN MUSIC
    Copyright Renewed
    This arrangement © 2013 JAZZ HORN MUSIC
    All Rights Controlled and Administered by SONGS OF UNIVERSAL, INC.
    All Rights Reserved Used by Permission
    Reprinted by Permission of Hal Leonard Corporation

"John McLaughlin"
By Miles Davis
©1969 JAZZ HORN MUSIC
    Copyright Renewed
    This arrangement © 2013 JAZZ HORN MUSIC
    All Rights Controlled and Administered by SONGS OF UNIVERSAL, INC.
    All Rights Reserved Used by Permission
    Reprinted by Permission of Hal Leonard Corporation

"Sanctuary"
By Wayne Shorter
© 1971 Miyako Music
    Copyright Renewed
    This arrangement © 2013 Miyako Music
    All Rights Administered by Songs of Kobalt Music Publishing
    All Rights Reserved Used by Permission
    Reprinted by Permission of Hal Leonard Corporation

"Miles Runs the Voodoo Down"
By Miles Davis
©1969 JAZZ HORN MUSIC
    Copyright Renewed
    This arrangement © 2013 JAZZ HORN MUSIC
    All Rights Controlled and Administered by SONGS OF UNIVERSAL, INC.
    All Rights Reserved Used by Permission
    Reprinted by Permission of Hal Leonard Corporation

Music Credits

"Spanish Key"
By Miles Davis
©1968, 1970 JAZZ HORN MUSIC
    Copyright Renewed
    This arrangement © 2013 JAZZ HORN MUSIC
    All Rights Controlled and Administered by SONGS OF UNIVERSAL, INC.
    All Rights Reserved Used by Permission
    Reprinted by Permission of Hal Leonard Corporation

"Pharaoh's Dance"
By Josef Zawinul
    © 1969 & 1970 by Zawinul Music, a division of
    Gopam Enterprises, Inc. Renewed
    All Rights Reserved. Used by Permission

Index

Adderley, Julian, 31, 33
"Agitation" (song), 23
Alias, Don, 41, 48, 53, 74, 76
Allman, Gregg, 6, 186
Armstrong, Louis, 37, 53, 131–32, 159
Avakian, George, 98, 110, 113, 128
Avedon, Richard, 161
Avery Fisher Hall, 126, 139, 166
"Ascent" (song), 32
At Fillmore (album), 24, 103, 129, 144, 186
"Autumn Leaves" (song) 23, 35

Balakrishna, Khalil, 142–43
Baraka, Amiri (LeRoi Jones), 131
Bartz, Gary, 129, 149
Bass ostinato, 24
Baumstein, Morris, 117, 119
Beatles, 5, 17, 26, 98, 108, 131
Belden, Bob, 29, 61, 98, 117, 184
Benson, George, 65
Berg, John, 124, 167, 186
Big Fun (album), 26, 142, 179, 189
"Big Green Serpent" (song), 143
Birth of the Cool (album), 4, 23, 51
Bitches Brew (album): after market, 108–10; band reaction, 49; *Call it Anything*, 51; cultural backdrop, 3–4; improvising techniques, 53–55, 58–59, 64–65, 76, 79, 95; instrumentation, 39–42, 47–49; legacy, 154–59; *Listen to This*, 122–23; marketing, 117–19, 122, 124; musical cues, 55–56; post-production, 97, 101–10; recording process, 100–101; rehearsal process, 44–46, 74–76; response, 113, 115, 127–30; session schedule, 43; writing process, 43–47, 52–53, 61–62, 68, 86–87, 95
Bitches Brew (painting), 123–24, 186
"Bitches Brew" (song): compositional structure, 56; Davis's directorial approach, 58–59, 61; Davis's soloing approach/analysis, 56–61; studio banter, 56, 99; tonal center, 53
Blakey, Art, 65, 67
Blood, Sweat, and Tears, 118
Bloomfield, Mike, 11
Blues scale, 29, 65
Blumenthal, Bob, 129
Boyd, Brandon, 157
Brooks, Harvey: after leaving Davis, 154; edited solos, 107; joining Davis's band, 41–42, 47; November 1969 sessions, 141–43; on "Bitches Brew," 102; working with Davis, 58, 85, 160
Brown, James: biography, 14–15, 18; influence on Davis, 7, 24, 36–37, 45–46, 51–52, 79, 96, 127, 129, 132

Carnegie Hall, 126, 128, 152
Carter, Ron: "Eighty-One," 28; *Live-Evil*, 148; November 1969 sessions, 142–43; precursor to Michael Henderson, 48; with Davis's second quintet, 5, 115, 131
Cellar Door, 143, 148–50, 190
Central Park (performance), 152
Chambers, Joe, 32
Chertok, Connie, 39, 111
Chicago (band), 118

197

"Circle in the Round" (song), 24
Cobham, Billy, 44–45, 55, 141, 143, 146
Cole, George, 108
Coltrane, John, 5, 129, 182
Columbia Records: capitalizing on jazz fusion, 155; Columbia Studio B, 31, 39, 42, 45, 97, 140, 143, 175; *Complete Bitches Brew Sessions*, 108; contract with Davis, 4; financial negotiations/agreements with Davis, 37, 105, 111, 135–37, 139, 193; "Great Expectations" (single), 143; handling *Jack Johnson*, 144; Lost Quintet, 32; marketing Davis, 117–19, 122, 126; "Miles Runs the Voodoo Down" (single), 76; pressure on Davis, 4, 116–17; reissue campaign, 110; relationship with Davis, 185; relationship with Teo Macero, 103–4; sale to Sony, 167; staff engineers, 100, 109; state-of-the-art studio, 97
Complete Bitches Brew Sessions (album), 108, 189
Corea, Chick: joining Davis's band, 33–35, 40, 48, 141–42, 148; keyboard style/approach, 61, 68, 73–74, 76, 79, 83, 95; return to Forever, 154; working with Davis, 43–44, 87; working with electric piano, 27, 57–59
"Corrado" (song), 142
Coryell, Larry, 153
Cosey, Pete, 30, 44, 55, 191
Costello, Del, 115, 118
"Country Son" (song), 25
Coyne, Wayne, 156
Cream, 5, 26, 173
Crouch, Stanley, 111, 115, 128, 131–32
Cuscuna, Michael, 101, 108, 119, 127, 184

Dark Magus. *See* Carnegie Hall
Davis, Clive: Columbia resignation, 155; corporate interferences with Davis, 104, 115, 117; financial arrangements with Davis, 37, 112, 135, 139; marketing Davis, 122, 127
Davis, Miles Dewey, III: Ahmad Jamal inspiration, 11; album and song titles, 24, 51; arrests, 18–19, 151; boxing, 6, 34, 96, 145–48, 153, 164, 169–70; childhood, 4, 19–20; drug problems, 14, 151–54; early career, 4–5; emphasis on rhythm section, 27–28; expanded instrumentation, 26–27, 31, 140–42; fashion, 6, 168–69; Ferrari, 18–20, 91, 132, 135, 164–66, 170; finances, 37, 111–12, 135–39; influence on Rap and Hip Hop, 156; influence on young listeners, 20; introduction to rock, 6–7; James Brown inspiration, 24, 52–53; Jimi Hendrix inspiration, 29–30, 37, 74, 117, 127, 132; modernity/postmodernity, 35, 126; as music director, 46–47, 56–58; persona, 5, 18–20, 37, 39–40, 51–52, 56–58, 62, 159–61, 163–66, 168; relationship with Teo Macero, 51–52; relationships with women, 6, 19, 51, 122, 149, 153–54, 164–65, 168; retirement, 150–54; sellout, 20, 116–17, 132–34; Sly Stone inspiration, 24; use of amplified trumpet, 30, 126; use of rock rhythms, 28–31; use of vamps, 23–25
Davis, Miles Henry, 4, 19–20
Dean, Walter, 135–37
DeJohnette, Jack: drum style/approach, 28, 33, 48; joining Davis's band, 33, 40–42, 143, 148–49; leaving Davis's band, 150; working with Davis, 43–44, 52–53, 74, 76, 96
"Directions" (song), 25, 31
"Dolores" (song), 28
Doo-Bop (album), 154
"Double Image" (song), 143
Douglas, Stella, 6, 123, 186
"Duran" (song), 146

Dylan, Bob, 9, 10–12, 15, 39, 41, 111, 124, 131, 167, 173

"Early Minor" (song), 32
"Eighty-One" (song), 28
Ellington, Duke, 30, 37, 98, 131–32, 164
E.S.P. (album), 25
Evans, Gil, 4–5, 23, 26, 133

Fender Rhodes, 26–28, 39, 105, 110, 158
Filles de Kilimanjaro (album), 27, 36, 117, 189
Fillmore East and West: Charles Lloyd, 33; Clive Davis proposing Davis shows, 122; Davis performances at Fillmore East, 124–26, 140–41, 144; East Village neighborhood, 6
"Flamenco Sketches" (song), 23, 25, 32
Fortune, Sonny, 129–30, 152
Foster, Al, 48, 150, 154, 191

Gahr, David, 170
Gaye, Marvin, 13–14
Get Up With It (album), 151
"Ghetto Walk" (song), 32
Giddins, Gary, 111, 126, 149–50, 152
Gillespie, Dizzy, 37, 159, 160
Gleason, Ralph, 124, 131
Gleason's Gym, 6, 164, 170
Gold, Jack, 103
Goldstein, Laurie, 142, 191
Graham, Bill, 33, 122, 125
Grateful Dead, 12, 125
"Great Expectations" (song), 142–43
"Guinevere" (song), 143

Hancock, Herbie, 26–27, 46,142, 146, 148, 154, 155; with Davis's second quintet, 5, 115, 131; Fender Rhodes, 26–27; *Head Hunters*, 154–55; *Jack Johnson*, 146; *Live-Evil*, 148; November 1969 sessions, 142; *On the Corner*, 46
Head Hunters (album), 154–55

Henderson, Michael: Cellar Door, 149; joining Davis's band, 48, 149, 190; leaving Davis's band, 152; working with Davis, 46, 55
Hendrix, Jimi: *Are You Experienced* (album), 17; blues influences, 5; early career, 17; funeral, 19; guitar innovations, 26, 126; influence on Davis, 29–30, 37, 74, 117, 127, 132; influence on John McLaughlin, 95; meeting with Davis, 6–7; Monterey Pop Festival, 12, 16–17; public persona, 16, 164; Woodstock, 12, 15, 20
Hershorn, Tad, 162, 166, 171
Holland, Dave: bass style/approach, 49, 61, 65, 87; joining Davis's band, 33–34, 40, 42, 48; last show with Davis, 190; playing with Jimi Hendrix, 29; thoughts on *Bitches Brew*, 102; time after Davis, 154; working with Davis, 43, 45–46, 100
Holzman, Adam, 131, 150
Hopkins, Lightnin', 11
Hubbard, Freddie, 129, 155, 191

"I Fall in Love Too Easily" (song), 23, 34
In a Silent Way (album): cultural backdrop, 32–33; Davis's profits, 111, 127; instrumentation, 26, 62–63; origins of *Bitches Brew*, 21, 25, 30–32, 41, 44, 100; post-production, 34; rhythmic emphasis, 27; working titles, 31
In Concert. See Philharmonic Hall
Inokuchi, Teppei, 152, 162–64, 166, 169–70, 190
Isle of Wight, 125, 141, 164, 166, 190
"It's About That Time" (song), 31–32

Jack Johnson (album), 148–49, 189
Jagger, Mick, 153
Jamal, Ahmad, 23
James, Bob, 155, 191

Jarrett, Keith, 27, 41, 48, 133, 148, 150
"John McLaughlin" (song): soloing approach, 65; song structure, 61–63, 102; tonal center, 53
Johnson, Jack (boxer), 144–45, 147–48
Juilliard School, 4, 39, 98, 100, 111

Kind of Blue (album), 5, 23, 32
King, Martin Luther, 12, 16, 32
Klarwein, Mati, 18, 123–24, 148, 186
Klarwein, Serafine, 123

Laico, Frank, 100–101, 104, 109, 180
Lawrence, Azar, 54–55, 128, 133
Led Zeppelin, 5, 26
"Like a Rolling Stone" (song), 11–12, 17, 131
Linear Development, 54
"Little Blue Frog" (song), 143
Live-Evil (album), 26, 111, 148–49, 173, 179, 186, 189
Lloyd, Charles, 33
Lombardi, Fred, 162–64, 166–68
Lombardo, Dave, 156
"Lonely Fire" (song), 143, 189
Lost Quintet, 32–35, 40, 65, 79, 179
Lucas, Reggie, 30, 55
Lundvall, Bruce, 104, 117, 124, 184

Mabry, Betty: *Bitches Brew*, 180; influence on Davis, 6–7, 122; Isle of Wight, 164; at Jimi Hendrix's funeral, 19; Klarwein painting, 148; marriage to Davis, 6, 149, 164–65, 168; personal life, 192; working with Teo Macero, 41
Macero, Teo: artistic involvement, 106–7, 117; biography, 98; Davis reissue campaign, 108–10; Davis's finances, 37, 111, 135; executive decisions, 102, 104; handling Davis's feedback from fans, 129, 188; *In a Silent Way*, 31; *Jack Johnson*, 146–47; preparing for *Bitches Brew*, 39–40, 43, 100–101; producing/editing *Bitches Brew*, 59, 73, 79, 86, 97–99, 100–102, 105, 184; production style, 109; thoughts about producer's role, 108; working relationship with Davis, 44, 56, 74, 86, 97, 99, 160; working with Harvey Brooks, 41
"Mademoiselle Mabry" (song), 29
Mahavishnu Orchestra, 154
"Masqualero" (song), 23, 35
Maupin, Bennie: on "Bitches Brew," 59; after Davis, 154; biography, 41–42; on "John McLaughlin," 65; joining Davis's band, 41–43; on "Pharaoh's Dance," 95, 102; on "Spanish Key," 83, 85; reactions to *Bitches Brew*, 49; working with Davis, 44–46, 56, 141, 143
McLaughlin, John: on "Bitches Brew," 58–59; on *Jack Johnson*, 146–49; on "John McLaughlin," 65; joining the band, 41–42, 62–63, 182; leaving Davis's band, 63, 68, 154; November 1969 sessions, 141; on "Miles Runs the Voodoo Down," 76; on "Pharaoh's Dance," 87, 95; on "Spanish Key," 83; post-production problems, 110; working with Davis, 45–46; working with Jimi Hendrix, 29
McLean, Jackie, 33, 41–42
"Mercy, Mercy, Mercy" (song), 31
Miles, Buddy, 30, 76, 147, 189
Miles in the Sky (album), 26, 28
"Miles Runs the Voodoo Down" (song): Davis's soloing approach, 76–79; discrepancies with drum beat, 52–53, 74, 76; Jimi Hendrix inspiration, 30; live performances, 35; recording process, 74; samples of, 191; tonal center, 53
Milestones (album), 5, 23, 34–35
"Milestones" (song), 34–35
Miller, Steve, 124–25

Mimram, Colette, 6, 123
Mingus, Charles, 98
Modes (modal improvisation), 21, 23, 25, 29, 31, 53, 117
Monk, Thelonious, 45, 98, 109
Monterey Pop Festival, 12, 16–18
Montreux Jazz Festival, 129
Moore, Ray, 100, 104, 107, 110, 185
Moreira, Airto, 141, 143, 148–49
Morgan, Lee, 42
Morgenstern, Dan, 126, 169
Motown (record company), 5, 28, 51, 127, 149
Mtume, James, 48, 55, 129

Nas, 157
"Nefertiti" (song), 28, 65, 99, 100, 183
Newport Jazz Festival, 12–13, 129, 163, 170
Nicholson, Stuart, 155
Nyro, Laura, 125

OK Computer (album), 135, 157–58
On the Corner (album), 31, 46, 48, 151, 165, 185
"Orange Lady" (song), 74, 142, 143

Palmer, Robert, 152
Pareles, Jon, 54
Parker, Charlie, 4, 7, 65, 164
Pascoal, Hermeto, 148
Penn, Irving, 161–62
Persson, Jan, 161, 163, 166, 168–69
"Pharaoh's Dance" (song): analysis, 92–96; legal disputes between Zawinul and Davis, 91; origin/interpretation, 87; original lead sheets, 88–90; presenting to Davis, 43; recording/editing style, 46, 86, 97, 102; start of recording, 74, 85; tonal center, 53
Philharmonic Hall (New York), 125–26, 127–28, 129
Phillips, Sam, 9–10

Playboy, 113
Presley, Elvis, 5, 9–10, 14, 20
Prestige, 4

Quine, Robert, 144

Radiohead, 135, 155, 157–58, 191
"Recollections" (song), 143
Redding, Otis, 9, 12, 17
Return to Forever, 154, 155, 173
"Right Off" (song), 146–47
Robinson, Sugar Ray, 145
Rock and Roll Hall of Fame, 158–59
Rock music, 5, 26
Rockwell, John, 126
Rolling Stone (magazine), 113, 119, 122, 124, 146, 163, 164, 167
Rolling Stones (band), 5, 17, 26, 128
Rollins, Henry, 156, 191
"'Round Midnight" (song), 23, 34–35
Roy, Badal, 46, 47, 48
Rubin, Rick, 104, 184–85

"Sanctuary" (song): analysis, 68, 73, 142; Davis's approach on, 68, 95; in Davis's repertoire, 150; Davis's solo, 69–73; disputes between Wayne Shorter and Davis, 147; harmonic movement, 53; inspiration, 65, 67–68; original lead sheets, 66–67
Santana, Carlos, 6, 12, 26, 32, 34, 37, 111, 118, 156, 167
Santos, Jumma (Jim Riley), 41, 48
"Selim" (song), 148
Sharma, Bihara, 142
"Shhh/Peaceful" (song), 31–32
Shorter, Wayne: alcohol problems, 43; *Bitches Brew*, 40, 46–47; "Bitches Brew," 59; with Davis's second quintet, 5, 115, 131; leaving Davis's band, 68, 91, 95, 154; Lost Quintet, 33; "Masqualero," 23; "Miles Runs the

Voodoo Down," 76; November 1969 sessions, 142–43; "Sanctuary," 65–73, 147; "Spanish Key," 83; writing styles, 27–28
Simone, Nina, 41
"Sivad" (song), 148
"Sleepwalk" (song), 142
Slugs, 41–42
"So What" (song), 23–24
Sony Records. *See* Columbia Records
"Spanish Key" (song): analysis, 83, 85; Davis's soloing approach, 79; harmonic structure, 53; keyboard setup, 48; musical cues, 79–80
"Star Spangled Banner" (Hendrix version), 15–16
Stone, Sly: biography, 12–14; influence on Davis, 6–7, 24, 37, 51, 127, 152
Stratton, Bert, 113, 128
Szantor, Jim, 113

"Take It or Leave It" (song), 143
Taylor, Creed, 155
Taylor, Francis, 6, 151
Terry, Clark, 113, 115
There's a Riot Goin' On (album), 13
Tone color, 25–26
Tonkel, Stan, 100, 104, 109–10
"Trevere" (song), 143
Troupe, Quincy, 3, 18, 127, 159
Tyson, Cicely, 153–54

Vietnam War, 12, 32

Wah-wah, 30, 125–26, 142
Warner Brothers, 4
"Water on the Pond" (song), 27
Weather Report, 95, 154
Wein, George, 13, 139, 153
White, Lenny: drum style, 28, 48; joining Davis's band, 33, 41; on Davis making a rock record, 117; Return to Forever, 154; troubles on "Miles Runs the Voodoo Down," 52–53, 55, 74, 76; working with Davis, 43, 45–46, 48–49, 57, 102
Whittemore, Jack, 86, 91
"Wild Thing" (Hendrix version), 16–17
Wilder, Mark, 101, 109, 184
Williams, Tony: "Nefertiti," 28; referring Chick Corea to Davis, 34; referring White to band, 41; Tony Williams Lifetime, 33, 62; with Davis's second quintet, 5, 115, 131
Wilson, John, 125–26
"Wind Cries Mary, The" (song), 29
Winter, Johnny, 6
Wolman, Baron, 163–68, 170, 192, 193
Wonder, Stevie, 149
Woodstock, 3–4, 12, 15–16, 18, 20, 141
Wyatt, Hugh, 128

"Yesternow" (song), 147
Young, Larry, 41, 48, 143, 182

Zawinul, Josef: "Double Image," 143; "Great Expectations," 142; "In a Silent Way," 32, 62; joining Davis's band, 31–33, 41–42; legal disputes with Davis, 147; "Orange Lady," 74, 143; "Pharaoh's Dance," 74, 87–88, 91–96; "Sanctuary," 68; Weather Report, 154; working with Davis, 43, 48–49, 58